COMPLETE
BOOK OF

HOME
WORKSHOPS

Books by

DAVID X. MANNERS

Plumbing and Heating Handbook

Handyman's Concrete and Masonry Guide

Projects You Can Make for Outdoor Living

Home Improvements You Can Do

Handyman's Handbook

Written in collaboration:

How to Build Outdoor Fireplaces and Furniture

How to Make Plumbing Repairs

How to Repair Appliances

Handyman's Concrete and Masonry Handbook

COMPLETE
BOOK OF

HOME
WORKSHOPS

DAVID X. MANNERS

Popular Science
Publishing Co.

Harper & Row
New York, London

This book is dedicated . . .

Not to the craftsmen of yesterday and the
old ways of doing things, but to Paul, Jon,
Mike and Tim and all the craftsmen of tomorrow
who will be doing things better than their fathers
and grandfathers.

Contents

Special thanks to ...

For permission to photograph their workshops: Henry Weiman, G. Harry Stine, Wendell H. Stickney, Jerome Osadnick, Donald Weill.

For help in supplying photos and data: Edward C. Benfield (The Stanley Works), Gene Sliga (Rockwell Mfg. Co.), Carl Starner (Black & Decker Mfg. Co.), William E. Kotzenberg (Skil Corp.), Kenneth Roche (Ridge Tool Co.), Thomas P. O'Hara (Nicholson File Co.), Jules Swerdlin (Simmon Omega), Herbert Perkins (Masonite Corp.), R. Hugh Love (American Plywood Asso.), D. Donald Lonie (Western Wood Products).

For editing: Henry Gross. For drawings: Carl Sigman (Sigman-Ward). For photo processing: Syd Greenberg (Weiman & Lester Photoservices). For preparation of the manuscript, encouragement, and preparation of refreshments at critical times: Ruth Ann Manners

For permission to use material which appeared in a different form: the Editors of *Popular Science Monthly*.

For conceiving the idea of the book: William Sill.

Part 1

DESIGNING and BUILDING YOUR WORKSHOP

1

Ten Places
to Put a Workshop

Every homeowner needs a workshop to keep his house in good shape. Even if a shop did not pay for itself in the money you save doing your own repairs, it would be worthwhile for the pleasure it offers. But usually a shop does help you save money. When repairs must be made you are at no one's mercy. You may mangle a few jobs at first, but you will be learning, developing your skills. Also, you will be better prepared to oversee those jobs you assign to others, and a better judge of workmanship and cost. In this age of technology a man is handicapped if he's baffled by a malfunctioning dishwasher, a balky oil burner, or the intricacies of a printed circuit.

There are at least ten good places you can put a shop. There are countless ways to create space where there seems to be none. In planning where to put a shop, think of the kinds of jobs you want to do in it.

The maintenance of a house involves carpentry, plumbing, electrical work, metalwork, painting and paperhanging, masonry, landscaping and gardening, roofing, and repairing and refinishing furniture. A place may be needed for hi-fi, ham

An orderly, attractive shop makes working a pleasure. Such a shop could be built in a garage, basement, or spare room. Inexpensive pine boards and decorative iron hardware lend a pleasant appearance.

radio, or electronics, working with plastics, leather, old clocks, or antique toys. Other activities may include gunmaking, modelmaking, welding, repairing gasoline engines, automobiles, and boats. A shop may be a creative center for the entire family, with workbenches for the children, girls as well as boys.

BASEMENT SHOPS.   More shops are in the basement than anywhere else. It has major advantages as well as some drawbacks. On the plus side, it is warm in winter, cool in summer. It is quiet, and you can mess it up. It may also be dark, dingy, cobwebbed, damp, or subject to periodic flooding. A damp basement creates rust problems. A flooded basement can be a disaster. But these are difficulties that can be overcome.

New foam boards can be used to insulate basement walls and check dampness. Applying epoxy waterproofing to walls from the inside, grading slopes away from the basement walls on the outside, and repairing leaking gutters and downspouts may be all that is required to prevent flooding. A good sump pump is added insurance. A false ceiling can hide plumbing, wiring, and ductwork. Ceiling panels may be removed for access. A load-bearing cabinet can support a weak or sagging floor overhead.

A basement shop benefits from sufficient light and air. If basement windows are below grade, recessed in a well, this areaway can sometimes be extended and additional windows installed. On walls paralleling floor joists, stock 18″-by-32″ windows can be set in a continuous ribbon, using 2″-by-8″ or 2″-by-10″ verticals to support the first-floor plates. You can even install windows in walls which support floor joists by inserting supports, such as 3″ pipe, every few feet, If your basement does not have good access to the outdoors, provide one. Prefab stairway assemblies and low-cost metal doors for the entrance make the job easier.

Some basements are difficult to remodel because they were

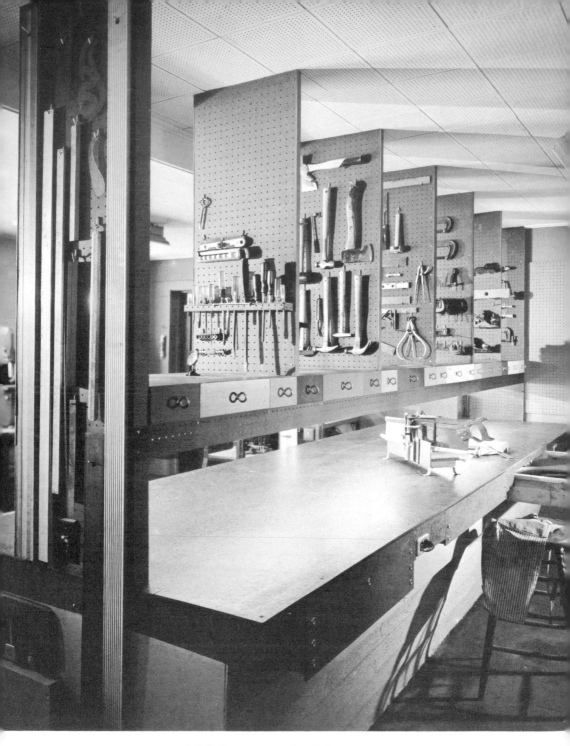

A full basement is divided with a two-way workbench in the shop of architect Paul R. MacAlister. Openness of design improves lighting and aids ventilation.

White walls and drawer
fronts lend a light, cheerful
accent to this basement shop.
Heating system in the basement keeps it warm and dry.

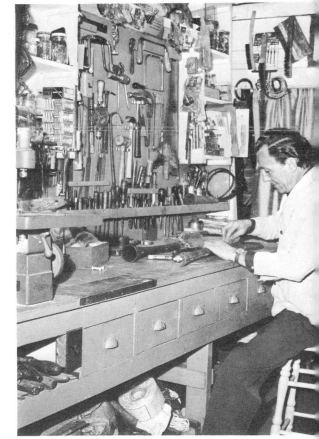

Replacing old, bulky heating
plant with a compact modern
system frees basement space
for a shop. This one is in a
former coal bin.

5

built improperly. If you are building or buying a house here's what to watch for in a basement:

• If basement walls are of concrete block, they should be at least twelve blocks high. The usual basement is built only eleven blocks high and this produces a ceiling just over 7' high, too low for a good shop. The added cost is only about $100.

• Pipes and electrical cables should run between the joists instead of below them. Keep warm-air ducts at the perimeter of the basement.

• Be sure the basement is waterproofed correctly. The exterior block walls should receive a coating of cement plaster. A heavy coating of asphalt waterproofing compound should go over this. The first two courses of block should be solid, and if there is any question at all about drainage, install a line of drain tile around the wall's footings, to lead off the water.

GARAGE SHOPS.   Getting a shop in a single-car garage is difficult. If you have 3' at one end it can be managed: A 2' bench leaves 1' clearance for working. If you have 3' to spare on one side, you can install a compact shop along this wall. Tools and sawhorses can be moved to the main area for large projects. If a garage isn't wide enough to accommodate a shop, you can add a bay to increase its width.

Switching to a compact car can free space in the garage for a shop. Storage is an important part of any shop. Space above the hood of a car is ordinarily wasted. Use it. In building locker space over the hood, allow a 6" clearance. Storage lockers on one or both sides of the car can help support the crossing structure. Use sliding panels on the lockers, and you won't have to worry about swing space. Make the panels of ¼" plywood or hardboard. Sliding track for the panels is available at your lumberyard.

Create loft storage under a pitched roof. Hang storage from the rafters. It's a good place for ladders. Get the most out of space by categorizing it: lawn and garden tools in one place, camping equipment in another, and barbecuing gear in a third.

BEFORE. This garage was nothing but a wasted space for haphazard storage. Converting it into a workshop with organized storage is really a simple job.

AFTER. Storage and organization bring order out of chaos and put waste space to work. Walls and cabinetwork are of knotty Ponderosa pine. *Courtesy Western Wood Products.*

In this garage shop, sander and grinder are mounted on brackets attached to the doors to use space that would otherwise be wasted.

Table saw and band saw occupy center of the same shop, with workbench and storage cabinets along the far wall. Combination cabinet-work support stores accessories for table saw.

By adding a carport, a double garage becomes available for a shop. One of the garage doors was replaced by two windows, the other was left intact to facilitate moving materials and projects in and out.

Christmas decorations, luggage, and dead storage can go on the highest shelves. If the storage is closed off by doors, it can present a neat appearance.

A garage shop is ideal if you plan to work on your car. A drain pit is important in such a setup. A typical size is 32" by 60", with depth to accommodate your height. Masonry blocks are an easy-to-use material. At the bottom of the pit, a 2'-by-2'-by-2' hole filled with gravel can provide drainage. The pit should be covered with a door when not in use.

If you need more light in your garage, but don't want to expose the interior to outside view, use textured glass. Prefab window units come in many sizes, and installation requires only the preparation of an opening. In a frame garage, simply install panes of glass between the studs, using molding strips. If desired, glass can be run all the way up to the gabled peaks. Again, use textured glass to block the view.

To get added light into the garage, place glass in some of the panels in a solid garage door. Cut out the panels, set in glass with quarter-round molding.

Prefab plastic skylight units are another way to bring light into the garage shop. Most skylights require no flashing or special framing. A ribbon of mastic is placed around the prepared opening, and the skylight is nailed through its flange directly to the roof.

An important advantage of the shop in a garage is that trucks can deliver materials directly to it.

An easy way to enlarge a garage is to extend one roof slope 8'. An 8'-by-16' extension not only provides space for a workshop, but also for storing garden tools and outdoor equipment.

Here is how to figure how much space your garage can spare for shop or storage: Your car requires its full width, plus the width of one door fully opened. It also requires its full length plus 2'. The rest of the space is yours. If garage walls are open studs, insulate them and cover them with half-inch plasterboard before building cabinets.

You may find it advantageous to build a carport for your car and take over the garage for your shop. In some cases a car may not even demand shelter. A garage offers prime space for conversion into a shop. Drive around town and look for garage conversions. The best will be hardest to spot.

ATTIC SHOPS.   Attics are often hot in summer and short on headroom. It is difficult to transport materials and supplies to and from an attic, and the noise of a shop and its dust carry down into the rest of the house. But these are drawbacks that can be lived with, or in some cases overcome.

If the attic is hot, install a ventilating fan. It will not only reduce the attic temperature, but will cool off the rest of the house. Painting the roof white can also reduce attic temperature. Special paints are available for the purpose.

You can cut down on noise by mounting power tools on rubber mats. Indoor-outdoor carpeting can muffle noises through the floor.

If your garage has a steeply pitched roof, there may be

Well-insulated attic workshop has workbench in the
center and near window, most
power tools along the eaves
(above). Deep storage cabinets are built into the other
low-headroom side (right).

enough space under it for a shop. For a 12′ span, 2″-by-6″ joists on 16″ centers are usually adequate to support the floor. A quick floor can be made of sheathing-grade plywood. An inexpensive folding stairway can give access to the deck.

ENCLOSE A PORCH.   Many porches are seldom used. Often, only part of a porch is needed to provide adequate shop space and the rest left open for entry purposes. Enclosing a porch is neither as difficult nor as expensive as building a complete structure. Roof, floor, and one or perhaps two walls already exist. Filling in the rest is a cinch.

A porch may provide ample space for a shop. The floor, roof, and one wall already exist; only three walls must be added. This porch shop features a workbench built on top of a steel filing cabinet.

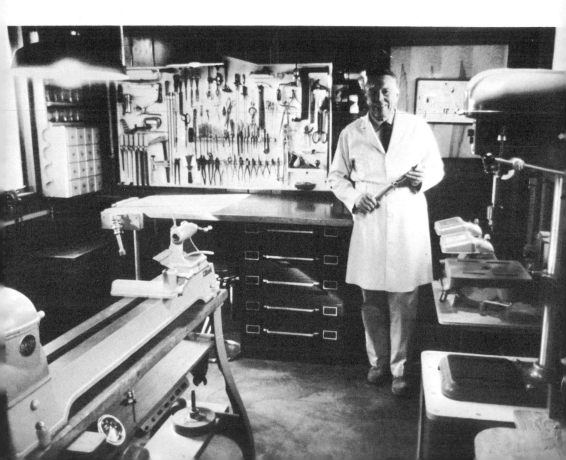

SPARE-ROOM SHOPS.   A bedroom, or any other spare room, can be taken over for a shop. The two big problems are noise and dust. Rooms are difficult to soundproof, which may limit your activities at some hours. They are also difficult to dustproof. A tight-fitting door may help, but how about the sawdust you track out on your shoes? And how will the dust that clings to the windowpanes look from outside the house?

Good light, heat, and ventilation are some of the happier assets of the spare-room shop. It often provides a more alluring aspect than having to descend into the basement or trek out to the garage.

Spare room in a city apartment was turned into a complete workshop with acoustical tile and wood paneling to soften noises. Shop is illuminated by overhead recessed fluorescent lights, even has a built-in sink for washing up.

CLOSET SHOPS.   With a little ingenuity, an amazing amount of tool storage and work space can be fitted into a closet. Highly productive shops have been hung on the back of a closet door, with work tables that fold down to reveal an array of hand tools neatly stored on panel of perforated hardboard. It's not an ideal solution, but it's a beginning. There may be space under a stairway or at the end of a hall that can provide comparable accommodations.

OUTBUILDING SHOPS.   If a house is small, without a basement, and there is no room in the garage, a separate building may be the answer. In it you can work late at night or in the early-morning hours without disturbing anyone. A precut garage may be an inexpensive way to get such a shop. Or how about a trailer?

One man bought a 10′-by-14′ chicken house for under $150 and used this prefab package for his shop. The 2″-by-3″

In mild climates tools can be kept in a storage house and wheeled out on sun-shaded platform for use. A cramped garage shop can be similarly extended outdoors.

and 1″-by-4″ roosts made shelves and benches. An intercom links it to the house. Such a structure is ideal for boatbuilding and other large projects.

Existing barns and outbuildings may afford prime shop space. Insulation and heating may have to be provided, possibly a power line run out to it, but it is only a remodeling job. Most people would rather remodel than attempt to build from scratch. In some areas, codes may stop you from adding an additional structure on your property, but an existing structure doesn't pose any problem.

OUTDOOR SHOPS.   If you live in a mild climate, you can keep power tools and bench inside in storage spaces and roll them out when you want to work. A blacktop or concrete slab is a necessity for easy rolling and simple cleanup.

THE CABINET TRICK.   That fine piece of furniture you see in someone's apartment living room may not be what it appears to be. It may open up in several directions to reveal a complete workbench. Plans for a cabinet-workbench are included in Chapter 3.

DOUBLE UP.   Make single space do double duty. A laundry room often has possibilities as a shop. A hinged fold-down workbench can go over the washer and dryer. True, a hinged workbench has drawbacks; you have to clear it before you can fold it out of the way. A family recreation room also has shop possibilities. There will be dust and noise, but some families will go along with it.

2

Planning
the Layout

You want a shop that is easy to work in, and this can be achieved only by an efficient and logical organization of tools, storage, and work areas. A shop should be organized in centers —everything for a particular function grouped together. If the main function is woodworking, there may be subsidiary areas for planning, painting and finishing, electronics, metalwork, and crafts.

In placing major power tools, the chief considerations are clearance and frequency of use. The most common arrangement is to have a table saw, and perhaps a jointer, in the middle of the shop area. This makes it easier to handle long work, and these tools need clearance on all sides. A radial saw needs clearance on three sides only, so it may be placed against a wall.

Another factor to consider in planning placement of tools is the natural order of their use. Work usually proceeds from storage to cutting to assembly to finishing, just as in a kitchen the sequence is from refrigerator to sink to stove. A well-designed shop should follow this principle.

Placement of the workbench, stationary saw, and storage is most important. Other tools can be placed with a freer hand, provided they have the necessary clearance for safe and comfortable operation. Of course, many major power tools can be placed on retractable casters and moved out for use.

Place hand tools nearest the point of most frequent first use. If tools are used in more than one area of the shop, have duplicates. Point-of-use-storage also makes tools easy to find.

Consider handling of materials. Direct and easy access to the shop from outdoors is the ideal arrangement, but it is not always possible. Ceiling height is important, as you'll discover the first time you try to flop a 12′ board.

Let's look at three shops designed by experts. In a multipurpose shop created by Hubert Luckett, an editor at *Popular Science* magazine, the woodworking center is focused around four tools: table saw, radial saw, jointer, and belt-disc sander. By concentrating the work area around them, many steps are saved.

These tools are all used in the basic cutting and fitting of parts. Assembly is at a nearby center-island bench. Small tools are stored on wall racks behind panels that drop down to serve as work tables. All benches and tabletops are the same height so they can function as added supports for long work. An extension table, hinged to the wall, folds down so it can serve both the radial and the table saw. Reserving the radial saw for crosscut work, and the table saw for ripping, permits each tool to do the kind of job it handles best, and eliminates changing blades and saw position.

The second major area in the shop is a metalworking center. Drill press, band saw, and bench grinder are grouped here because they are used more for metalworking than for woodworking. Strictly for metalworking are a 9″ metal lathe, a forge, anvil, quench tub, gas and electric welders, and a welding table topped by ½″ boiler plate. A hooded exhaust fan discharges fumes from both forge and welding table. Everything needed for auto work is stored in a roll-about cart.

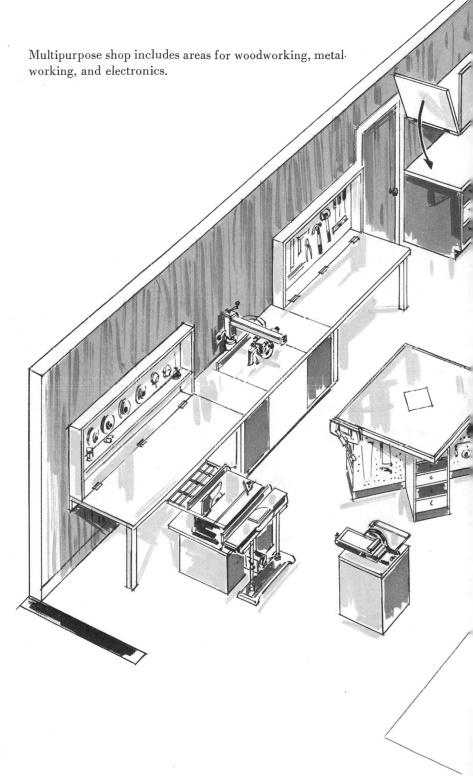

Multipurpose shop includes areas for woodworking, metal-working, and electronics.

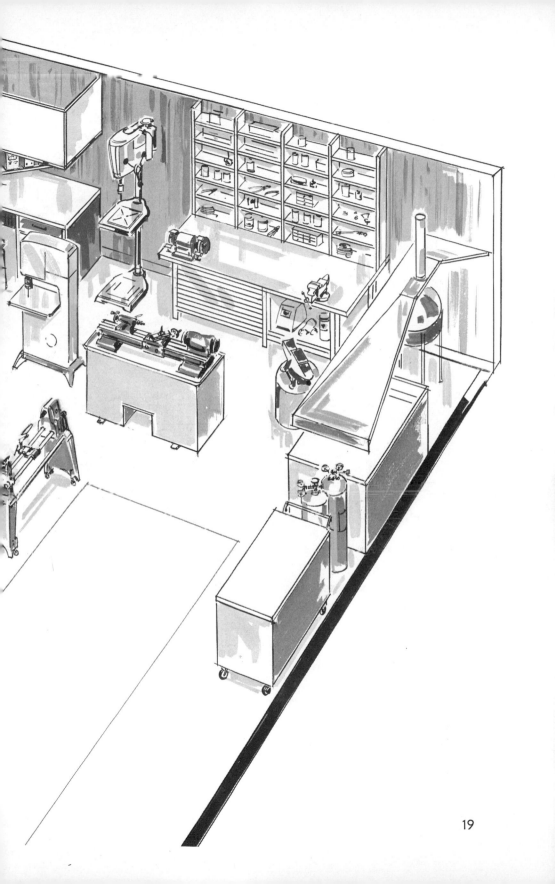

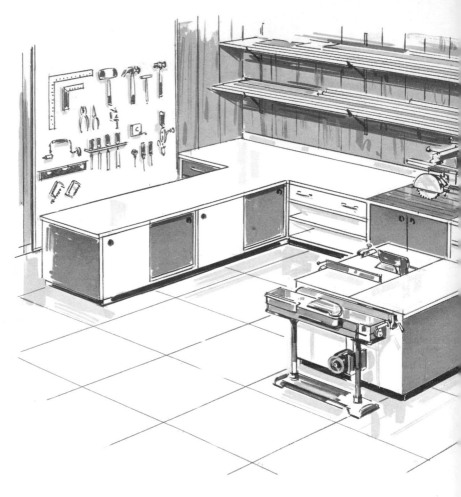

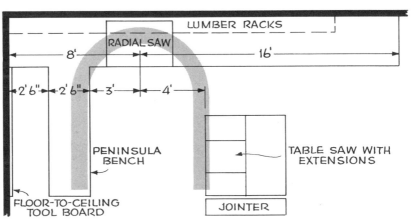

LUMBER RACKS

RADIAL SAW

8'

16'

2'6" 2'6" 3' 4'

PENINSULA
BENCH

TABLE SAW WITH
EXTENSIONS

JOINTER

FLOOR-TO-CEILING
TOOL BOARD

U-shaped shop saves steps, can fit in a small basement or single-car garage.

The third major area is an electronics work center. Located in a rear corner, it has an L-shaped rather than a conventional straight bench. A chassis can be tested on either leg of the bench with important testing instruments always in easy view. These instruments are on shelves that run diagonally across the corner.

A U-shaped plan is the most popular in kitchens, and it works extremely well in a shop, too. Everything is always within easy reach. Such a shop, designed by Jackson Hand, well-known expert, has its horseshoe shape formed by a radial saw built into a wall bench, a peninsular bench that extends

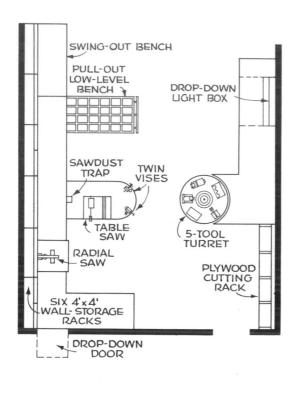

SWING-OUT BENCH

PULL-OUT
LOW-LEVEL
BENCH

DROP-DOWN
LIGHT BOX

SAWDUST
TRAP

TWIN
VISES

TABLE
SAW

5-TOOL
TURRET

RADIAL
SAW

PLYWOOD
CUTTING
RACK

SIX 4'x4'
WALL-STORAGE
RACKS

DROP-DOWN
DOOR

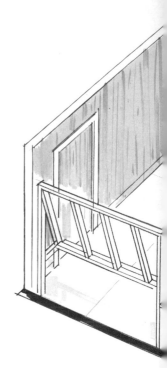

out from it at right angles, and a table saw and jointer on the third side.

Mr. Hand places his radial saw 8′ from one end of the bench and 16′ from the other. This permits cutting 16-footers at the middle or the ends. Lumber is stored on wall racks just behind the saw, instantly at hand for selection and use. A tool storage board is run from floor to ceiling. It not only concentrates a great variety of tools in one spot, but it eliminates stretching across a bench to get them.

For space saving, several small power tools may be grouped on a revolving turret. A circular turret in a shop designed by former *Popular Science* editor Sheldon M. Gallagher holds a drill press, jigsaw, belt-disc sander, bench grinder, and small shaper. The central pedestal is 3″ pipe with a spring latch that locks the turret in any desired position.

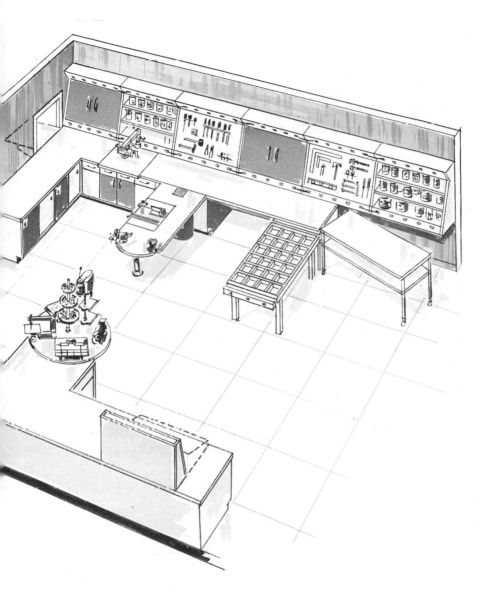

Focal point of this shop is the five-tool turret. A quick turn delivers any tool to your fingertips.

DRAWING PLANS.   It is advisable to draw plans for the shop. You can't keep it all in your head. Once you have something on paper, over a period of time you can incorporate changes as new ideas occur. The plan doesn't have to be fancy, but it should be done to scale. A good scale is ¼″ to the foot. If you have trouble keeping lines at right angles, or calculating scale, use graph paper that has ¼″ squares. Layout includes more than just a flat floor plan. It must also include what will go on the walls and be suspended from the ceiling.

The first thing to get on paper is the exact space available. Indicate locations of windows, posts, doors, stairs, heating plant.

Make an inventory of your present tools and those you plan to get. You will have to plan a place for each of them. If you can, leave a little extra space for such expansion that may not be foreseeable now.

Tool symbols shown are in ¼″ scale. Duplicate them as cardboard cutouts, and you will have a handy means for testing various arrangments. You'll find it easier to move cutouts made this size on your own drawing than to shove the actual tools around on your shop floor site. Each tool has its light and clearance requirements. Provide for them.

When the arrangement of all elements in the shop is set, you will have a basis for deciding where lighting fixtures, power outlets, vacuum system, etc. should go. Remember such needs as a ventilating fan, telephone, intercom, TV outlet, waste bins, possibly a washbasin. If you like to relax to music as you work, provide a place for speakers.

By using a trolley track or lighting duct, you can have light and power anywhere in the shop. Power tools can plug into the track from middle-of-the-floor locations, and it's safer not to have power lines snaking across the floor.

If the workshop is being developed as part of a larger overall improvement project, don't plan it piecemeal. If you are remodeling a basement, and the workshop is only stage one, with a playroom, sewing room, or other facilities to come later,

Long, narrow basement space accommodates woodworking shop and darkroom. Portable tools are stored on shelves under stairway.

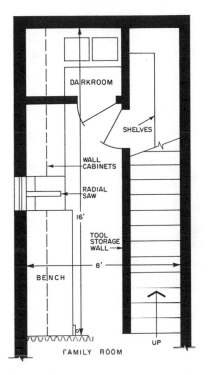

Garage "bustle" shop, 6' by 15', is large enough for most jobs. For big woodworking projects, tools are rolled into the garage. Twin storage doors swing open flat against walls, out of the way. Lumber is stored on overhead racks in garage. For added bench space, the lathe may be hinge-mounted to swing up against the wall.

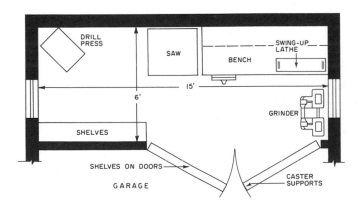

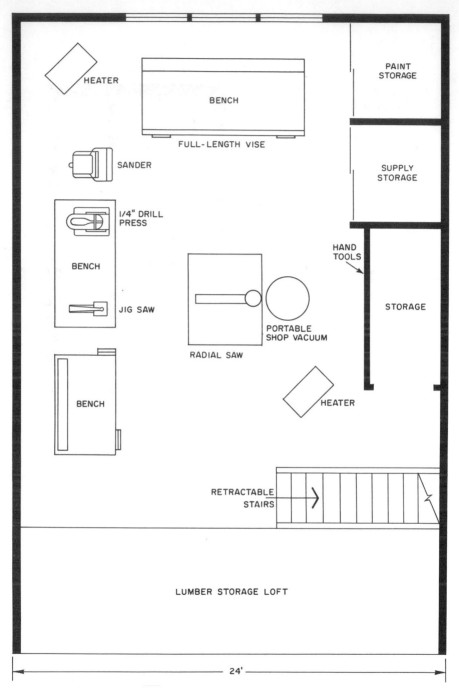

HEATER

BENCH

FULL-LENGTH VISE

SANDER

1/4" DRILL PRESS

BENCH

JIG SAW

BENCH

RADIAL SAW

PORTABLE SHOP VACUUM

HEATER

PAINT STORAGE

SUPPLY STORAGE

HAND TOOLS

STORAGE

RETRACTABLE STAIRS

LUMBER STORAGE LOFT

24'

Attic shop uses low-headroom space on one side for storage, on other for recessing benches and equipment. Radial saw is partially enclosed by hood which connects to portable shop vacuum behind it.

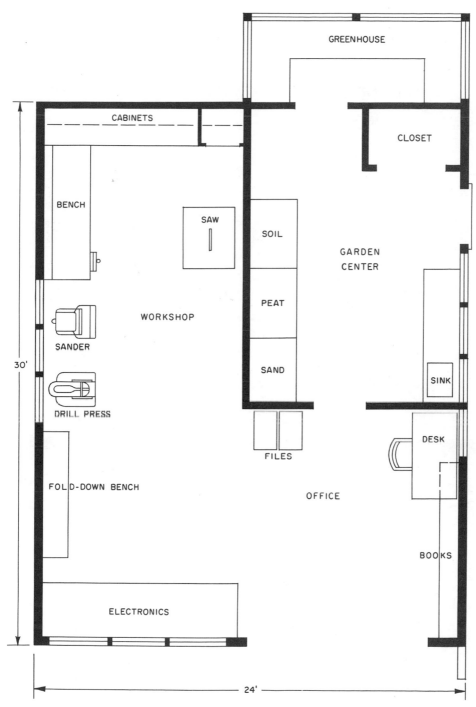

Double garage converted to shop, office, potting room, and greenhouse. One garage-door opening remains to permit passage of large projects and materials.

SPACE AND LIGHT REQUIREMENTS FOR POWER TOOLS

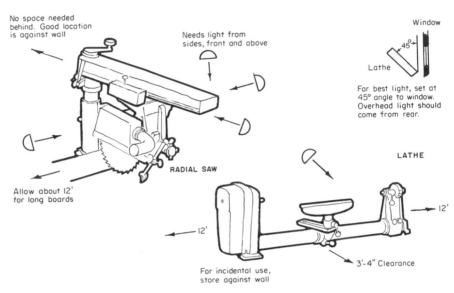

No space needed behind. Good location is against wall

Needs light from sides, front and above

Window

45°

Lathe

For best light, set at 45° angle to window. Overhead light should come from rear.

LATHE

RADIAL SAW

Allow about 12' for long boards

12'

12'

3'-4" Clearance

For incidental use, store against wall

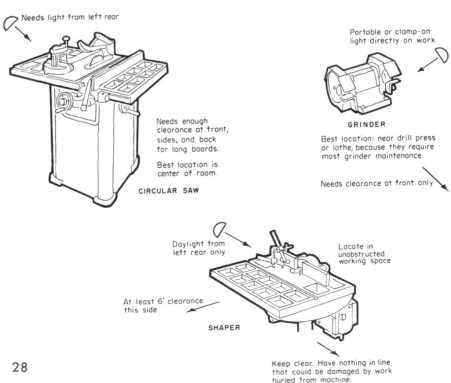

Needs light from left rear

Portable or clamp-on light directly on work

GRINDER

Best location: near drill press or lathe, because they require most grinder maintenance.

Needs enough clearance at front, sides, and back for long boards.

Best location is center of room.

CIRCULAR SAW

Needs clearance at front only

Daylight from left rear only

Locate in unobstructed working space

At least 6' clearance this side

SHAPER

Keep clear. Have nothing in line that could be damaged by work hurled from machine.

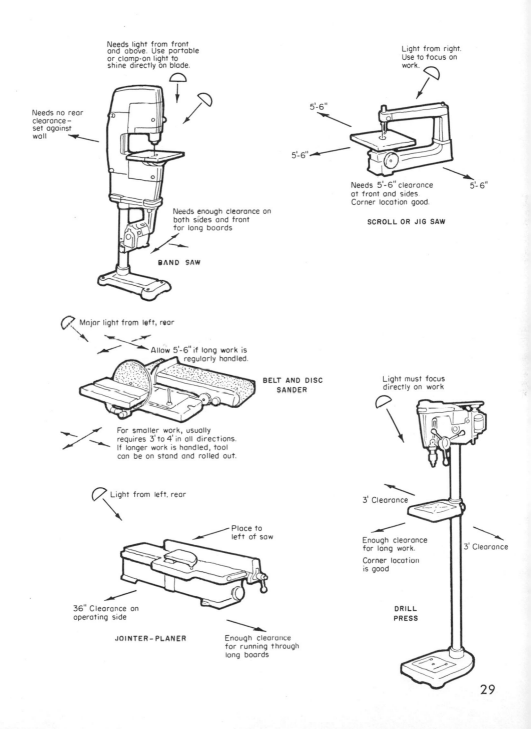

Needs light from front and above. Use portable or clamp-on light to shine directly on blade.

Needs no rear clearance – set against wall

Needs enough clearance on both sides and front for long boards

BAND SAW

Light from right. Use to focus on work.

5'-6"

5'-6"

5'-6"

Needs 5'-6" clearance at front and sides. Corner location good.

SCROLL OR JIG SAW

Major light from left, rear

Allow 5'-6" if long work is regularly handled.

BELT AND DISC SANDER

For smaller work, usually requires 3' to 4' in all directions. If longer work is handled, tool can be on stand and rolled out.

Light from left, rear

Place to left of saw

36" Clearance on operating side

JOINTER-PLANER

Enough clearance for running through long boards

Light must focus directly on work

3' Clearance

Enough clearance for long work.

Corner location is good

3' Clearance

DRILL PRESS

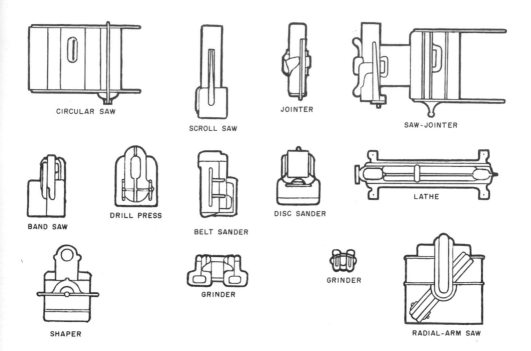

CIRCULAR SAW

SCROLL SAW

JOINTER

SAW-JOINTER

BAND SAW

DRILL PRESS

BELT SANDER

DISC SANDER

LATHE

SHAPER

GRINDER

GRINDER

RADIAL-ARM SAW

These symbols, drawn on a scale of ¼″ to a foot, are the approximate size of power tools you now have or will want for your shop. Trace over them and make handy cutouts to help you visualize various shop layouts. Arrange your cutouts on a plan of your shop site, drawn on a ¼″ to a foot scale and showing the location of windows, posts, stairs, and other permanent features.

make a master plan that will show exactly what is to go into these other areas.

A typical workshop starts small, grows through the years. Every few years it may require reorganization to accommodate new tools, new supplies, and expanded interests. If you are a renter, or on the move, plan your shop for easy disassembly.

To sum up, here are seven rules to follow in planning your shop:

1. Organize each activity with its own work center.
2. Have principal work surfaces the same height.
3. Put large power tools on casters so they can be moved.

4. Provide duplicate hand tools at each place they are needed.
5. Use continuous strip wiring to let you plug in tools anywhere.
6. For safety's sake, provide your shop with adequate lighting.
7. Keep arrangements flexible. Plan for expansion.

3

Workbenches

If there is one indispensable item in a shop it is the bench. You'll spend more time here for most projects and repairs than anywhere else. A shop without a bench is like a kitchen without counter space.

A workbench usually is from 24″ to 30″ wide and from 4′ to 7′ or more long. Height ranges from about 30″ to 34″, depending on how tall you are. The top should be even with your hip joint, to permit you to work without stooping.

A bench should have at least 18″ clearance at each end. If you don't have clearance at an end, you can't work there. If there isn't enough space along one wall for the bench, you can turn the corner with it, but ends should be clear. The corner can have a lazy-susan arrangement under the counter for storage.

Some men prefer to place their bench in the center of the shop, giving access from all four sides. Instead of being confined to a small board above the bench, tools can be stored on the entire wall nearby.

A bench must not become a catch-all for tools. Provide space for storage under the bench top. If drawers or cabinets extend to the floor, you won't have the problem of debris collecting underneath.

Don't attach power tools permanently to the bench top, especially a grinder or machinist's vise. The bench top is actually too high for a grinder. Mount the vise on a 9"-by-9"-by-2" block, and when you need the vise, clamp it in place in your wood vise. You'll also find a wood vise handy for holding a sharpening stone. The stone should be mounted in a wood block to protect it from breaking.

Be sure your bench is level lengthwise and crosswise. Your floor may not be level and adjustments may have to be made in the length of the bench legs to compensate for it.

For convenience, provide enough electrical outlets at the bench so that you don't have to string extension cords. The tangle of power-tool cords can also be avoided by using an overhead cord system.

Steel-framed workbench can be purchased in parts and assembled at home. The top is of tough compressed board; the back panel holds an assortment of hand tools. *Courtesy Hirsh Mfg. Co.*

Somewhere on the bench nail a yardstick with a stop at its end. It comes in handy for measuring and marking boards for rough cutting.

There are good inexpensive benches you can buy. A sturdy steel-framed bench made by S. A. Hirsh Mfg. Co. has a 24″-by-48″ top of 1″ compressed board. It has a perforated back panel with a double-tier tool rack, a drawer, and a bottom shelf. The bench comes disassembled and can be assembled at home.

A somewhat more expensive bench is available from Sears, Roebuck Co. It has a 48″-by-60″ top and an all-steel frame, five drawers on one side, a lockable door concealing two shelves on the other. The top is hardboard-covered flakeboard. For a little extra you can get the bench with a power strip which has three sets of outlets, plus switches, safety lights, and a fuse.

Haunt the house-wreckers' yards and secondhand shops if you want to pick up the makings of a bargain bench. Old desks and chests need only the addition of a more durable and spacious top to become a workbench with an array of ready-made drawers.

In the following section are plans for building several practical workbenches, from a simple model that can be constructed in a couple of hours, to more elaborate types that will challenge your skill and provide you with a complete work center when you have finished.

FIVE WORKBENCHES
YOU CAN BUILD

1. Beginner's Workbench
2. Lock-Up Workbench
3. Power-Tool Workbench
4. 4-Way Workbench
5. Living-Room Workbench

BEGINNER'S WORKBENCH

This simple bench can be built in a short time with only hand tools and will serve as a solid and durable work surface in a small shop. The frame is made of 2-by-4s; the top and shelf of ¾" plywood; and the back and sides of ¼" ply. The plywood gives maximum rigidity to the frame. For details on building the tool rack see Chapter 5. *Courtesy American Plywood Assoc.*

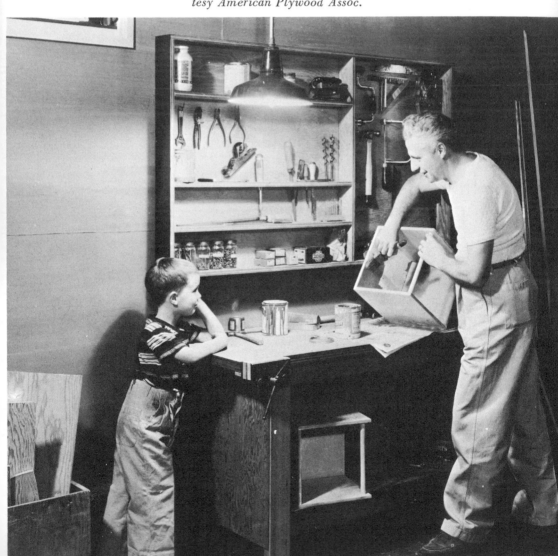

Plans for Building
the Beginner's Workbench

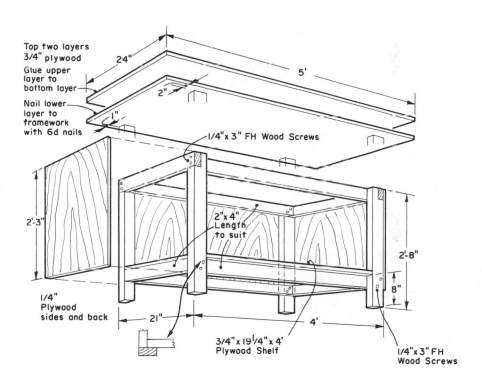

Top two layers 3/4" plywood

Glue upper layer to bottom layer

Nail lower layer to framework with 6d nails

24"

5'

2"

1"

1/4"x 3" FH Wood Screws

2'-3"

2"x 4" Length to suit

2'-8"

8"

1/4" Plywood sides and back

21"

4'

3/4"x 19 1/4"x 4' Plywood Shelf

1/4"x 3" FH Wood Screws

3/4" Plywood, BD Cutting Diagram

Shelf

Top

Top

First step in building the bench is to draw cutting diagrams on ¾″ and ¼″ plywood panels using a straightedge and square. Then mark the pieces (sides, back, etc.) and cut them out, allowing for saw kerfs.

Cut all 2-by-4s, notching one end of each leg; drill screw holes; and assemble the two end frames with glue and screws. Countersink screw holes for best results.

Nail and glue the side panel to one end frame, then join the two end frames with long 2-by-4s, using glue and screws. Other side panel goes on after shelf's in place.

Insert lower shelf through open end frame and glue and nail it in place. Then glue and nail lower top panel to the top rails. Glue the top panel to the lower panel and keep under pressure until dry. This eliminates screws or nails in the bench top and gives a smooth finish.

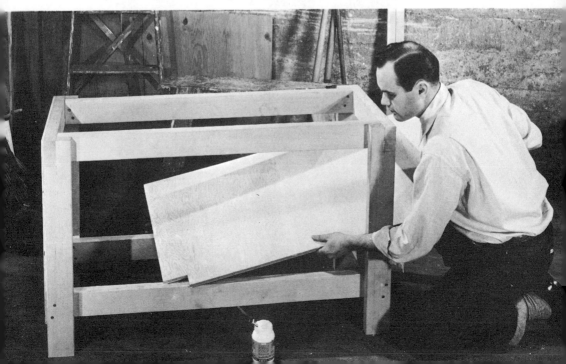

LOCK-UP
WORKBENCH

This workbench allows you to keep tools locked behind sliding doors, protected against rust and the curious hands of children. The ¾″ plywood side panels support a husky top of glued-up 1¾″ hardwood strips. Fluorescent lamps behind the valance supply excellent illumination, and an outlet strip along the front of the bench provides connections for power tools at point of use. In this version, a pullout storage shelf for portable power tools was installed in one bottom cabinet; the other was left open for storage.

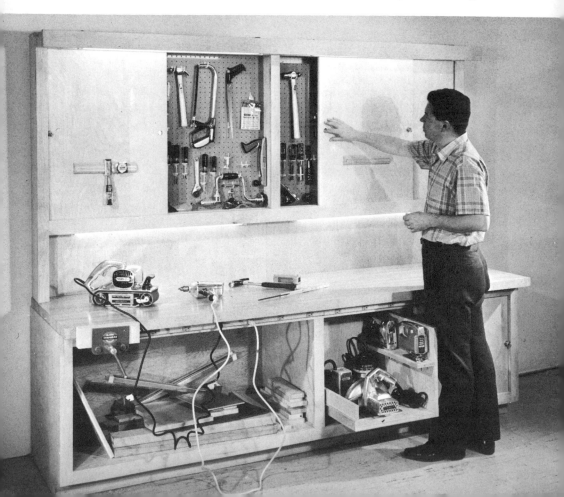

Plans for Building
the Lock-up Workbench

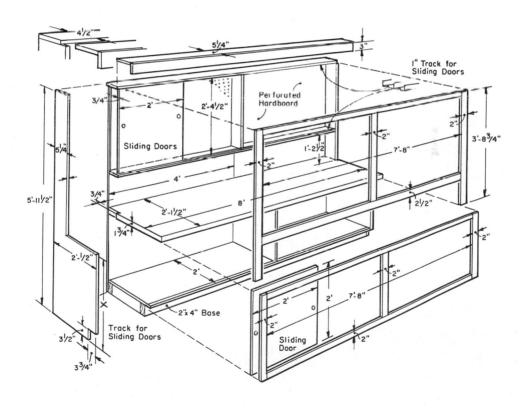

Measurement "X" on the side panels is optional, depending on the height of the user.

POWER-TOOL
WORKBENCH

Here's a workbench designed especially for hand power tools. The tools are stored in a locked cabinet, and are equipped with quick-disconnect fittings which plug into a single overhead cord that winds up when not in use. The unit features a 4'-long stand-up bench with tool chest; a smaller work table with a pullout bench for sitting or sawing; and a storage shelf for bulky items.

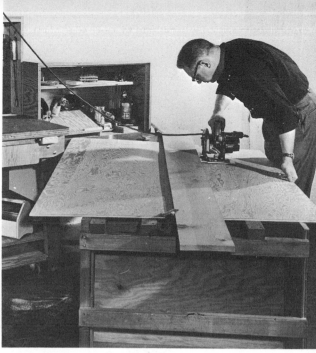

Door of tool cabinet, supported by a hinged leg, serves as a work table (left), the rolling bench as a stool, or a platform for cutting panels (right).

Frame of 2-by-6s is assembled first. After building the two sides, attach the rear rail and the left rear leg; then add the front rail.

Turn the bench upside down after adding the bench top and tool cabinet. This makes it easy to install the drawer runners, lower rear rail, and bottom shelf.

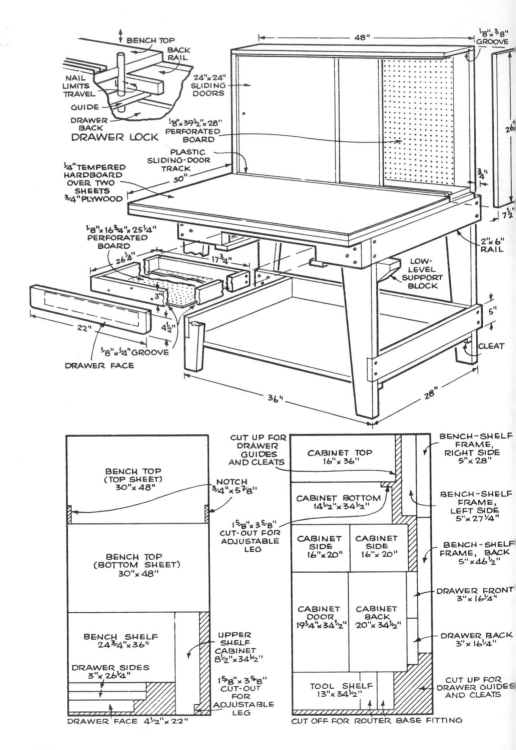

BENCH TOP
BACK RAIL
NAIL LIMITS TRAVEL
GUIDE
DRAWER BACK
DRAWER LOCK

1/8"x39 1/2"x28" PERFORATED BOARD

24"x24" SLIDING DOORS

48"

1/8"x3/8" GROOVE

26"

1/4" TEMPERED HARDBOARD OVER TWO SHEETS 3/4" PLYWOOD

PLASTIC SLIDING-DOOR TRACK

30"

3/4"

7 1/2"

1/8"x16 3/4"x25 1/4" PERFORATED BOARD

26 1/2"

17 3/4"

2"x6" RAIL

LOW-LEVEL SUPPORT BLOCK

3"

22"

4 1/2"

1/8"x1/4" GROOVE

DRAWER FACE

5"

CLEAT

36"

28"

BENCH TOP (TOP SHEET) 30"x48"

CUT UP FOR DRAWER GUIDES AND CLEATS

NOTCH 3/4"x5 7/8"

CABINET TOP 16"x36"

BENCH-SHELF FRAME, RIGHT SIDE 5"x28"

CABINET BOTTOM 14 1/2"x34 1/2"

BENCH-SHELF FRAME, LEFT SIDE 5"x27 1/4"

BENCH TOP (BOTTOM SHEET) 30"x48"

1 5/8"x3 5/8" CUT-OUT FOR ADJUSTABLE LEG

CABINET SIDE 16"x20"

CABINET SIDE 16"x20"

BENCH-SHELF FRAME, BACK 5"x46 1/2"

CABINET DOOR 19 1/4"x34 1/2"

CABINET BACK 20"x34 1/2"

DRAWER FRONT 3"x16 1/4"

BENCH SHELF 24 3/4"x36"

UPPER SHELF CABINET 8 1/2"x34 1/2"

DRAWER SIDES 3"x26 1/4"

1 5/8"x3 5/8" CUT-OUT FOR ADJUSTABLE LEG

DRAWER BACK 3"x16 1/4"

TOOL SHELF 13"x34 1/2"

CUT UP FOR DRAWER GUIDES AND CLEATS

DRAWER FACE 4 1/2"x22"

CUT OFF FOR ROUTER BASE FITTING

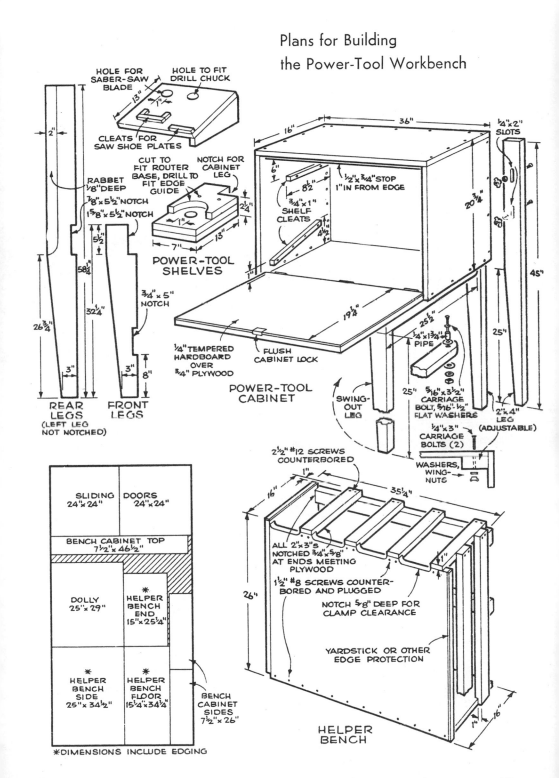

Plans for Building the Power-Tool Workbench

HOLE FOR SABER-SAW BLADE

HOLE TO FIT DRILL CHUCK

CLEATS FOR SAW SHOE PLATES

13"

1"

2"

CUT TO FIT ROUTER BASE, DRILL TO FIT EDGE GUIDE

NOTCH FOR CABINET LEG

2¼"

1"

7"

13"

POWER-TOOL SHELVES

RABBET ⅛" DEEP

⅞" x 5½" NOTCH

1⅝" x 5½" NOTCH

5½"

58¾"

32¼"

¾" x 5" NOTCH

3"

26¾"

3"

8"

REAR LEGS
(LEFT LEG NOT NOTCHED)

FRONT LEGS

16"

36"

6"

8½"

½" x ¾" STOP 1" IN FROM EDGE

¾" x 1" SHELF CLEATS

4½"

20¾"

¼" TEMPERED HARDBOARD OVER ¾" PLYWOOD

FLUSH CABINET LOCK

19¼"

POWER-TOOL CABINET

SWING-OUT LEG

25"

25¼"

¾" x 1¾" PIPE

¼" x ⅜" CARRIAGE BOLT, ⅝" - ½" FLAT WASHERS

¼" x 3" CARRIAGE BOLTS (2)

¼" x 2" SLOTS

45"

25"

2" x 4" LEG (ADJUSTABLE)

WASHERS, WING-NUTS

SLIDING DOORS 24" x 24"

DOORS 24" x 24"

BENCH CABINET TOP 7½" x 46½"

DOLLY 25" x 29"

*HELPER BENCH END 15" x 25¼"

*HELPER BENCH SIDE 25" x 34½"

*HELPER BENCH FLOOR 15¼" x 34¾"

BENCH CABINET SIDES 7½" x 26"

*DIMENSIONS INCLUDE EDGING

2½" #12 SCREWS COUNTERBORED

1"

16"

35¼"

26"

ALL 2" x 3"s NOTCHED ¾" x ⅝" AT ENDS MEETING PLYWOOD

1½" #8 SCREWS COUNTERBORED AND PLUGGED

NOTCH ⅝" DEEP FOR CLAMP CLEARANCE

YARDSTICK OR OTHER EDGE PROTECTION

1"

16"

HELPER BENCH

4-WAY
WORKBENCH

This sleek workbench conceals a couple of surprises. In addition to its ample work surface, it contains a lathe, and a scrap bin that doubles as a bench for sawing and gluing.

Scrap bin with hinged frame-work top makes use of ordinarily wasted space.

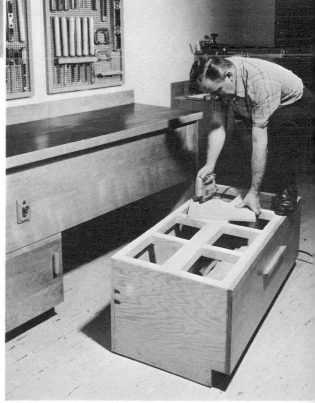

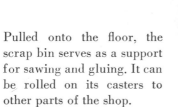

Pulled onto the floor, the scrap bin serves as a support for sawing and gluing. It can be rolled on its casters to other parts of the shop.

48

Hinged bench top swings up, revealing the lathe stored
sideways inside.

Lathe is pulled into position with a sturdy lever. The
hinged platform on which the lathe is mounted swings up,
pushing up rear flap, which then slips under it and acts as
a brace.

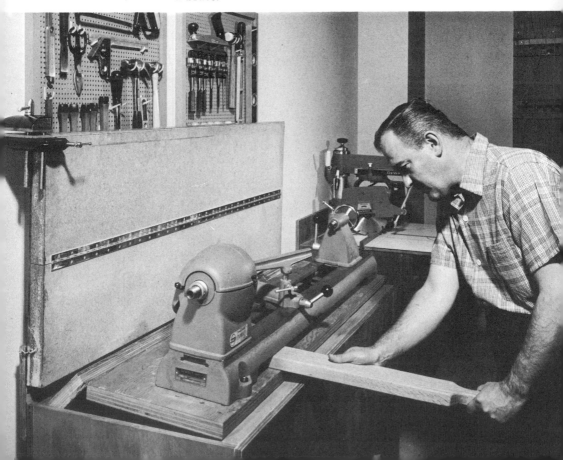

Plans for Building the 4-Way Workbench

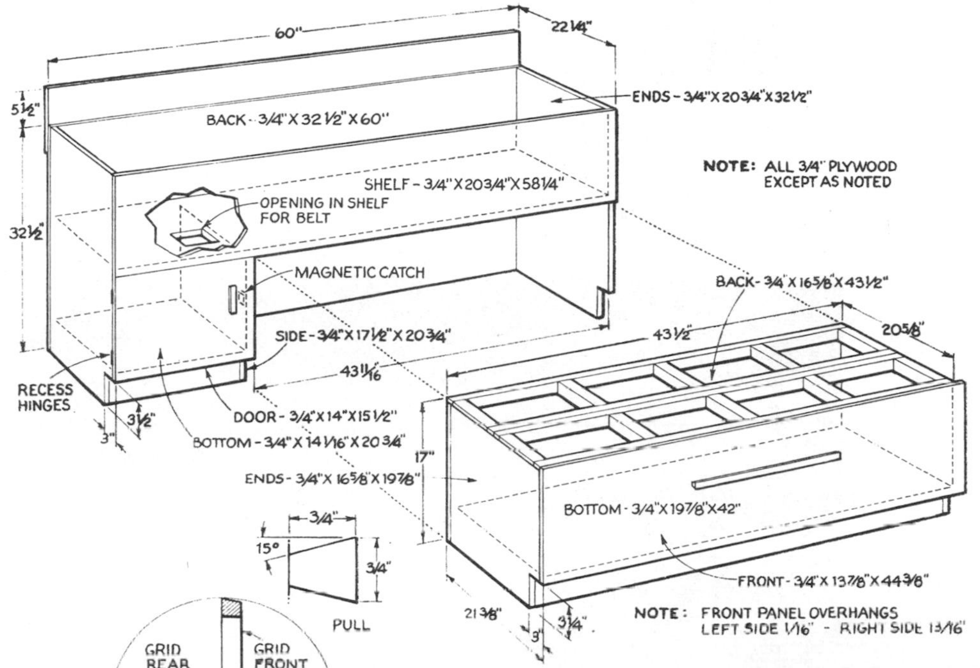
60"
22¼"
5½"
32½"
BACK - 3/4" X 32 1/2" X 60"
ENDS - 3/4" X 20 3/4" X 32 1/2"
SHELF - 3/4" X 20 3/4" X 58 1/4"
OPENING IN SHELF FOR BELT
NOTE: ALL 3/4" PLYWOOD EXCEPT AS NOTED
MAGNETIC CATCH
BACK - 3/4" X 16 5/8" X 43 1/2"
SIDE - 3/4" X 17 1/2" X 20 3/4"
43½"
20⅝"
43 11/16
RECESS HINGES
3½"
3"
DOOR - 3/4" X 14" X 15 1/2"
BOTTOM - 3/4" X 14 1/16" X 20 3/4"
17"
ENDS - 3/4" X 16 5/8" X 19 7/8"
BOTTOM - 3/4" X 19 7/8" X 42"
3/4"
15°
3/4"
PULL
FRONT - 3/4" X 13 7/8" X 44 3/8"
21⅜"
3¼"
3"
NOTE: FRONT PANEL OVERHANGS LEFT SIDE 1/16" - RIGHT SIDE 13/16"

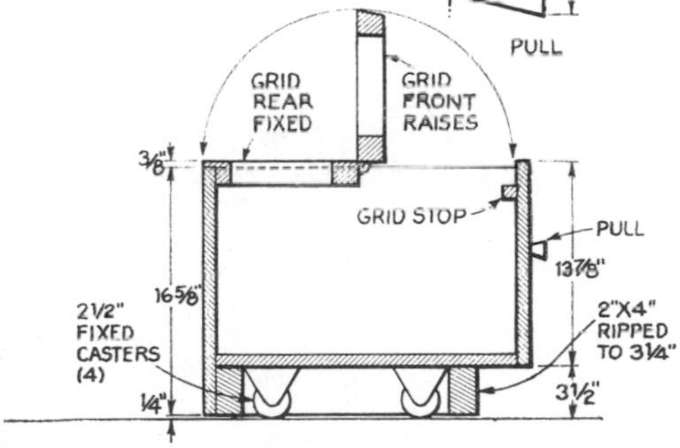
GRID REAR FIXED
GRID FRONT RAISES
3/8"
GRID STOP
PULL
13⅞"
16⅝"
2 1/2" FIXED CASTERS (4)
2"X4" RIPPED TO 3¼"
1¼"
3½"

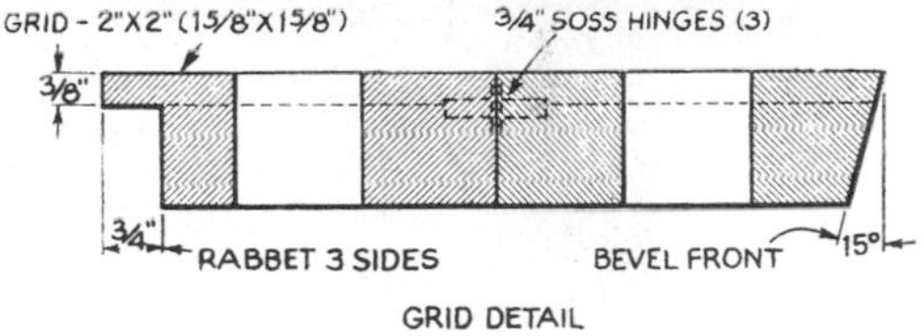
GRID - 2"X2" (1 5/8"X1 5/8")
3/4" SOSS HINGES (3)
3/8"
3/4"
RABBET 3 SIDES
BEVEL FRONT
15°
GRID DETAIL

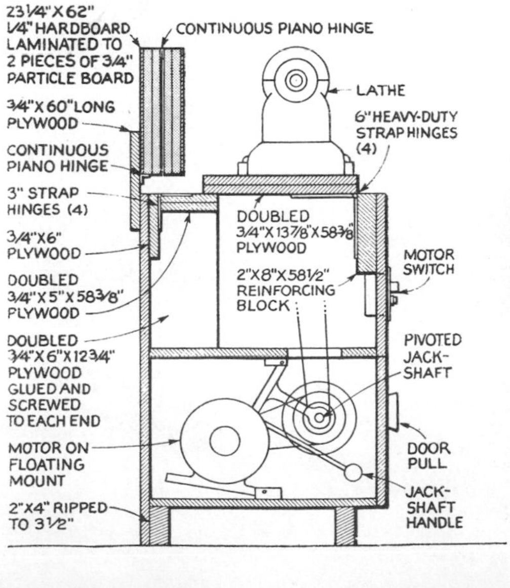
23 1/4"X62" 1/4" HARDBOARD LAMINATED TO 2 PIECES OF 3/4" PARTICLE BOARD
CONTINUOUS PIANO HINGE
LATHE
3/4"X60" LONG PLYWOOD
6" HEAVY-DUTY STRAP HINGES (4)
CONTINUOUS PIANO HINGE
3" STRAP HINGES (4)
DOUBLED 3/4"X13 7/8"X58 3/8" PLYWOOD
3/4"X6" PLYWOOD
MOTOR SWITCH
DOUBLED 3/4"X5"X58 3/8" PLYWOOD
2"X8"X58 1/2" REINFORCING BLOCK
DOUBLED 3/4"X6"X12 3/4" PLYWOOD GLUED AND SCREWED TO EACH END
PIVOTED JACK-SHAFT
MOTOR ON FLOATING MOUNT
DOOR PULL
2"X4" RIPPED TO 3 1/2"
JACK-SHAFT HANDLE

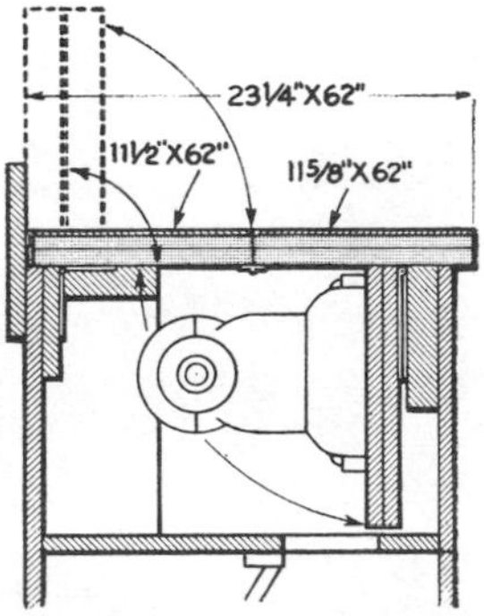
23 1/4"X62"
11 1/2"X62"
11 5/8"X62"

LIVING-ROOM
WORKBENCH

Handsome cabinet looks like a respectable piece of furniture, but it's actually a complete workshop. Hinged top opens to display ample assortment of hand tools (right).

Narrow panel on front of
cabinet hinges up and work
table slides out, supported by
screw-on legs that are stored
in the interior. The inner
sides of the cabinet doors
hold bits, blades, sandpaper,
and fastenings.

With doors open, a drawer on heavy-duty slides pulls out. It holds planes, hand brace, clamps, metal cutters, etc.

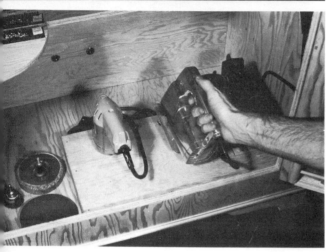

Portable power tools fit into holes cut in a ½" plywood shelf at the front of the cabinet bottom.

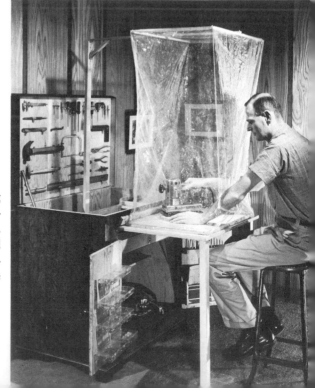

Frame holds plastic sheeting over workbench for controlling sawdust when sanding. Holes in plastic reinforced with masking tape provide access for hands and electric cord from power sander.

52

Plans for Building
the Living-Room Workbench

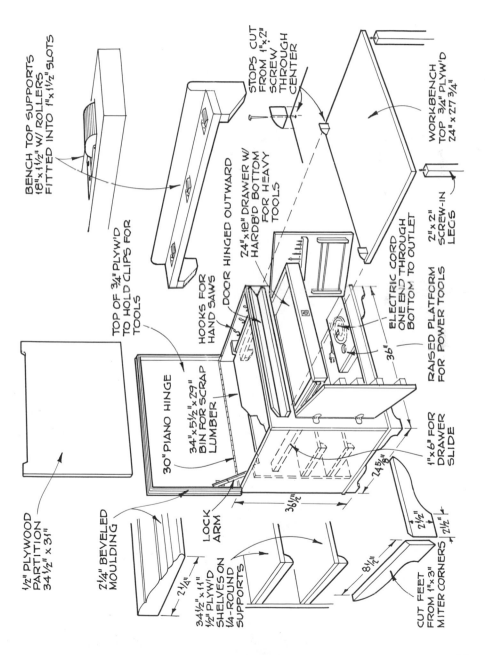

BENCH TOP SUPPORTS
18"x1½" W/ ROLLERS
FITTED INTO 1"x1½" SLOTS

TOP OF ¾" PLYW'D
TO HOLD CLIPS FOR
TOOLS

STOPS CUT
FROM 1"x2"
SCREW
THROUGH
CENTER

24"x18" DRAWER W/
HARDB'D BOTTOM
FOR HEAVY
TOOLS

DOOR HINGED OUTWARD

HOOKS FOR HAND SAWS

WORKBENCH
TOP ¾" PLYW'D
24" x 27 ¾"

2"x2" SCREW-IN
LEGS

ELECTRIC CORD
ONE END THROUGH
BOTTOM TO OUTLET

RAISED PLATFORM
FOR POWER TOOLS

36"

1"x6" FOR
DRAWER
SLIDE

30" PIANO HINGE

34"x5½" x 29"
BIN FOR SCRAP
LUMBER

½" PLYWOOD
PARTITION
34½" x 31"

2¼" BEVELED
MOULDING

LOCK
ARM

34½" x 11"
½" PLYW'D
SHELVES ON
¼-ROUND
SUPPORTS

CUT FEET
FROM 1"x3"
MITER CORNERS

2¼"

36½"

24⅝"

2½"

2½"

8½"

4 | Shop Construction

WORKSHOP WALLS. All basements and many garages are of masonry construction. If these areas are used for a shop, their walls require special treatment to keep them from getting damp and cold. Basement walls may get damp because of seepage from outside, or because of moisture condensation on their cool surface during hot, humid weather.

If seepage is from outside, first check to see that rainfall is diverted away from the walls. If the ground does not slope away from the walls, regrade so that it does. Lead the water from downspouts away from the house, either to storm sewers or to sloping runoff areas.

After heavy rainstorms, check for points where water is entering and mark them with a grease pencil. The most frequent point of entry is a crack where walls meet floor. Squeegee or sponge-mop water away to create a dry spot; then you can trace the location of the leak.

Cracks and holes through which water is entering can be immediately plugged with hydraulic cement. Follow the manufacturer's directions. Regular patcher is easier to use. If you can wait until walls dry out, you'll do a more satisfactory job.

Block walls are porous. To seal them against seepage, after active holes and cracks have been plugged, coat walls with at least two coats of scrubbed-in powder-type block filler and sealer. Special brushes are available for the purpose. The kind with a handle is easiest to use. Follow manufacturer's instructions. A tank-type garden sprayer is good for fogging the walls with moisture. Walls should be damp but not wet.

When basement walls and floors are subjected to water under pressure, the pressure can be relieved and the basement secured against flooding by the installation of an automatic sump pump. To install a pump, first recess into the floor a section of clay sewer pipe 16″ to 24″ in diameter and 2′ to 4′ long. The pump is set into this pit. Install a pipe from the pump to take the discharge from this sump either to a point of runoff outside the house or to a sewer. If the pipe is connected to the sewer, a check valve must be used to prevent backflow. The pump, plugged into an ordinary electrical outlet, will come on automatically whenever the water level rises in the sump. In some cases it is necessary to jackhammer trenches in the floor around the wall perimeter, and crossing the floor, and install drain tiles leading to the sump.

Masonry walls tend to be cold. Your body radiates heat to these cold surfaces and you feel chilled even though the air temperature may register 72 degrees. To avoid this radiant-heat loss, warm up basement walls by covering them with paneling, either boards or sheet material.

Basements that are subjected to water under pressure can be made safe and dry by installing a sump pump. Plugged into an ordinary electric outlet, the pump will come on automatically whenever the water level rises in the sump.

Some manufacturers recommend vertical furring strips for attaching paneling, others horizontal. Furring can be attached to masonry walls with special adhesive, and panels attached to the furring with the same adhesive. Tapping panels with a padded block insures adhesion.

Paneling pointers.　Paneling is applied over 1″-by-2″ furring strips which can be attached to masonry with a special adhesive available at your building supply dealer. They can be fastened to block walls by driving spiral nails into mortar joints, but do this only where there is no danger that nail holes will cause leakage.

Place furring strips horizontally, 16″ apart, measured from the center of one strip to the center of the next. When using 4′-by-8′ panels, also apply furring strips 48″ on centers vertically to correspond to panel joints. Allow ¼″ space where vertical and horizontal furring strips meet. If walls are uneven, level out furring strips by placing flat wood wedges at low spots. Pieces of cedar shingles are ideal for the purpose.

Before applying paneling, staple vapor-barrier paper or polyethylene film over the furring strips to prevent moisture from penetrating.

Sheet material can be applied to the furring strips with adhesive, or can be nailed. All four edges of each panel should be attached to the furring. There should be no "floating" edges.

Start paneling in a corner of the room. To achieve a perfect fit at out-of-plumb corners and around projections, place the panel in position and with a pair of compasses scribe

In some cases, as in a garage, it may be desirable to insulate masonry before applying paneling. Use 2"-by-2" furring strips to allow for thickness of insulation.

a line from the top of the panel to the bottom, with one leg of the compass following the wall and the other on the panel. Cut along the line with a coping or saber saw. To get a neat fit where panels intersect, bevel their edges slightly toward the rear with a plane.

When applying tongue-and-groove board paneling, start at a corner after scribing and face-nail the board at top and bottom. Use galvanized finishing nails 1½" long. The tongue of the board should be facing away from the corner. Subsequent boards are nailed at an angle through the tongues. Continually check the plumb of boards as you nail. Stop the paneling ¼" short of floor and ceiling to allow ventilation from behind. Where humidity conditions are excessive and

These 16"-wide Marlite planks have tongue-and-groove joints which conceal all fastenings.

Tongue-and-groove boards provide an inexpensive and attractive finish to a basement shop. Here the boards are being nailed to studs set on 24″ centers, and nailed to each other at an angle through the tongues.

there is a possibility of condensation on walls even after paneling is applied, install midget louvers every 6″ along the floor and ceiling.

Basement walls may be covered with gypsum wallboard if it is the kind that is backed with foil. The foil prevents vapor from penetrating the wallboard.

In some cases, 2″-by-3″ studs are a more desirable support than furring strips for paneling. If walls are irregular, studs are much easier to plumb. They also make it easier to frame around pipes and other obstructions. There is more space behind a stud wall in which to place wiring. A stud wall need be fastened at only the floor and the ceiling joists overhead. If joists run parallel to the wall, bridge the space in between with a 2-by-3 every 4′. Anchor the floor 2-by-3s with concrete nails. If the concrete is too hard to nail into, use lead anchors set in ¼″ holes about 1½″ deep, or use adhesive. Sight along studs to be sure they are straight before you put them in the wall. If they are crooked, discard them, or use them where it doesn't matter. A bowed stud means a bowed wall.

Frame around water, gas, and electric meters, but when you apply paneling, provide small doors for access. If there is a shut-off on a pipe, provide either a small door or a sliding panel.

Partitions.   There are advantages in dividing a basement. You may wish to use only part of the basement for the shop. Dividing helps keep noise and dust from spreading. And it makes it easier to lock the shop, a safety factor where children are concerned.

If you are taking half of a double garage as a shop, partitioning will make the shop area easier to insulate and give it more wall space. When partitioning an attic, you don't have to finish all of it if you only need part for your shop.

In many cases, because a partition wall is self-supporting, a minimum of framework is required. If you use V-joint tongue-and-groove boards, usually 1″-by-6″ in size, and install them vertically, you need 2″-by-4″ studs no closer than on 12′ centers. Boards are nailed to a 2″-by-4″ plate attached to the floor with adhesive, and to a 2-by-4 nailed to the ceiling joists. If the partition runs parallel to the ceiling joists, locate it directly under one of them.

To determine how many square feet of boarding you need for your partition, calculate the wall area and then add 25 percent. If the wall is to receive paint or stain, apply it before boards are nailed in place. Then when they dry out and shrink,

Partitioning a basement or attic can provide room for a workshop. Partition studs are placed on 16″ centers and nailed to 2-by-4s at floor and ceiling (right).

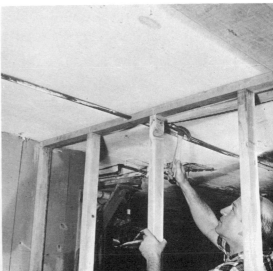

Perforated hardboard is an excellent material for creating partitions in shops, and may be applied on only one side of a stud wall. When nailing panels to studs (below) use spacers so holes over stud are saved for hanging tools.

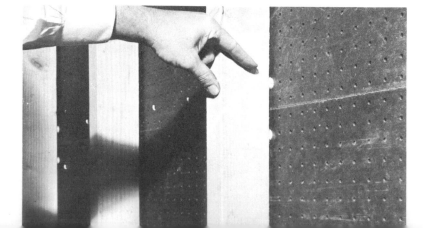

you won't have raw wood showing where the tongues become exposed.

If boards cut off necessary light and air, make your partition of metal mesh. This low-cost material comes in rolls 24" wide and 50' long, galvanized or coated with colorful plastic.

Perforated hardboard, commonly known as Peg-Board, is a most popular wall and partition material for shops. In applying it, use fiber spacers to offset the panels ¼" from the surface. Otherwise holes for hooks and other fixtures will be blocked.

A 4'-by-8' panel of hardboard will expand 3/16" across its width and 3/8" in length. Keep the panels where they are to be used for a few days and they'll expand to the normal moisture content of the area. To take care of additional expansion you need leave only about 1/16" space between panels and at sides.

Hardboard is available in prefinished attractive colors. You can use solid hardboard panels in some areas and matching perforated ones in others. Hardboard, in both the 1/8" and ¼" thicknesses, makes good sliding door panels for cabinets. You can get tracks for these panels at your lumberyard.

In an attic, build the walls under the sloping roof far enough out so that they are at least 4'6" high. The space under the eaves can be used for storage. This is a good place for sliding-door cabinets.

In finishing off the attic, don't obstruct eave louvers that provide ventilation. If you install a flat ceiling under the roof peak, there should be a ventilating louver at each gable end.

Attic partition walls should be built of 2"-by-4" studs on 16" centers. Studs are nailed to a 2"-by-4" sill set flat on the floor and to a 2"-by-4" cap at the ceiling level. Use double studs on either side of a door opening.

Plasterboard, also known as gypsum wallboard, is one of the least expensive raw materials. Get the ½" size for maximum rigidity and sound control. For top noise absorption, you can install sound-deadening board as a base for it. This board is ½" thick and comes in 4'-by-8' panels. For best results, wallboard should be attached with adhesive to the sound-deadening board.

Gypsum wallboard is available surfaced with vinyl in a choice of colors. It can be cleaned with soap and water. It can be cemented in place or nailed with color-matching nails.

Where added thermal insulation is a critical factor, use insulation board as a wall-covering material. It comes in 4′-by-8′ panels, either ⅜″ or ½″ thick. Where fire control is paramount, use asbestos cementboard panels. These 4′-by-8′ panels come in ⅛″, ³⁄₁₆″, and ¼″ thickness.

CEILINGS.   The best kind of ceiling in a basement is a suspended one. It is also the easiest to put up. As a special advantage, it gives you access to any plumbing pipes and heating ducts that may be covered.

In a typical installation, you just nail or screw wall angles around the perimeter of the shop space at the height you want the new ceiling. Usually you must allow at least 3″ between the framework and the lowest part of the old ceiling so that you can insert panels. But you can get one variety that installs without any appreciable loss of headroom.

In addition to the perimeter angles, other supports are hung 2′ apart at right angles to the joists. Crosspieces between these supports complete the framework. You lay the panels on the framework and the job is done.

Ceiling panels are 2′-by-2′ or 2′-by-4′ in size and have a variety of surface finishes, usually vinyl. Generally made of fiberglass or other acoustical material, the panels don't prevent sound from going through to the floor above, but they do keep most of the sounds that strike their surface from bouncing back at you.

In a suspended ceiling, you can combine translucent panels with the acoustical ones and install lights behind them. Used with fluorescent fixtures, the translucent panels diffuse the light and reduce glare. They come in a variety of styles. Some are white vinyl with prism or grid designs; others are of polystyrene.

Suspended ceiling is an excellent overhead finish for a basement shop. Metal supports are fastened around the perimeter of the basement wall; then cross supports are suspended by wire from screw-eyes in the joists.

Lightweight 2'-by-4' ceiling panels are simply laid in place in the metal grids. They are easily removed for access to concealed plumbing, heating, and wiring.

If there is no headroom to spare in the basement, an acoustical ceiling can be applied to 1″-by-2″ furring strips nailed to the joists. It's important that furring strips be straight, not wavy. Wedge-shaped pieces of shingle driven under strips can remedy irregularities. The tiles are attached to furring strips with a staple gun (right).

For nonsuspended ceilings, you can get acoustical tiles in 12″ and 16″ squares. These can be applied by stapling to furring strips. You can borrow a stapler where you buy the tiles.

For stapling tiles to a gypsum wallboard ceiling there are special "piggy-back" staples. The first staple toes in, the piggy-back staple flares out, providing needed holding power.

You can also install tiles by slipping them, without nailing or stapling, into special angled metal strips that you attach to joists or an existing ceiling.

FLOORS.   A concrete floor in a garage or basement is a durable shop surface, but it is strictly utilitarian. You can make it more attractive with paint or tile.

Before painting a floor, it must be cleaned. First, use latex concrete patcher to repair any holes or cracks. Then, clean and degrease the floor with trisodium phosphate or any other cleaner made specifically for concrete.

If the floor has a hard fiinish, to achieve a good bond it may be necessary to etch it. Muriatic acid is a good etching solution. First, scrub the surface with a solution of 1 part concentrated muriatic acid and 3 parts water, using a stiff fiber brush. (*Caution:* Muriatic acid is corrosive. Mix in a glass or polyethylene container, wear rubber gloves when applying it, and don't spatter on clothes or furniture.)

Allow about 1 gallon of solution to each 100 square feet of surface. Let it remain until all bubbling stops and then flush it off thoroughly with plain water. If the surface has not dried uniformly within a few hours it means that some of the acid still remains, so flush it again.

The floor will dry in several hours, depending upon the porosity of the surface, or it may take a day or more. As soon as it is completely dry, you can paint it.

Use a paint specially made for concrete. Some of the best are latex paints. Easiest application is with a 9″ floor roller with a 40″ handle.

Water can rise through cracks in a basement floor. First step in repairing the leak is to chisel out the cracks to a depth of ½".

Patch the chiseled-out crack with cement mixed with latex. Follow the manufacturer's directions for mixing patching material.

Most common point where water enters is at the joint between floor and wall. Chisel out the weak mortar and apply patching compound.

The toughest finish for concrete is epoxy enamel. It is expensive but long-lasting. Whichever floor finish you use, follow the manufacturer's directions exactly.

Halfway between a paint and a tile is seamless floor covering made of a clear acrylic or urethane plastic in which colorful plastic or metal chips are suspended. It is applied over a base coat that goes on like paint. On this base coat, the plastic is applied. While the plastic is wet, color chips are spread over its surface. Another coat of plastic goes over the top of the flakes and then a final finish coat. The result is a floor that never needs waxing, and because it has no dirt-catching cracks is extremely easy to maintain.

To provide a smooth base for a tile floor in an attic, nail 4'-by-4' underlayment panels to the rough subfloor with cement-coated nails.

The best kind of tile floor for a shop, whether it goes over concrete or wood, is vinyl asbestos tile. It is low in cost, attractive, and easy to maintain. Avoid tile thinner than $\frac{1}{16}''$. The thicker the tile, the less chance floor irregularities will "ghost through."

The best adhesive for vinyl asbestos tile rolls on and dries clear. Another variety dries black. It is less expensive, but there is a problem of black smudges. For installing vinyl asbestos tile over a radiant-heated floor, there is a special vinyl adhesive. When installing tile over strip wood floors, duplex lining felt is laid first. It has its own special adhesive.

Good system for installing floor tiles is to divide a room into approximate quarters by snapping chalk lines at right angles to each other. A "dry run" placement of tiles will show you where to place lines to minimize cutting.

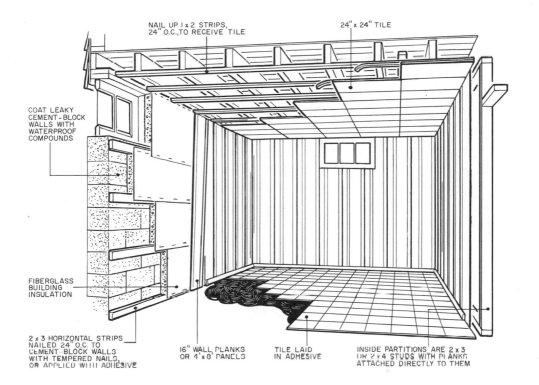

NAIL UP 1 x 2 STRIPS, 24" O.C.,TO RECEIVE TILE

24" x 24" TILE

COAT LEAKY CEMENT-BLOCK WALLS WITH WATERPROOF COMPOUNDS

FIBERGLASS BUILDING INSULATION

2 x 3 HORIZONTAL STRIPS NAILED 24" O.C. TO CEMENT-BLOCK WALLS WITH TEMPERED NAILS OR APPLIED WITH ADHESIVE

16" WALL PLANKS OR 4'x8' PANELS

TILE LAID IN ADHESIVE

INSIDE PARTITIONS ARE 2 x 3 OR 2 x 4 STUDS WITH PLANKS ATTACHED DIRECTLY TO THEM

All the components for finishing a basement are included in this drawing. Horizontal strips of 2-by-3s are used here as backing for fiberglass insulation and wood paneling. Acoustical ceiling tiles are stapled to 1"-by-2" strips; the floor tiles are laid in adhesive. One wall is a partition framed of studs and covered with paneling.

To provide a base for tile over an attic subfloor, underlayment panels are required. These come in 4'-by-4' sheets, slightly less than ¼" thick. They are nailed down with cement-coated nails every 6" on lines 6" apart.

In ordering floor tile, allow about 10 percent extra for waste. If the floor is uneven, use special leveling compound available where you buy the tile.

You can buy in kit form everything you need for a tile installation—a disposable roller, an adhesive scoop, a sharp cutting knife, and a 25' chalk line.

STAIRS.   Direct access from the shop to outdoors is invaluable. You don't have to go through the house to get to the shop, and moving lumber and other materials is simplified. It is especially important in a basement shop.

Creating a new entrance to the basement from outdoors requires digging out the earth at the point the stairway is to be installed and breaking through the masonry basement wall. The excavated well, typically 4′ wide and 5′ long, is lined with walls of masonry block or poured concrete, on a poured

New entrance to a basement shop was created here by digging a well and lining it with poured concrete. Stair stringer was cut from 2″ lumber, but steel stringers are available which can be nailed to the side walls and fitted with wood treads.

These basement stairs contain ample storage area underneath, closed off by hinged doors of tongue-and-groove knotty pine. Minimum headroom for a stairway is 6′6″.

Installing a disappearing stairway in an attic requires cutting joists to make an opening. Joists must then be reinforced by a header nailed to the ends and those at sides.

If there is sufficient headroom in the attic, you can make your own disappearing stairway. Counterweight makes it easy to move stairway up and down in sliding track of 2-by-2s (below). Stringers and treads are cut from 2-by-8s.

concrete base a minimum of 3½″ thick. If the well is to be covered by an all-steel door, make it a size that will fit the units available in your area. Steel stair-stringers are available which can be nailed to the side walls of the well. Treads of 2″-by-10″ lumber can then be tapped into the stair slots with a hammer. For the entry through the basement wall, you can buy an exterior door frame complete with sill. A door 3′ wide is recommended.

If there are no stairs leading to your attic or the loft above your garage, the simplest solution is a folding stairway. A spring mechanism does most of the work of folding and unfolding. Get the largest size that will fit your available space.

If there is no hatchway to the attic space where the stairway is to be placed, you will have to cut one. This may require cutting one or more joists. Support the cut ends with doubled headers made of the same stock as the joists. Nail the headers securely to joists on each side as well as to the cut-off ends.

INSULATION.   In an attic, or in a frame garage with exposed studding, the easiest kind of insulation to install is a type of fiberglass that requires no stapling. It comes in preformed batts and fits by friction. Push it into the stud spaces and it stays there. Use 3″ thickness in walls, 6″ in ceilings or roof areas.

All insulation requires a vapor barrier on its interior or warm side. With friction-fit fiberglass, use 2-mil polyethylene film. You can get it 8′ wide, which means an almost complete elimination of joints.

In places where batt insulation can't be used, try pour-type fiberglass or vermiculite. You can rake it between attic joists to any depth desired.

On masonry walls in basement or garage you can use urethane panels. Urethane is one of the best insulators known. Apply furring strips at top, bottom, and between the ¾″-thick panels. So that the furring strips can serve as nailers for wall finish applied after the insulation is in place, trim the 4′-by-8′

Preformed bats of fiberglass insulation fit between attic stud space and require no stapling. Ventilation is provided by triangular louver which fits at roof peak where hot air would otherwise collect.

insulation panels 1½″ on one side and end to allow for the width of the furring strips.

BUILDING AN EXTENSION.   An easy kind of shop to build is a lean-to against the house or garage. The existing structure serves as one wall and you have only three to add.

The lean-to should be located on a "non-bearing" wall. This is a wall on which the existing roof rafters do not rest. When you saw an opening in this wall, cut studs so that you can bridge the opening with a 4″-by-8″ header (two 2-by-8s spiked together). This header will serve as a base for the 2-by-4s that

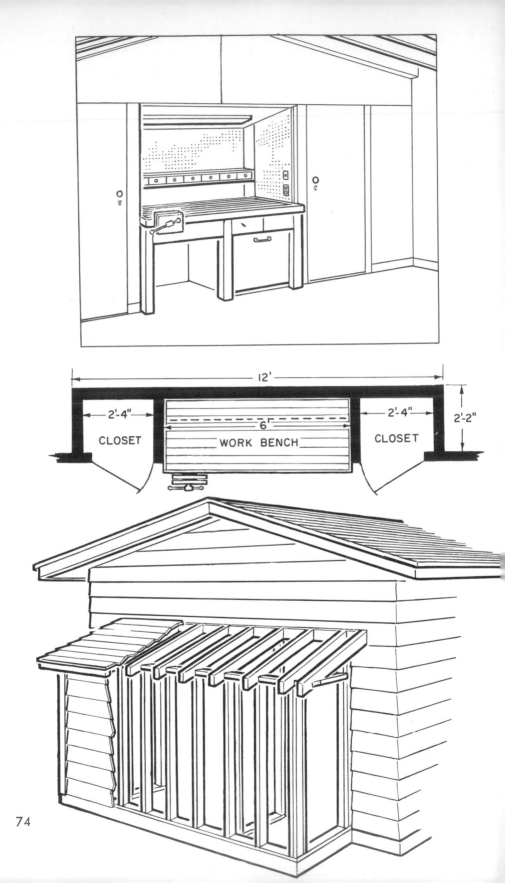

12'

2'-4" CLOSET

6

WORK BENCH

2'-4" CLOSET

2'-2"

go the rest of the way to the roof and also as a nailing base for the 2″-by-4″ rafters of the lean-to. Use triple studs as support at the header ends.

Because the lean-to is light in weight, its foundation can be minimal. It can be a concrete slab poured in a securely staked 2″-by-4″ form over a 6″-deep bed of coarse gravel for drainage. In cases where the garage floor is above grade, it may be necessary to prepare a supporting foundation wall to match that of the existing structure.

In attaching the lean-to, first remove shingles, clapboard or other exterior finish from the existing structure. Do it carefully; you may be able to salvage much of it for use on the new addition. Frame the structure with 2-by-4s on 16″ centers. Notch the 2″-by-4″ rafters where they cross the 2″-by-4″ cap that tops the stud wall. Where the rafters attach to the existing structure, they should rest on a 2″-by-3″ ledger strip nailed to the bottom of the 4″-by-8″ header which bridges the opening. Nail the rafters to the header.

You can enclose the structure with ⅜″ plywood sheathing. Finish sidewalls and roof to match the existing structure. Before applying roofing, flash joints between roof and wall with aluminum or copper sheet to seal out the weather.

Example of an extension lean-to built on the non-bearing wall of a garage to allow for a workbench and closets.

5 | Storage: Walls / Shelves

PERFORATED HARDBOARD. The most commonly used system for storing tools is to hang them on walls of perforated hardboard. A variety of special hooks and hanging devices are available that fit in the perforations. For average service, ⅛″ hardboard is satisfactory, but for hanging heavy items like sledges, chain saws, and shelves, ¼″ panels are recommended. Panels are available prefinished in a number of attractive colors.

Most hanging devices are of metal or plastic. Many of the metal hangers require special stabilizers so they won't pull out of the holes every time you unhook a tool. But even with stabilizers, devices tend to pull out of holes. Plastic devices hold fairly well without stabilizers but are apt to break, especially if moved from one set of holes to another.

Don't skimp on hangers. If you don't have the right types, or enough of them, you can't make efficient use of the available storage space. Often, after removing a tool, there may be some doubt as to which hanger it belongs on. For this reason, it is often helpful to label tool locations or to draw outlines of the tools on the storage board.

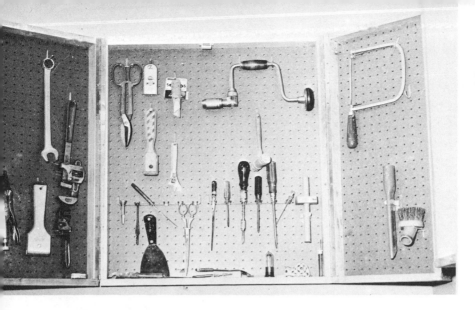

Perforated hardboard is ideal for hanging hand tools over a workbench. Here a hinged cabinet backed with the material keeps a variety of tools within reach but when closed protects them from dust and rust.

This garage was paneled with perforated hardboard, and garden tools and paint supplies neatly stored on hangers and shelves. For heavy tools like these, ¼″ board should be used. Light hand tools can be hung on ⅛″ board.

Special hangers are available for hanging all kinds of items on perforated hardboard. These shelf hangers support heavy paint cans and even lengths of lumber.

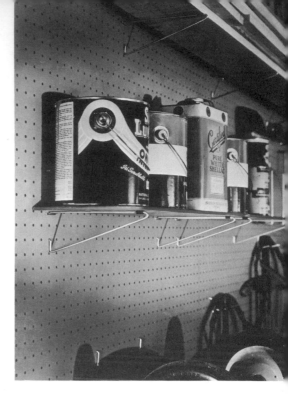

Space that might otherwise be wasted at the end of a workbench can be used for tool storage by installing a panel of perforated hardboard. A door backed with same material doubles the storage area and keeps tools clean.

Here a panel is mounted on the side of a table saw to hang saw blades, tools, and accessories needed in this area.

Holes drilled so close to the edge of a plywood strip that they break through the front make convenient hangers for handled tools on this perforated hardboard storage wall.

79

Perforated storage panels can go places other than walls. They can line the inside of cabinets, several can be set in a series of slots and individual panels pulled out for tool access, or they can be framed and hinged so they can be opened like the pages of a book. The hinging arrangement makes it possible to hang several layers of tools on one wall space.

When perforated panels are set flat against the wall, they should be offset sufficiently so that hooks can be inserted through the holes.

SOLID STORAGE WALLS.   Walls of ¼″ plywood, or of tongue-and-groove boards, make a superior surface for hanging tools, especially with screw-in devices. Large clothesline hooks can handle big, heavy tools and equipment. Cup hooks can manage smaller items. To hang an electric drill from a cup hook, tighten a screw eye in its chuck.

In this shop, walls of solid board paneling serve as a complete tool storage area. By using a variety of screw-in devices and wooden racks, the shop owner was able to hang his hand tools in a neat and convenient arrangement.

Wooden blocks shaped to fit the handles or frames of saws serve as efficient hanging devices on this storage wall. L-screws and broom clamps are also good hangers.

On a plaster wall, scrap pieces of plywood provide the necessary backing for attaching hanging devices. Broom clamps and dowels on the plywood are used effectively to store handsaws.

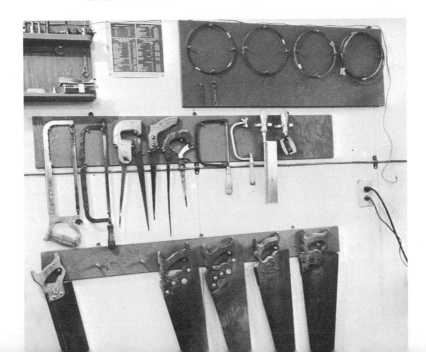

This paneled wall of Ponderosa pine deserved a set of elegant hangers. Strips of $\frac{5}{4}''$ sugar pine were dadoed and doweled to accept hand tools.

Clothesline hooks come as screw-in or plate-and-screw types. Other available hooks include clothes hooks, steel hooks that screw in, utility hangers, and hammock sets (in which hooks are set on a swivel).

As an aid in hanging items, you can get handle holders commonly used for hanging brooms. They can be tapped on with a hammer; some types attach with only adhesive. Swing-out racks and dryers, commonly used in bathrooms and kitchens, are other useful storage devices which are easily attached to a wood wall.

Wood blocks, custom-shaped to fit saws, pliers, snips, scrapers, nail pullers, and a variety of other tools also make highly satisfactory hanging devices on wood walls. Saw hangers should have a turnbuckle arrangment so the saw won't slip off. This is especially important when a saw is mounted on a door.

Old garden hose cut in short pieces and attached vertically is good for small tools like screwdrivers. Cut the hose at an angle and the short lengths are easy to tack up. Use a pair to receive plier handles. For tools too wide to drop through a hose opening, slit the hose down the front.

Attractive hangers that will accommodate many kinds of tools can be made from 2"-by-2" boards slotted at 1½" or 2" intervals. Or similar strips may be drilled to receive screwdrivers, files, pliers, nail sets, etc.

For tools like chisels you can make dado cuts in ¾"-by-2" board, and mount the board so the cuts are against the wall. Dowels set into backing strips at a slight tilt make excellent holders for hammers, snips, etc.

Most men prefer open tool panels for tools that are in frequent use. In planning such storage, provide not only for tools you now have but for others you will acquire in the future.

A window and its frame were utilized to the full as a tool storage area in this shop.

Space under the eaves that would be wasted in this attic shop is filled with a plywood panel on which tools are hung on broom clamps, dowels, and screw-in hooks. Area behind the panel is also used for storage and is closed off by a door.

Magnetic holders made for cutlery are convenient for keeping light tools like putty knives within easy reach on the side of the workbench.

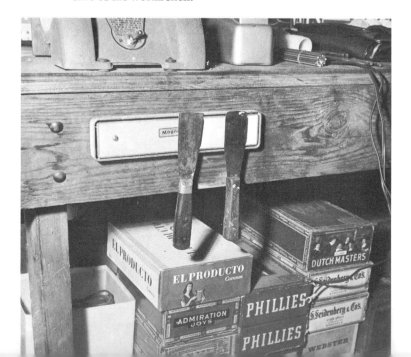

SHELVES.   For many tools and most supplies, shelves are the answer. Shelves can be hung on walls, can serve as room dividers, and can be installed inside and on top of cabinets and under benches. They can go on the back of closet doors, between studs, or be hung from rafters. Most shelves are hung level, but to display tools like chisels and screwdrivers they can be set at a front-to-back slant.

Pine shelving is the most popular for use in a workshop. It's expensive if you buy top grades, but the price plummets when you get down to #3 grade. It comes as wide as nominal 12", which is actually about 11½". This width can be increased slightly by nailing strips on either side. When you do, reinforce the ends of the shelf with a ¾"-by-¾" strip. Where a shelf

Shelves between two beam-supporting posts in a basement shop store tiers of numbered boxes and glass jars. Contents of boxes are listed in an index according to number.

width much greater than 11½″ is desired, a good solution is to use plywood.

Shelves made of ¾″ stock should not span more than 30″. Heavy tools and supplies will make any shelf longer than that sag. To stiffen a shelf board against sagging, glue and nail a 1½″-wide strip to its front edge.

The simplest support for a shelf is a cleat at each end. A cleat along the rear edge gives added strength and support. Cleats can be of ¾″ half-round molding, 1″-by-2″ boards or equivalent. Ends can also be supported by rests of metal or plastic. These rests push-fit into holes drilled in wood side-supports. By providing a vertical series of holes, you can quickly move a shelf to a new position. Shelf rests may fit into vertical metal standards.

Metal standards can also be used to support brackets for shelves. Brackets come in sizes from 6″ to 14″. Tension-pole standards can be set between floor and ceiling for supporting shelves.

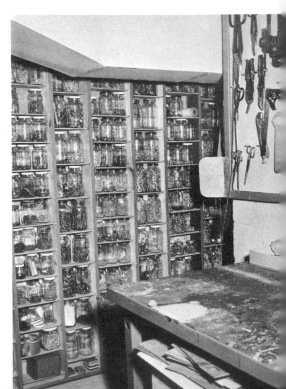

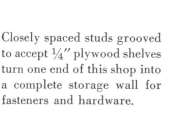

Closely spaced studs grooved to accept ¼″ plywood shelves turn one end of this shop into a complete storage wall for fasteners and hardware.

Cabinet to hold jars for small parts storage has shelves of ⅛″ hardboard supported on quarter-round moldings. Strips across the shelf fronts keep jars from slipping off.

Metal standards with clip supports are available in hardware stores and make shelf installation an easy job.

If a shelf adjoins a window, round off its corner and it won't be an obstruction.

The small parts rack in the shop of Marshall W. Geletee has ten shelves, each with five jars for screws, bolts, etc. When not in use the rack folds up between the floor joists, leaving the area clear.

Brackets which are inserted in the holes of perforated hardboard are another type of shelf support.

For shelves on the back of a door, nail a ledge along the front to keep things from falling off when the door is swung. You can increase the storage capacity of shelves by nailing a wide board ledge across their front and converting them into bins. Such a bin is ideal for keeping wiping rags, plumbing fittings, nails, and miscellaneous tools.

Metal shelving is low in cost and excellent for shop use. It can be bought in knockdown kits, with shelves spaced as you desire. You can buy additional shelves if closer spacing is required. Some steel storage units are available with strong card-

This tool rack was designed to fit the Beginner's Workbench in Chapter 3. The rack can either be fastened to the bench top or hung on the wall over the bench. *Courtesy American Plywood Co.*

Plans for Building
the Beginner's Workbench Tool Rack

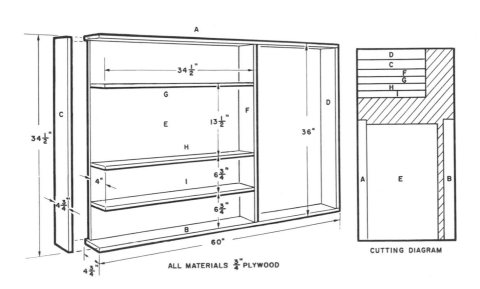

ALL MATERIALS ¾" PLYWOOD

CUTTING DIAGRAM

board boxes, good for many storage uses.

Instead of using boards for shelves between exposed wall studs, you can use rain gutters. They are especially good for a miscellany of screws, nails, nuts, and bolts.

You can get high utilization from shelves by designing them to accommodate jars and boxes. Cigar boxes, peanut-butter jars, cans are only a few of the kinds of containers that may be used. So that you'll know what's in boxes (not easy to remember when you have a hundred or more), give each a number and have an index listing what each number contains.

Circular saw blades can be stored in shelves divided like a record cabinet. A divider should separate each blade.

Shelves for the storage of light bulbs can have holes drilled in them to accept the bulb screw-base. Along the shelf edge, place a label to clearly identify bulb type and size.

When making shelves that are fastened permanently to side supports, the preferred technique is to make a dado or groove in each side. When the shelf is inserted in the dado, fasten it there with glue, and screws or nails. As an added touch, if you don't want the dado to show, make it a "stopped dado," ending it just short of the front face of the upright support.

6

Storage: Cabinets / Chests

Workshop cabinets and chests should be simple and rugged, but they can also be attractive. Avoid the urge to plunge in and build a single cabinet or chest before you decide what the whole shop is going to be like. First establish an overall plan; otherwise you'll end with a mishmash. A makeshift shop won't be pleasant or relaxing to work in. It is just as easy to create a shop with a degree of uniformity.

Restrict yourself in the use of materials. Try to keep storage units similar in appearance. If your cabinets have flush doors, don't put lipped fronts on the drawers, and try to use matching hardware throughout.

Perhaps you have old kitchen cabinets, secondhand desks, shabby bookcases—all of which would be handy to use in the shop. If some are tall, others short, some narrow and some deep, overcome these discrepancies by cutting the big ones down to desired size and building the little ones up. Differences can be deemphasized by application of unifying features. Base cabinets can be unified by giving them all a common, continuous top. Drawers that don't match can be unified by painting them all the same color and giving them matching hardware. If nothing else, line up the tops of doors and drawers. If a piece is beyond remedy, you can still salvage its parts.

Whether you are building new storage units, or readapting old ones, plan your design to serve specific needs. Measure shelves and divide drawers to accommodate specific tools and supplies. Plan their locations so these tools and supplies are near their point of most frequent use. Avoid "general storage." Plan storage for portable power tools, plumbing tools and supplies, for concrete and masonry tools and supplies, for electrical/electronic tools and supplies, for painting equipment and supplies, etc.

Open shelves are the easiest to build, but doors offer protection against dust and rust, hide clutter, and can give security against unauthorized use. If you build shelf units, it's usually easy enough to add doors later.

BUILDING THE BOX.   A storage unit is essentially a box. In this box you place shelves or drawers. The box can be any shape. It can rest on its own bottom, or on legs or a base.

The materials you use for building storage units will be mostly ¾″ fir plywood or 1″-by-12″ shelving boards. For economy, the plywood will be interior grade, good one side (G1S); the shelving will be #3.

The advantage of plywood is that it offers widths up to 4′ without the necessity of piecing. The disadvantages are that

A cabinet or chest is basically a box in which shelves or drawers are installed. It can be assembled with butt joints or, as shown here, with a rabbet joint at the top and a dado joint at the bottom. Be sure to use glue with nails or screws on all joints.

Plywood is the ideal cabinet material because it comes in panel sizes, but this craftsman decided to save money by using #3 pine shelving. Two 1-by-12s joined with white glue and corrugated fasteners make a wide panel.

To protect the interior against dampness and make cleanup easier, the base of the cabinet is off the floor. It fits in dadoes cut in the sides.

Hardboard back gives a cabinet rigidity and seals out dust. It can be nailed directly to the edges of the case, or set in a rabbet ½" wide and ¼" deep for a neater finish.

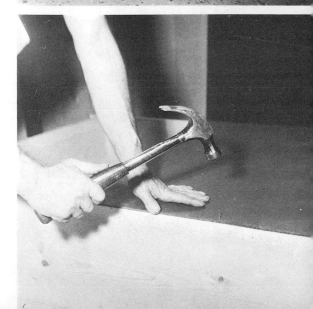

it is a little harder to assemble (because of the problem of edge nailing), it shows edge grain that is unsightly, and it may delaminate in areas subject to excessive moisture.

The advantage of boards is that they are easier to handle, join, and paint. The disadvantages are that usually they don't come wider than 11½", they have a tendency to warp and twist, and they aren't as strong as plywood.

Tempered hardboard has a place, too. Because of its smooth surface, it makes unexcelled drawer bottoms. Because of its panel size and economy, it makes excellent cabinet backs. You'll want cabinet backs. They add rigidity and seal against dust, moisture, and small animals.

You can cover base cabinets with a top to provide a working surface. Typical stand-up height would then be 32", sit-down height 28". Depth (distance from front to back) can be 18" to 30". If a hanging cabinet is to go above it, the clearance between the two would be about 15".

If cabinets run from floor to ceiling, plan upper shelves for dead storage or seldom-used items. You can't see into a drawer whose top is more than chin high, so plan accordingly.

Once the case has been constructed, the interior can be divided according to your needs. Cleats can be used to support shelves or drawers.

Rear view of chest assembly shows how drawer slides and guide strips are constructed. Back of each drawer is notched to ride on guide strip.

Cabinets may be built as free-standing units or, as here, built-ins. Proper use of a level may spell the difference between success and failure. Keep *construction* level and plumb, disregarding slope of walls and floor.

To make a cabinet turn a corner, miter the shelves with glue and corrugated fasteners. This joint is stronger than a butt joint.

WOODWORKING JOINTS.   There are all kinds of joints, but only a few have significant application in constructing shop furnishings. Strength and rigidity are the prime considerations. The butt joint and the dado joint can handle almost everything. Occasionally you can use a half-lap, spline, and lock mortise.

Regardless of whether the top of a cabinet overhangs its ends and front or fits flush, it can be attached with a simple butt joint. If it overhangs, you gain a little something by making it a dado joint.

Simple dado cuts in the sides of a cabinet offer the best joint support for a shelf. If you use a butt joint for shelves, you can gain strength by resting the shelf on a wood strip. A cabinet back can be applied flush, but you'll gain in rigidity by recessing it in a rabbet. Secure all joints, wherever they are, with white glue *and* nails or screws. In most cases, use 2″ finishing nails or 1¼″ #8 flat-head wood screws.

Cabinets can be supported on legs, which you buy and attach with screws, or on a base. A simple sturdy base is a 2-by-4 running along the back, with other 2-by-4s recessed 2½″ for toe space at front and sides. The cabinet bottom is nailed or screwed to this frame. Cabinet sides also can run to the floor, being notched at the front to receive the toe-space board.

HOW TO BUILD DRAWERS.   If a cabinet is a box, a drawer is merely a sliding box. A workshop needs numerous drawers, so you ought to know how to build them.

A drawer front may be inset flush with the frame, or it may have a lip. The inset drawer is easier to build, but is much harder to fit. A drawer needs ¹⁄₁₆″ clearance. A lip hides this gap so that clearance differences aren't apparent.

The biggest strain on a drawer is at its front joints. Yanking on a drawer tends to pull its front loose from its sides. Most commercial drawers have dovetail joints at their front, and if you have a router and a dovetailing kit, this is a good chance to enjoy the pleasure of making these joints.

The easiest drawer-front joint to make is a simple butt joint with the drawer sides overlapping both front and back. For appearance and added security, a facing of ¼″ plywood is applied over the front, or ½″ plywood if the facing extends to make a lip.

You can substitute dowels for dovetail joints on drawer fronts. First, apply glue to the joint and tack the parts together with a couple of nails. Then drill holes the size of the dowel to a depth of at least three times the thickness of the drawer's sides. Apply glue to the dowels and drive them into place. Use grooved dowels. If you use smooth dowel stock, flatten one side by sanding, or cut a groove on it and taper the dowel-end slightly. If you don't flatten the side or cut a groove, excess glue or trapped air can't escape and the dowel won't fill the hole properly.

A third type of joint can be made by cutting dadoes in the drawer front into which the sides are fitted and angled nailed and glued.

The backboard of a drawer should be recessed in a dado cut in each side to a depth that is half the thickness of the side. The dado should be ½″ to ¾″ from the rear edge. If you don't have the tools or know-how to make a dado joint, a butt joint here will suffice.

One way to attach the drawer bottom is to groove the inner face of the front and sides (but not the back). The drawer back is not cut as deep as the sides. Its bottom edge is flush with the tops of the grooves cut in the sides. This makes it possible to slide the drawer bottom into place under it.

A drawer bottom can be ⅛″ or ¼″ tempered hardboard or ¼″ plywood. The groove into which it fits should be cut at least ¼″ up from the bottom of the sides and should be a shade wider than its thickness. The groove's depth should be a shade less than half the thickness of the side. Plane the edges of the bottom panel slightly if the fit is too tight. The bottom will extend over the drawer back and should be attached to it with small nails. The bottom is not glued anywhere.

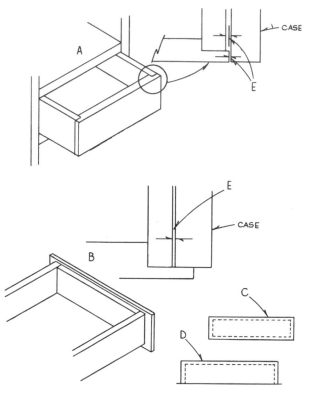

Drawer front can fit flush with the case edges (A) or over-hang the edges (B). Rabbet joints are used in both instances. If the sides are simply butted against the front, and a front panel applied, the overlap can be on four edges (C) or three (D). Provide clearance of $\frac{1}{16}''$ (E) so drawer works smoothly.

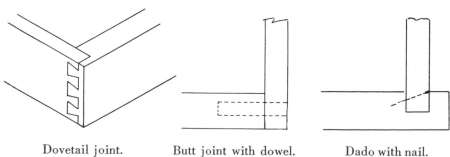

Dovetail joint.   Butt joint with dowel.   Dado with nail.

The ½" sides of this drawer are attached to the ¾" front by recessing them in dadoes. Glue, and finishing nails driven from the side at an angle, provide satisfactory holding power.

The sides and back of this drawer, or tray, are higher than the front, making the contents easily accessible. It's all built with butt joints. Note groove along the side. The tray will slide on angled supports which will be inserted into this groove.

Dividing a drawer helps to keep it neat and provides sections for different types of equipment. Slots for the partitions should be cut before the drawer is assembled.

If slots have not been cut in the drawer before assembly, an insert arrangement can be made of ½″ stock without losing much storage space.

When dividers cross each other, use a half-lap joint to fit the pieces together.

Here is a completely divided drawer. The small tray slides on top of the lower divided section, providing access.

Drawer rests and slides on this divider frame. Middle member of the frame is a guide to keep drawer straight and prevent jamming. The bottom edge of the drawer back is notched to fit the guide, as shown in a previous photo on page 95.

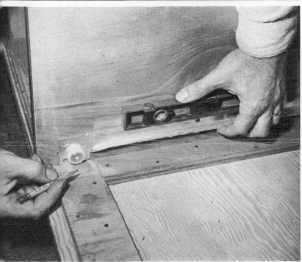

When drawers are big, and will be required to bear heavy loads, manufactured slides are recommended to insure satisfactory operation. One part of the slide is attached to the side of the chest and the other to drawer (below).

If you don't have a power tool for cutting grooves, you can nail and glue the drawer bottom directly to the edges of the sides, front, and back. In this case, you don't have to cut the drawer back shorter than the sides. To enable the drawer to move easily, nail two ⅛″ strips to the bottom, one on each side.

It is difficult to maintain an orderly drawer unless it is partitioned. Nor will it accommodate as much. Deep drawers can be partitioned to provide two storage levels, with a sliding tray as the upper level. If a drawer is to be divided, dividers may be made of hardboard, plywood, or ½″ solid stock. They are inserted into dadoes cut in the drawer sides. Plan for dividers before you build the drawer. You can't readily cut dadoes after it is assembled. To make dividers for an existing drawer, make a complete slip-in unit of ½″ stock.

A drawer moves on a divider frame, or on slides, and is kept straight by strips called guides. A drawer doesn't rest on the guide but on the frame or slides, which should be lubricated with soap or melted paraffin for easier action. Since shop drawers are usually heavily laden, for easiest operation attach ball-bearing slides.

For economy, you can attach runners to the drawer sides and cut grooves in the case sides. The alternative is to cut the

Technique for handling heavy bottom drawers is to put them on casters. Drawer bottom will be a loose, removable panel.

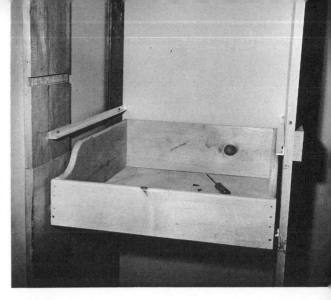

Here is completed tray (shown in previous photo) resting on its slides. By attaching each pair of slides only after the drawer below is installed, proper fit and clearances are assured.

grooves in the drawer sides and attach supporting strips to the case sides. The latter is a technique for adding a drawer to an existing case. Instead of wood strips, you can use aluminum angle as supports.

When there is no means of side support, as when you wish to hang a drawer under a counter or bench top, you can use an aluminum channel attached to the top. Drill screw holes through both sides of the channel and you won't have difficulty making the attachment. Or you can cut an L-shaped hanger from ⅝″ stock. Easier still, make the L out of two separate pieces.

Good small drawers for small parts can have sheet-metal bottoms. Let the side edges of the bottom project so they can slide in saw-kerf slots cut into a box frame.

Once you know the principles, you can make such improvisations as a chest in which the drawers are all cigar boxes.

CABINET DOORS.   The two basic kinds of shop doors are those that slide and those that swing. Sliding doors are easier to install, but they provide access to only half a cabinet at a time. You can buy sliding-door tracks of wood, metal, or plastic for ⅛″, ¼″, or larger panels. Panels may be of hardboard, plywood, plastic, or glass. The top track has deeper grooves than the lower one, and panels are inserted by lifting them into the upper grooves and then dropping them into the lower ones.

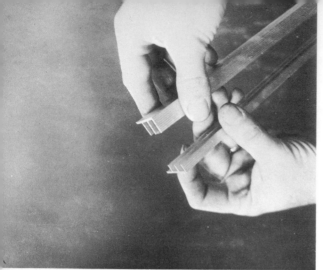

Sliding door tracks, whether of aluminum, plastic, or wood, come in pairs. The upper track has deeper grooves to permit inserting and removing the panel.

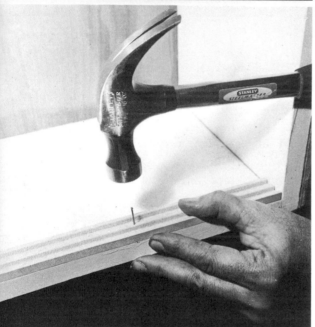

Wood track can be quickly installed in a cabinet with finishing nails, whereas metal track requires screws. Finishing wood track to match the cabinet presents fewer problems than with metal.

To mark a sliding panel for size, raise it all the way into the upper track, then mark for cutting even with the top of the bottom track.

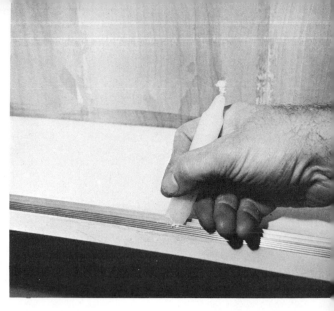

Lubricating track with paraffin eases operation of sliding panel. Secret of building smooth-working doors is to have perfectly square panels and parallel tracks.

You can rip your own track out of wood strips, cut integral grooves into the frame of your cabinet, or create grooves with surface-mounted wood strips.

A popular type of pull for sliding panels is a shallow cup which fits into a hole drilled in the door. For convenience, insert a pull of this kind at the end of each panel.

If you have a shelf unit that you want to put behind sliding panels, it may be necessary to extend the top, bottom, and sides so they extend forward of the shelves and allow clearance for the sliding panels.

The simplest swing doors for shop cabinets are ones that overlap the front edges of the case. They are preferably hung with pin hinges, but you can use butt-hinges.

Swing doors may be inset within a case. These are harder to fit than overlapping doors, but some people prefer their style. These can be hung with mortised butt hinges, surface hinges, hinges with an exposed barrel, or semiconcealed hinges. You can get no-mortise butt hinges and save yourself some work. Continuous-style hinges give superior support to recessed doors and have a distinctively handsome appearance.

A third type of swing door for shop cabinets is lipped. The lip may partially overlap the opening, or may completely cover the front edges of the case. There are several types of semiconcealed hinges for lipped doors.

Though some hinges are "self-closing" and stay shut without a catch, in most cases you will need some type of catch to

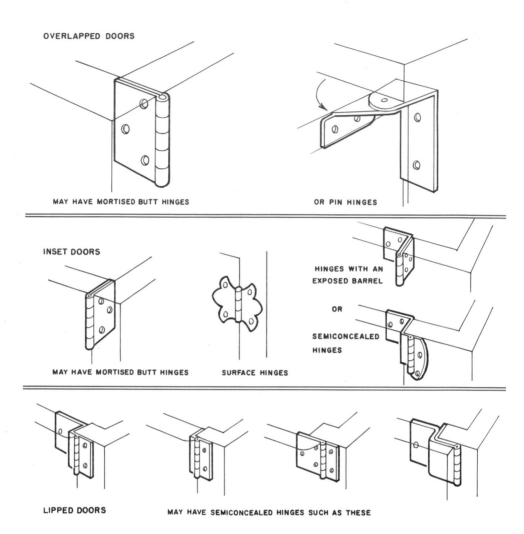

OVERLAPPED DOORS

MAY HAVE MORTISED BUTT HINGES

OR PIN HINGES

INSET DOORS

MAY HAVE MORTISED BUTT HINGES

SURFACE HINGES

HINGES WITH AN EXPOSED BARREL

OR

SEMICONCEALED HINGES

LIPPED DOORS

MAY HAVE SEMICONCEALED HINGES SUCH AS THESE

Methods of hinging overlapped, inset, and lipped doors.

keep doors closed. Two simple types are magnetic and double-roller friction catches. If you want to lock the doors, get a cupboard lock.

Single doors require a stop so they won't swing inward. A cleat does the job. If a cabinet has double doors, it needs a center-stile stop. For flush, inset doors the stile requires a cleat along each edge to act as a stop. Or the stile and door edges can be rabbeted so they form a half-lap joint where they meet.

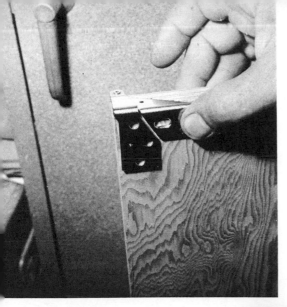

Pin hinges are almost invisible on overlapped doors. Top of door must be mortised slightly to receive this style of hinge.

When pin hinges are attached to the side of a door, one half must be recessed in a slot.

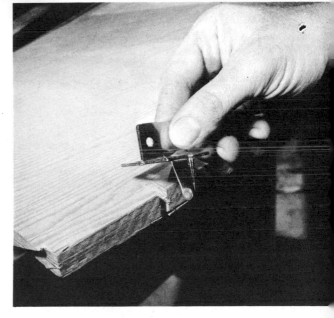

STORAGE-BENCH COMBO. Accompanying drawings show a complete workshop that grows on a modular plan. All units are based on the construction details for the Lock-up Workbench in Chapter 3. First, you build unit A. It provides storage, lighting, and a working surface at which you can stand or sit. Next, you can build B. It provides additional storage as well as more working surface. Units C and D provide a variety of other kinds of storage. All units are coordinated and combine to create an harmonious shop environment.

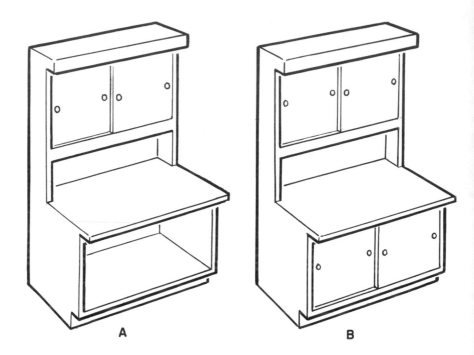

A   B

Complete workshop grows with modular units that provide
bench and storage space. Construction details are the same
as for Lock-up Workbench in Chapter 3 except that units
are built half the size.

For economy, you can build the units of fir plywood. Birch
is better looking and more durable, but costs considerably
more. You may find it worth the difference.

You can make the work surface 30″, 32″, or 34″ high,
which ever best suits your size and work habits. You can install
sliding or swinging doors on the base cabinet of unit A, or leave
it open to provide storage for lumber shorts, folding sawhorses,
or a toolbox.

CONSTRUCTION TIPS

• If, instead of making freestanding storage units, you're
making built-ins, use your level religiously. Don't forget that
your floors may slope and your walls may be out of plumb. A

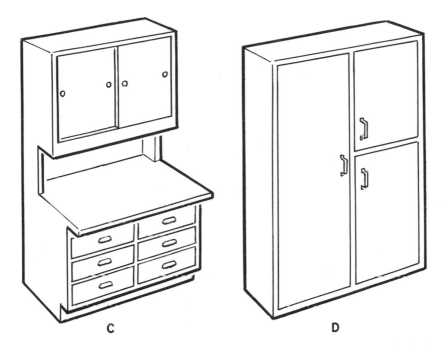

C   D

level is insurance that you'll get true horizontals and verticals. If you build out of plumb, shelves will slant, drawers may roll open, and doors refuse to fit. Use shims wherever needed to make your structure level. Wood shingles, because of their wedge shape, make especially good shim material. Use a pencil compass to transfer the irregularities of a wall to a board or panel that is being butt-fitted against it.

• If you are working with plywood, carefully lay out parts needed on each panel to minimize waste and confirm that your grain directions are right.

• If you have swing room, hinge doors give maximum accessibility. Don't overlook the possibility of using bottom-hinged cabinet doors and special drop-leaf supports. They can provide extra working space.

• If you want to reinforce a butt joint, you can do it easily with dowels and glue. It doesn't matter if dowel ends show.

• Dowels are also a good way to overcome the lack of holding power in the end-grain of plywood. Insert with glue a

Some storage devices are so good and inexpensive that it pays to buy rather than to build them. Plastic drawer case shown here is one example. It is ideal for storing small parts.

Everything displayed on the floor is stored in this cabinet, which is mounted on casters and also serves as an outboard support for sawing long pieces of lumber. This illustrates how orderly storage can reduce clutter.

⅜″ dowel about ⅜″ back, and parallel to, the end of the end-grain piece. Pre-drill holes through the end-grain and into the dowel before driving screws.

• Miter joints aren't any stronger than ordinary butt joints, but it's easy to give them added strength. Cut 45-degree saw kerfs into edges of meeting pieces and set thin spline strips into the grooves.

• Instead of nailing through sides into shelves, toenail from underneath shelves into sides. In that way you avoid marring the sides of your cabinet with overzealous hammer blows or with holes you have to fill.

7

Power and Light

Few shops start out with enough power or adequate lighting. There are seldom enough outlets, or outlets in the right places. Lighting is makeshift rather than planned. To improve the situation in your workshop it may be necessary to do an elaborate job of rewiring, but you may be able to get by with only a few improvements requiring little skill and a minimum of equipment.

SIMPLE IMPROVEMENTS.   One of the easiest improvements to make in your shop is to replace existing two-prong outlets with grounded three-prong outlets. This eliminates the nuisance of having to use an adapter to fit power tools to two-prong sockets.

Another practical improvement is to replace single outlets with duplex ones. It's just a matter of substituting a new device and plate. Then you won't have to unplug a lamp when you want to plug in a drill.

A circuit is a power line that originates at the service center (fuse or circuit-breaker box). A minimum of two, preferably three circuits is required for a shop. If you now have a single circuit supplying both lighting fixtures and outlets,

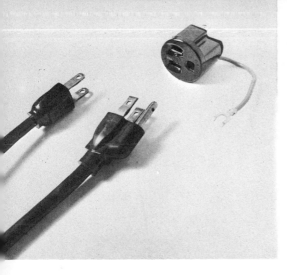

Most power tools have three-pronged plugs like the one at right. The adapter in front of it allows you to plug into a standard socket and ground the tool by fastening the end of the grounding wire, which is U-shaped, under a screw in the outlet faceplate.

adding a second circuit will enable you to keep light and power needs separate. This means you won't be left in the dark when one of your power tools blows a fuse or trips a circuit breaker, nor will your lights dim when you start up a motor.

A typical lighting circuit is designed to handle 15 amperes and is wired with No. 14 cable. A power circuit should be able to handle 20 amperes and be wired with No. 12 cable.

Installing some type of circuit-breaker system is a good way to guard against blown fuses. Circuit-breaker plugs are available that fit into three-pronged outlets. If an overload occurs, a button in the plug pops up and the tool is automatically disconnected. You can gain this same convenience by substituting screw-in circuit breakers for fuses in your fuse box. You can also ease the nuisance of blown fuses by installing a special fuse box within the shop to protect one or more branch circuits.

Adding plug-in facilities in your shop without actually adding new outlets is fairly simple. One method is to use an extension box, generally a 4″-by-4″ metal box wired with two duplex receptacles and covered by a plate. An extension cord connects it to an outlet. This gives four plug-in places instead of one. If desired, it can be combined with a switch controlling each duplex receptacle.

Another way is to mount a "power pack" on your stationary tool. It may include two three-prong outlets, an on-off toggle switch, and a safety light to indicate when power is on. Power packs are commercially available.

To bring more power into the shop, run a single 40- or 50-amp cable from the service entry to a sub-box.

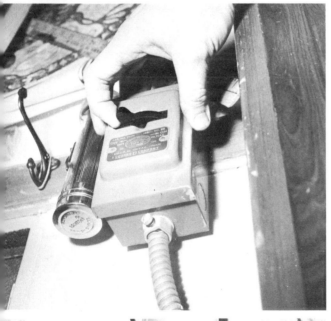

Installing a master switch in a closet or other hidden place enables you to shut off all shop circuits with a single flick—a particularly good idea when small children are apt to enter the shop.

Label power outlets clearly to be sure which circuit you are using and how much current it can supply.

If you have more than one circuit in the shop, you'll find it convenient to tag each outlet, so you know immediately which circuit it's on and which fuse controls it. The tag can also include data as to amps, voltage, cycles, etc.

Often service centers have one or more circuits that are not in use. In a circuit-breaker setup, you may be able to gain extra circuits by installing duplex breakers. If you have no spare circuits, and your house power is already inadequate, you may want to consider installing a new, larger service.

MORE POWER FOR YOUR SHOP.   A few years ago, a 60-ampere service was considered standard. Now, many home-owners are finding even 100-ampere service inadequate. With a dishwasher, drier, air conditioner, water heater, range, even the furnace and boiler being powered by electricity, more and more people are turning to 200-ampere service.

Power pack can be mounted on power-tool stand, provides extra outlets and an on-off switch. It has a light that glows to show if power is on.

Plug at left has its own built-in circuit breaker. Mini-Breaker, center, can replace an ordinary fuse like one at right and cut off power when overload occurs.

Installing a new service does not necessarily mean tearing out the old. For example, if you were to install a new 200-ampere entry, a 100-ampere breaker could be included in it and from it a cable run to "feed" the existing service. If you wish, the new service can be in a new location. There need be no disruption while the new service is being wired. The power company will run in new, heavier lines from the pole, but you may have to provide a new meter socket and cable from it to the service center box.

Typical cost of converting from 60 to 100 amps is about $150. In many areas, the power company will finance the job and charge monthly payments for a year or two on your regular electric bill.

Here's how to calculate how much power you need for your shop. A typical ½ hp motor draws 7 amps. Good practice requires that it be on a 20-amp circuit.

If you have ample current, provide a separate 20-amp circuit for every major stationary power tool. If you have, or plan to acquire, an arc welder, even the smallest requires a 30- or 40-amp circuit.

A 100-watt bulb draws 1 amp. If you are hard-pressed for power, substitute fluorescent tubes. They will give 2 to 4 times as much light for the same current.

If you have circuits without much on them, you can gain convenience by adding new outlets. At the workbench, one of the best arrangements is the use of Electrostrips. These are power-carrying strips into which you can snap receptacles at any point. Electrostrips can take off from an outlet box or a cable end. The strip can be nailed or screwed to any convenient surface.

If you have the money to spend, the best system of all is a "lighting duct." This is a kind of power system used in industry. It is an overhead track, about 1″ square in cross section, into which a variety of plugs, trolleys, or light fixtures can be connected. The duct can be mounted flush to the ceiling or suspended. The duct can be arranged in any pattern on the

Electrostrip along front edge of bench or on wall behind it brings power wherever it is needed. The strip can be connected to an outlet box or cable end.

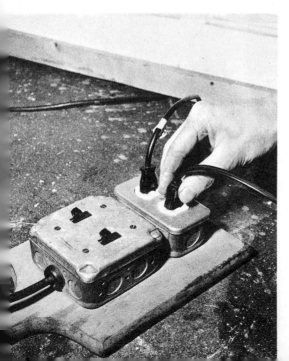

Duplex outlet with switches and extension cord can be mounted on a breadboard to make a mobile plug-in platform for power tools.

Outlet on the side of the house is convenient for outside jobs requiring power tools. Snap-up covers protect against dirt and rain. Make sure outlet is grounded.

When adding extra outlets, you can sometimes avoid difficulties in snaking cable through walls by installing outlets in the floor. Special types are available for the purpose.

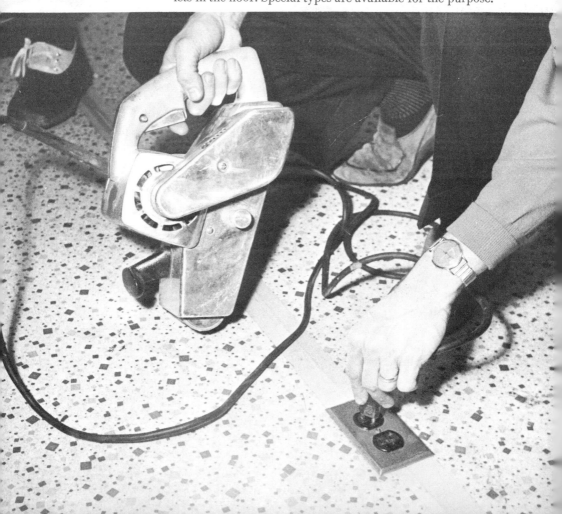

ceiling so that power is available anywhere in the shop. Power tools can be connected by drop lines in the center of the floor, eliminating hazardous trailing wires.

DOING YOUR OWN WIRING.   Most local codes permit the homeowner to do his own wiring, provided he has a permit. Your wiring will then be inspected for conformance to regulations. Often, an electrical inspector will offer you good advice on how your wiring may best be done. There are usually very sound reasons for every code requirement, even though it may not readily be apparent to the nonprofessional. Faulty wiring is a major cause of fire in the home. You may only be cheating yourself if you try to get away with a wiring violation.

Even though the existing wiring in your house may lack a grounding wire, it must be included with all new work. All new outlets must be grounded. Following is a list of do's and don'ts to bear in mind when undertaking a wiring job.

1. Be sure to insert a fiber or plastic bushing to protect wire from the cut end on BX cable.

2. Never bury a box. If you no longer have use for a box at its present location, don't cover it with plasterboard. If you can't convert it to an outlet, switch, or light, cover it with a blank plate.

If you add partitions when creating your shop, you automatically provide a good place for running electric cable. Outlet box with its own mounting strap is easily attached to a stud.

3. Don't crowd boxes with wiring. The typical outlet or switch box should have no more than one cable leading in and one leading out. Use a 4"-by-4" box when more than this must be accommodated.

4. Don't cut wire leads short. Allow enough length so that a switch or outlet can be pulled completely free of the box when it is connected.

5. Don't connect more than one wire under a switch or outlet screw. If more than one wire is to be connected to a screw terminal, connect a single wire to the terminal and then join this wire to the other wires by means of a solderless connector.

6. Never work on a box when it is live. Shut off the power. Don't assume that all wiring in a single box is from the same circuit. If you're in doubt about current being off, check terminals or wires with a test lamp before you touch them.

7. Don't mount fluorescent fixtures on combustible surfaces. The ballast inside can get hot enough to start a fire. Use metal brackets to allow an air space between the fixture and the surface. In some cases, mounting the fixture on asbestos board over wood is permissible.

8. Use no more than 80 percent of a circuit capacity. On a 15-amp, 115-volt circuit you have 1380 watts, not 1725 watts.

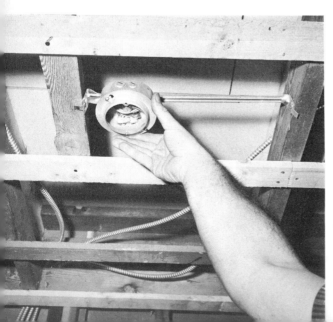

Outlets for ceiling fixtures and ventilators are mounted on a support between joists. Box can be positioned anywhere along the support.

9. Always connect black wires to brass terminals, white wires to chrome terminals. Except in switch wiring, always connect black to black, white to white, red to red.

GOOD LIGHTING.   There are three important reasons for having good lighting. First, and most important, is safety. When you can't really see what you are doing, you're inviting trouble. Second, is efficiency. It's easy enough to make errors in measuring, marking, and cutting even when the light is good. When you have to strain to see, you'll make more errors and you'll waste energy. Third, good lighting is more pleasant. A dingy shop is depressing, dull, uninspiring. Good lighting is stimulating and invigorating. You feel like working and enjoy it more.

Every ten years in this century business and industry have been doubling lighting levels in office, factory, shop. Brighter lighting does not mean glare. Outdoors, in the shade, it's ten times as bright as you would ever have it in your shop, yet there is no glare. Glare comes when there is excessive contrast between light and dark.

To avoid glare, no part of your shop should be more than three times as brightly lighted as any other part. To accomplish this uniformity of illumination, you first must have supple-

Gooseneck lamp attached to jigsaw stand focuses light on work area.

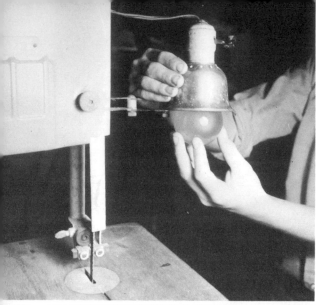

Band saw requires its own light, which can be swung aside when not in use.

Fluorescent desk lamp is adapted to wall use for lighting a specific area where much close work is done.

Never use bare bulbs in a shop. Reflectors are available that screw on the threaded end of socket adapters.

Industrial fluorescent light with its own reflector is first rate for shop use. It can be hung by a chain from an outlet box.

mentary lighting at power tools and at the workbench.

Don't worry about getting your shop too bright. What you do have to avoid is a few bright spots of light. Spread the light around with many low-intensity sources of illumination. Incandescent bulbs are good for spot illumination, such as at a band saw, because they pinpoint light. Fluorescent bulbs are good for general illumination because they spread light.

An industrial fluorescent fixture with two 40-watt lamps, approximately 48″ above the surface, gives good general illumination to a workbench area, but for close or precision work you will have to supplement it with another fixture. Gooseneck lamps are good. So are the clamp-on reflector lamps used by photographers.

Never use a bare bulb. Put a good reflector on it, and it will provide nearly twice as much light. The reflector will also spread light more effectively.

Lighting experts measure the level of illumination in footcandles. Theoretically, one footcandle is the amount of light one candle gives at one foot. An incident-light photographic meter can be used to measure footcandles. The noonday sun provides about 10,000 footcandles. General illumination in the home is typically about 10 footcandles, though kitchen or bathroom may be about 30. Benchwork requires a minimum of 70, with close work 100 to 200 or more. Remember, these are minimum standards. The best lighting is natural sunlight, and to match it in a woodworking shop, you would need about 1500 footcandles.

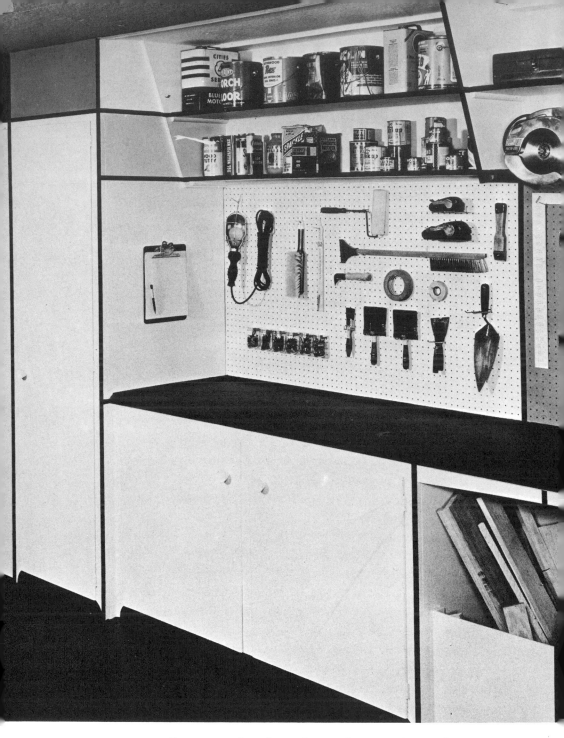

Painting tools and supplies are kept together in this shop corner. Base cabinet provides storage for belt and orbital sanders, sandpaper, paint sprayer, and a bin for rags.

8

The Paint Center

The tools and equipment for painting and paperhanging, for refinishing furniture, for the upkeep and repair of windows, floors, and walls—all these belong in one department. Call it the paint center, because painting and refinishing are the most important part of it, but it logically includes many subsidiary activities. The laying of resilient floor tile and the application of ceramic tile are part of it. So is the application and maintenance of plastic laminates. It is a good place to store all kinds of adhesives, though they might alternately go in the section for nails, screws, and other fastening devices.

The paint center is really not one area, but two. One is the shop section in which you store all the tools and equipment, and perhaps carry on finishing activities. The other is where you store paints, thinners, removers, etc. These materials need not necessarily be kept in the shop.

PAINT STORAGE. There are definite advantages in storing paints, solvents, and all flammable materials outdoors. The only concern need be for freezing—in the case of latex paints. But even these may include an antifreeze. Read the label for temperature requirements and be guided accordingly. Avoid

Tools and adhesives only are stored in this paint center.
Paint is kept in an outdoor cabinet. Slanting shelf holds
small items within sight and reach. Many supplies are
hung in their packages for quick identification.

storing paint supplies near heat or in confined cabinets the sun may turn into hot boxes. The cooler paint is kept, the better.

If you do keep paint and related supplies in the shop, store them on open shelves or in ventilated cabinets. Ventilate paint cabinets by using preforated hardboard as door panels or back panels, or by drilling holes.

Best storage is one-can deep and one-can high. Then you never have to move anything to get at anything else. You can have one or more shelves just high enough for pint cans, but be sure to have at least one shelf high enough for rectangular-shaped gallon cans of thinner, remover, and wood preservative. These cans are 10½″ high; a shelf to accommodate them should be 12″ high. Regular round gallon cans of paint are 8″ high, require a shelf 10″ high. Pint cans are 4″ high, require a 6″ shelf. The space between studs in a wall framed with 2-by-4s is deep enough to store aerosol cans, and you will undoubtedly acquire countless numbers of these.

Your paint dealer will write the color formula of specially color-matched paint right on the can. Add your own information on where in the house the paint was used. Then you won't have to waste time opening cans when you need matching paint for touchups. Don't worry about getting a few splashes or drips

Paints can be stored in a shallow, lockable cabinet mounted on an outside house or garage wall. Temperature requirements on cans of latex paint indicate whether they can be left out in the winter.

Space between wall studs is usually deep enough to accommodate narrow shelves holding paint supplies. Plywood doors should be drilled with ventilation holes.

of paint on the outside of the can. It helps in identification. Paint a patch of the paint on the label to improve the surface for writing.

Paint cans must be tightly closed to prevent deterioration in storage. Cover the can lid with a rag so you won't get splashed by groove paint, and hammer the lid on. After the hammering, turn the can upside down briefly to form an airtight seal.

BRUSHES AND ROLLERS.   Brushes can be stored by hanging them on nails, or keeping them in a drawer if they are first wrapped in brown paper or aluminum foil to maintain their shape. Never rest a brush on its bristles in a paint can.

Paint and brush storage center has an adjustable shelf and ¼″ dowels for holding brushes. Mounted on casters, it rolls out from under the workbench.

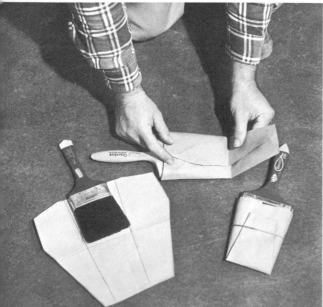

Underside of basement stairs is a handy place to hang paintbrushes on nails (above). If brushes are kept in a drawer, they should be combed and wrapped in brown paper or foil to maintain their shape (left).

Never immerse the brush bristles more than halfway in the paint. A brush can be suspended in a can of solvent by running a wire spindle through a hole drilled in its handle.

The best practice is to buy a good brush and take care of it. A cheap brush won't hold a full load of paint. The paint will run back over the handle onto your hand. Its bristles will shed, and paint won't flow smoothly from it. A good brush is not expensive if it lasts ten years or more.

What is a good brush? Brushes may be "natural bristle" or nylon. In a moderate price range, you'll do better with nylon. Good natural-bristle brushes, made of 100 percent Chinese or Siberian hog bristle, are rare and expensive. If a brush is only partly hog and mostly horsehair or other inferior material, don't buy it. Nylon bristle is best for latex paint. It doesn't absorb water and lose its shape. Natural bristle is superior only for oil paints, enamels, and varnishes.

But all nylon bristle isn't alike. Examine the nylon bristles of a good brush and you'll see that each is tapered so it comes to a fine point. These tapered filaments are the reason the paint flows so well. Cheaper brushes will have only some tapered bristles. In addition, a good brush will have a high proportion of "flagged" or split-ended bristles. These increase its paint holding and smooth-spreading qualities. Poor-quality brushes have blunt-ended filaments.

Run a wire through holes drilled in brush handles to keep bristles from touching bottom when they are being soaked in solvent.

You can also judge a good brush by the quantity of its bristles. Grasp the brush bristles in one hand and you can feel the thickness. Spread the bristles apart and look in the center and you can see just how much is bristle and how much is deception. Look at the brush tip. It should not be blunt across the end, but taper to a point.

Here are some of the brushes you'll probably want in your collection: For large, flat surfaces—a 4″ brush. For trim—a 2″ or 2½″ brush. For furniture, toys, etc.—a varnish or enameling brush 1″ to 3″ wide. A dusting brush is a good investment. So are throwaway brushes, often made of foam, for minor jobs that don't warrant the nuisance of cleaning a brush.

A good part of your painting may be done with rollers. These have different sleeves or covers, depending on whether they are to be used for smooth surfaces, rough surfaces, indoors, outdoors, with latex or oil paint. The most popular sizes have sleeves that are 7″ or 9″ wide, but you can get them 12″, 14″, even 18″. If you're painting a big surface, like a double-garage floor, you'll find a bigger roller a time-saver. You'll also want one with a long handle. Whatever the width of the roller, you need a pan and metal grid to accommodate it, though on a floor you can merely pour a pool of paint and then spread it.

Keep a supply of aluminum foil handy for wrapping brushes when you want to interrupt painting from one day to the next without cleaning them. It's also a good liner for pans. But be sure to remove the foil once the job is done. If you leave it on, drying paint may make it stick. You can also use brown paper as a pan liner. Only the oil will penetrate it.

You will need one or more 9′-by-12′ drop cloths of inexpensive paper or polyethylene. If you have two or three of them, you can cover all the shrubbery along one side of your house without the nuisance of having to shift one cover continually.

You will need scrapers. Those with double edges give you twice as much duty before dullness takes over. (Some have four edges.) Those with a single edge allow you to apply full pres-

There are no duplicates among these scrapers and knives. Blades may look alike, but one is stiff, the other flexible.

sure on the scraper end without having to contend with a cutting edge.

Putty knives, besides coming in various widths, also come with stiff or flexible blades. A flexible blade is often better for scraping. A stiff blade is better for such things as pressing filler into holes.

SPRAYING EQUIPMENT. It is easier to become expert with a spray gun than with a brush. A good sprayer enables you to apply a machine-perfect finish not possible by brush, and in half the time.

Spray painting is fast, but light-duty equipment won't do a big job. A paint tank that holds one gallon is preferable to a spray cup that holds only one pint. A quart size is a good compromise for average use. For a big job, you can rent a spray rig.

Paint sprayers are heavy, and in use have to be moved continually. A mobile unit permits you to roll the equipment with ease.

Small sprayers are for light duty. Don't expect them to handle standard heavy paints or to do a house-painting job.

This 2-in-1 painting outfit can be used either for spray or roller painting. Paint supply is kept in gallon can in which paint is purchased. Control button on roller handle regulates the flow.

The smallest sprayers are self-contained and use a vibrator rather than air to eject the paint. They are all right for small hobby work, but for average home use you need the compressor-and-gun type of sprayer. Compressors may be light, inexpensive diaphragm types, or piston models which work at higher pressures and can handle heavier paint.

Judge the capability of a spray outfit by the number of cubic feet it will deliver a minute (cfm), its pressure in pounds per square inch (psi), and the size of its spray pattern. A light-duty sprayer may deliver .4 cfm at a pressure of 20 psi, with a 3″ to 4″ pattern. A medium-duty sprayer may deliver 1.2 cfm at 20 psi, with a 5″ pattern. A heavy-duty sprayer may deliver 2.7 cfm at 35 psi, with a 6″ pattern. This is by no means the limit. You can get really large equipment that may have up to a 14″ pattern and deliver 7 or more cfm.

If you have a ⅓ or ¼ hp motor, you can get a compressor separately and save. Just bolt your motor to it. It will deliver about 2.1 cfm at 30 psi.

Instead of a gun, a sprayer may use a special roller. Paint is supplied to the roller by hose so there is no need to dip it in a pan. A fingertip control in the handle regulates the flow to the roller.

SHOP PAINTING.   Although many kinds of painting and finishing are done right in the shop, it's better, because of the dust problem, to use a separate room, or at least keep the work away from where most dust is generated. Good lighting, especially natural daylight, is an advantage. Good ventilation is always essential. You may want to provide a spray booth.

The whole point of a spray booth is to confine the paint mist and keep it from spreading. Attach large sheets of paper to lightweight wood frames and hinge the frames like shutters on each side of a window. Panels may also be cut from ⅛″ tempered hardboard. Use polyethylene film to protect any part of the window that is exposed. A panel roof for the booth can simply rest on top of the two extended side panels.

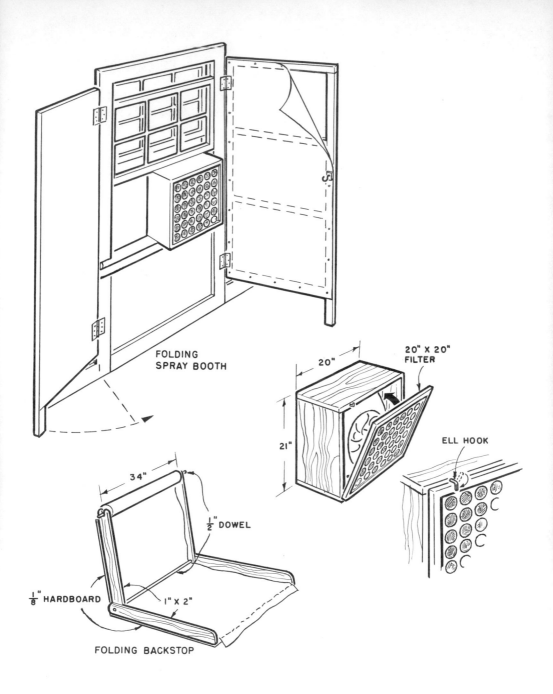

FOLDING
SPRAY BOOTH

20"

20" X 20"
FILTER

21"

ELL HOOK

34"

½" DOWEL

⅛" HARDBOARD

1" X 2"

FOLDING BACKSTOP

Spray booth for large jobs (upper left) consists of light-weight wood frames covered with paper and hinged to the sides of a window. The ventilator is a fan enclosed in a wood box equipped with a furnace filter to catch paint particles. For small jobs, a folding backstop (lower left) can be built to hold a roll of newsprint on a dowel.

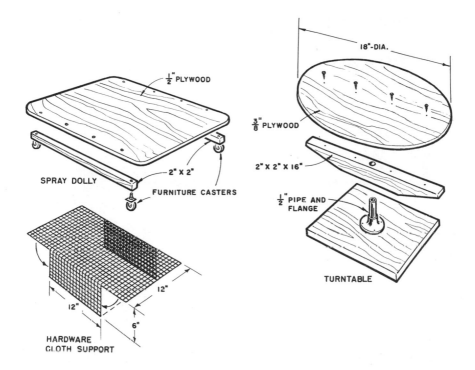

Three types of platforms for use in spray painting: a dolly on casters for large pieces; a turntable, for smaller items, which revolves the work and allows you to remain stationary; and a hardware cloth support for effectively covering all sides of small objects.

Ventilation is essential. Just having the window open may not be enough. A simple ventilator can be made by enclosing an 8″ or 12″ fan in a wood box. A 1″ furnace filter on its face will catch paint particles and prevent their discharge outside. Be sure the ventilating fan has a shaded-pole motor. One with sparking brushes can ignite paint vapors.

A revolving dolly or turntable allows you to rotate work so that you don't have to shift your own position as you spray. If you don't have a booth, you can make a simple backstop to catch overspray of a piece of fiberboard with newspaper thumbtacked to it.

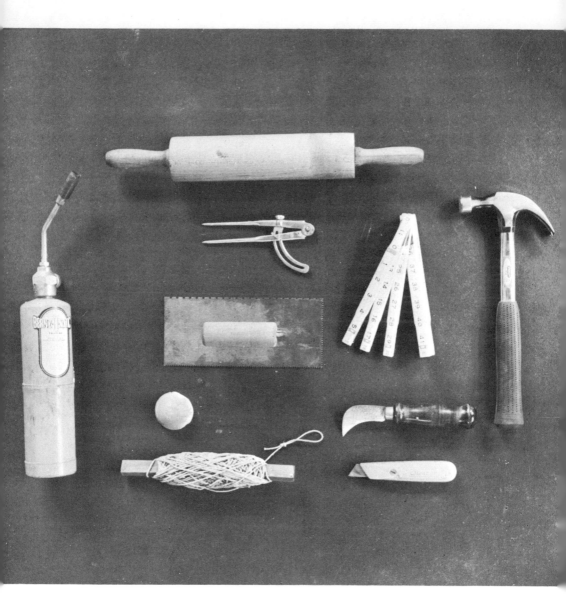

Typical kit for laying resilient flooring includes vinyl knives for cutting tile, rolling pin for flattening tile, scribers for fitting tile in irregular places, notched trowel for spreading adhesive, and a hammer, ruler, and chalk line. The torch is for working with asphalt tile, now largely supplanted by vinyl.

PAPERHANGING, OTHER JOBS.   You can buy or rent complete kits for paperhanging which usually include a 6″ paste brush, a smoothing brush, a seam roller, and a razor knife. In addition, you will need a 6′ straightedge (just a straight board), a stepladder, and a working table approximately 2′ by 6′. It can be a panel of plywood mounted on saw-horses or on a pair of card tables. If you are doing much paper-hanging, a wheel cutter and a wheel trimmer are helpful. You'll need a yardstick, and you may have to improvise a scaffold. A 2′-by-8′ plank between a pair of stepladders may do. For removing wallpaper, rent a steamer.

For laying resilient flooring, you'll need a pair of heavy shears for ducting today's lighter-gauge vinyl and vinyl-asbestos tiles. Solid-vinyl sheet materials are extremely tough and hard to cut, so you'll need a sharp vinyl knife. You'll need a notched trowel for spreading adhesive, or you can use a brush and brush-on adhesive. The latter is often better for it insures that you don't use too much or too little cement. For flattening down tiles, you can use an ordinary kitchen roller, but you'll be better off renting a heavy professional roller from the store where you buy your materials. A pair of scribing dividers is a useful tool. Other than that, there are no special tools—just the usual chalk line, level, square, and ruler or tape.

For installing ceramic tile, you will need a spreader, as recommended on the adhesive can. For 4″ wall tile, you will need a tile-cutting machine. It scores and breaks tiles up to ⅞″ thick with ease. You can buy a small one for about $10, or borrow one where you buy your tile. For cutting ceramic mosaic tile, get a pair of nippers—good ones. You will note that the jaws of tile nippers don't bite together.

For dry-wall or plasterboard taping you need a 5″ or 6″ knife with a flexible blade. For finishing, get a knife with an 11″ blade. Also useful is a "corner-taping tool." It makes inside corner taping fast and easy.

Glass cutting belongs in the paint department. Don't be afraid of it. It's simple—if you follow a few basic rules. One is to have a new, sharp cutter. The second is never go over a scored line. It ruins the cut and also the glass cutter. It may still score glass, but the glass won't break right. Finally—work on a thick pad of newspapers and keep your cutter well lubricated with mineral spirits. It doesn't hurt if you wipe a rag sopped with mineral spirits along the line of cut.

9

Electricity / Electronics Center

Count the number of electric appliances, motors, and electronic devices in your house and you'll see why electricity and electronics commands a special department in your shop. In addition to troubleshooting and repairing equipment, you may also be extending house wiring, adding new devices, putting together electronic kits ranging from garage-door openers to hi-fi sets.

There is a saying that any electrical repair you can't make with ordinary hand tools, you can't make at all. Don't believe it. With a convenient place to work, properly arranged and properly equipped, you'll breeze through procedures you otherwise wouldn't even attempt.

THE WORKBENCH.　A bench for electrical work is not the same as a woodworking bench. For one thing, it's lower. Because you'll be sitting down at this bench, make it 28" high. Leave the underside open so you can get your legs under, as if it were a desk. An old wooden desk, incidentally, makes an excellent bench. The drawers can store all kinds of supplies and equipment. The pullout leafs provide extra working space. And a desk swivel chair is good seating.

Old desk was transformed into a bench for electrical work by applying light-colored, heat-resistant linoleum to the top. The pullout leaves offer extra work surfaces, and drawers provide ample storage for small parts. Electro-strip outlets run along the wall near the bench top, and a perforated hardboard panel and shelves take care of tools and equipment.

Any light-colored material that's reasonably heat-resistant makes a good surface for an electricity/electronics bench. Small parts are easier to see on a light-colored surface, and light reflects better. Linoleum is a good choice; so is tough, light-colored particle board.

For convenience, you'll want a variety of tools, meters, and other test equipment within easy reach. Locate the bench in a corner, or create a cubby, with wall storage on one or both sides, and you'll find it easy to surround yourself with everything you need. Shelves will give you space to put everything without cluttering up the bench top. Provide a place for hanging wiring diagrams directly in front of you.

LIGHT AND POWER.   You need better than average lighting and electrical facilities in this shop center. Where 70 FC (footcandles) is good enough general lighting for many workshop operations, electronics requires 200 FC. In addition to a 4′ two-tube reflector fluorescent lamp hanging directly above the work surface, you'll also want a supplementary lamp that you can focus directly on the work at hand.

Some photo light meters will give you a direct reading in footcandles. If you have one with ASA readings, set its film speed dial to 100 and take your reading. If you have the required 70 FC general lighting, the EV (exposure value) scale

Weston light meter (left) gives direct reading of light level in footcandles. Electronic meter (right) was assembled from a kit.

on the meter will read between 10.5 and 11. Take another reading under your supplementary lamp. If this lamp builds the light up to 200 FC, the reading on the EV scale will be between 12.5 and 13.

You should have a least a half-dozen duplex outlets or equivalent within easy reach so you can keep testing equipment and regularly used electrical tools always plugged in. Make it a 20 amp circuit. The best setup is an Electrostrip running around the sides and back of the bench just above the bench top. You can locate outlets in it anywhere you choose, change locations when you want to.

In addition, you will want a fused "test" outlet. By separately fusing the test outlet (you can use a fused plug), you'll spare yourself the nuisance of finding yourself in the dark if you short a line. Further, it should be wired through an "isolation transformer" rated at 150 watts. In servicing electrical equipment, especially AC-DC devices, you expose yourself to more than average shock hazard. An isolation transformer eliminates direct physical connection between the outlet and the power source. It can literally be a lifesaver. Typically, it comes with a 6' cord, plug, and standard AC receptacle.

ELECTRICIAN'S TOOLS.   You'll want a variety of *screwdrivers* with electrician's, cabinet and Phillips blades. The electrician's and cabinet blades have tips the same size as the shaft so they can turn screws that are deeply recessed. You'll want an 0, 1, and 2 Phillips-head driver. You'll also want at least one offset screwdriver, and one or more fine-blade jeweler's screwdrivers.

Include at least one *screw-holding screwdriver*. There are many occasions when you can't hold a screw in place by hand when you're starting to drive it. Also, it lets you hold onto the screw when it's being removed so that it doesn't drop into the works.

To turn and crimp wires around terminals, to reach into tight situations to hold wires or retrieve fallen parts, you'll

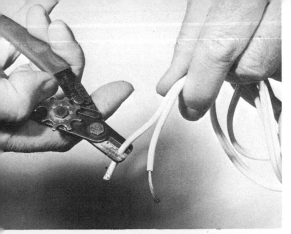

Wirestrippers adjust for removing insulation from various sizes of wire. The jaws will cut wire, too, but are not recommended for such use as they may become misaligned.

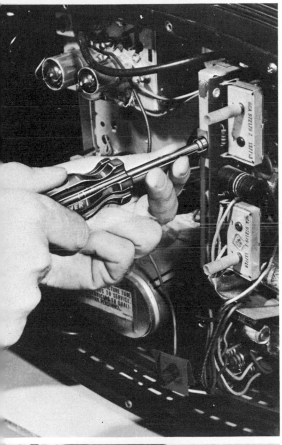

Nutdriver is a useful tool for electrical work. Some drivers fit a ratchet handle (below) for fast work.

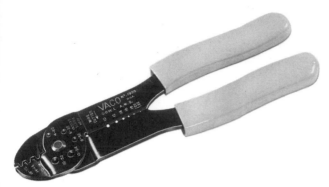

This tool cuts and strips wire and crimps solderless terminals to wire. It also cuts five sizes of bolts.

want a pair of standard *longnose pliers* and a *miniature pair*. Incidentally, there are also *pick-up tools* you can get to retrieve dropped objects. Press a plunger and the tool's jaws open; let go, and the jaws close. A pair of 10″ tweezers are also good reach-extenders.

For cutting wires to length, you'll want a pair of *oblique, side,* or *diagonal-cutting pliers*. The 5″ needlepoint are best for electronic projects. Also useful are needlenose end cutters. They'll get in and make cuts where nothing else can reach. They're especially good when you're taking old equipment apart for salvage.

You'll need a *wire stripper*. You can get an inexpensive pair that adjusts to various wire sizes so that you cut through the insulation without nicking the wire. In addition, you'll find a two-bladed *electrician's knife* useful. One blade is a combination screwdriver-wire-stripper. The other is a spear blade.

Nut drivers are useful. You can get one that adjusts to any size hex nut. If you get separate drivers, a ³⁄₁₆″, ¼″, ⁵⁄₁₆″, and ⅜″ will take care of most chassis work. Get ones with handles that are color-coded for quick size identification. Though sometimes awkward to use, a *dog-bone wrench* is a useful alternative. It will fit ten hex-nut sizes, but it often requires more swing room than is available.

SOLDERING EQUIPMENT. Consider getting both a soldering iron *and* a soldering gun. The iron has a resistance wire heating element coupled to a soldering tip. It takes a minute or two to heat up, because the tip is heated by conduction. In a typical soldering gun the heating element *is* the tip. When you pull the trigger, it heats up in three or four seconds.

The advantage of a gun is that it heats up fast. One advantage of an iron is that it holds its heat. This means you can use it to solder a joint on an electrical line after turning off the circuit. Another advantage is that you can get a pencil-type soldering iron that weighs only ounces. It won't ruin delicate jobs, such as soldering a phono cartridge. But it won't solder a heavy connection. For that you need a heavier iron or a gun.

The job of a soldering iron or gun is not to melt the solder but to heat the metal to be soldered. Solder isn't an adhesive. It performs a chemical action, dissolving metals from the material being joined and forming an alloy. The amount of heat a soldering tool delivers is usually determined by its wattage. For small and heat-sensitive work, a 40-watt tip is insurance against damage.

You can get guns with interchangeable tips, so you can match tip to work. The heavy tip may use 100 to 200 watts. The medium, 50 to 100, and the light 25 to 100. A power rating indicates the size of the joint a tool is capable of soldering, but it doesn't necessarily indicate its working temperature. Most of the jobs you'll want to do can be handled by a low-power iron.

Instead of a single-loop tip, some guns have a single-post design. It has an indirectly heated tip and uses a copper heating element. A single-post gun drawing 100 watts is said to deliver twice as much heat as the conventional iron. But it takes about twelve seconds to heat up—three or four times longer than the single loop.

Soldering tools can do more than soldering. There are special tips for cutting plastic, removing old putty, and for burning identification on wood handles. A smoothing tip can be used for welding plastic. It's also good for sealing freezer bags and taking dents out of furniture. In the latter case, put a damp

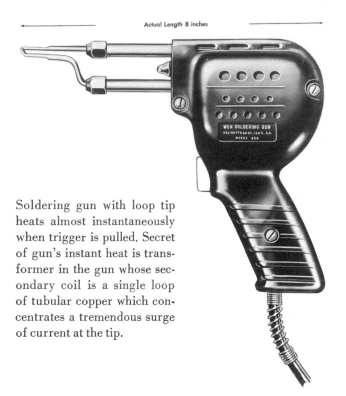

Actual Length 8 inches

Soldering gun with loop tip heats almost instantaneously when trigger is pulled. Secret of gun's instant heat is transformer in the gun whose secondary coil is a single loop of tubular copper which concentrates a tremendous surge of current at the tip.

rag over the dent, then touch it with the tip. The steam will make the wood fibers swell and the dent will disappear. The smoothing tip will also melt stick wax or shellac to seal scratches and nicks.

Solder is the alloy that holds the connection together. A mixture of tin and lead, when molten it has the capacity to dissolve (not melt) copper. The best solder for electronic wiring is about 60 percent tin and 40 percent lead. Joints to be soldered must be clean. Flux helps with this cleaning by dissolving surface oxides and it is often incorporated in wire solder as a core. Acid flux leaves corrosive residues that will ruin the operation of electronic equipment. For this reason rosin flux is recommended for electrical and electronic work. It doesn't present this problem.

You'll need a heat sink for soldering transistors, diodes, and other components that are readily damaged by heat. But

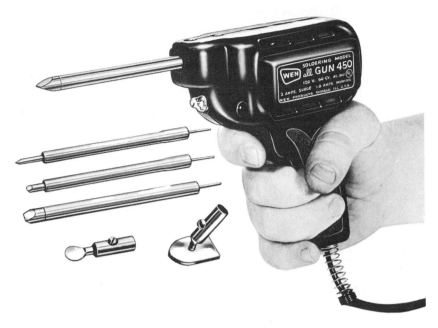

Single-post soldering gun is lighter than most single-loop guns, has readily changeable tips. Special insulation and a temperature-control switch enables it to use a copper heating element from which heat is conducted to the tip.

This is not a soldering gun but a pistol-grip soldering iron. It has no transformer; conduction from a resistance element heats the tip.

you probably don't have to buy one. One is likely to be included
in any kit you assemble.

TEST EQUIPMENT.   One of the most useful tools for
troubleshooting is a *continuity checker*. Wires burn out, break,
or become disconnected. A continuity checker will enable you
to tell if this has happened. It can tell you if a switch or fuse
is good. It can tell you if the windings in a motor armature are
intact. *Testing is always done on disconnected equipment,*
never on live circuits.

One of the simplest continuity checkers is a "clicktester."
It's easy to make. It consists of an earpiece, like that used on a
transistor radio, a C or D flashlight battery (even an old run-
down one), and some wire. Solder a 4″ piece of insulated wire
to the top center connection of the battery as a probe. As a
second probe, solder another similar length to one terminal
of a jack that will accommodate the tiny plug of the earpiece.
Run a short wire from the other jack terminal to the bottom of
the battery and solder. For convenience, tape the jack to the
battery. That's all there is to it.

Simple clicktester is made from a D cell and an earpiece.
Current has to travel through suspected part to make a click.
If there is no click the circuit is open.

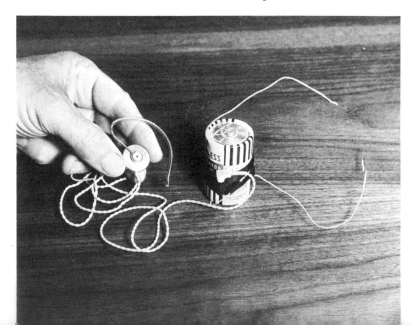

VOM meter enclosed in a box to protect it against damage. It is being used to test the output of an extension cord.

To test the condition of a switch, touch the two probes to the switch terminal screws. With the switch on, you should hear a click in the earpiece. With the switch off, there should be no click. You can test electric bulbs, fuses, motor windings, etc.

The clicktester has limitations. It can't distinguish between the extremely low resistance of a short circuit and the relatively low resistance of some normal circuits. For such accurate evaluation, you need an instrument such as a volt-ohm-meter (VOM). You can assemble one of these instruments yourself from an inexpensive kit. A VOM measures both volts and ohms, AC as well as DC.

In testing appliances and other equipment for malfunctions, you check the resistance in ohms against what the normal resistance should be. A variation indicates a malfunction. It's very valuable, for example, in checking the value of a resistor. You can tell immediately if it's gone bad. An electric clock, for another example, usually measures between 700 and 1000 ohms. Touch the probes to the prongs of the clock cord and you immediately know if the clock and motor winding are good. If the meter shows no reading, you know that either the cord or motor is open.

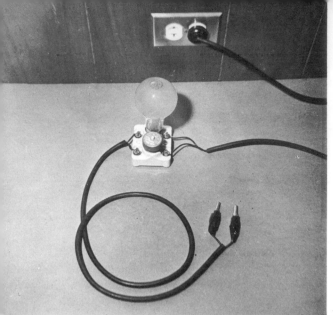

Test light works on the same principle as a clicktester, but requires more careful handling because of line voltage. Circuit breaker is handy for resetting in case of a short.

A socket and bulb, as shown here, can be used as a test light to determine when an outlet or circuit is live.

Neon test quickly indicates if the current is reaching motor terminals. Lack of light indicates trouble is in the cord or supply, not the motor.

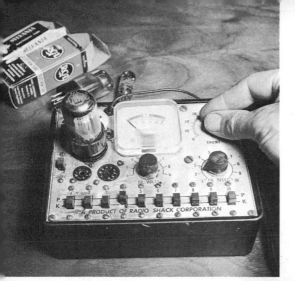

Simple electron tube tester like this one can be assembled from a kit.

A "cheater" cord performs the same connecting function as an interlock. It enables you to operate a TV with its back off, a great convenience in locating defective tubes.

A test lamp is another simple but invaluable aid in troubleshooting. You can make your own of a lamp and socket fitted with two test prods, or you can buy an inexpensive neon tester. You'll use it to determine when electricity is reaching a wall outlet, terminals, or any specified point along a line or circuit.

Other test instruments you may find useful in electronic work are a vacuum-tube voltmeter (VTVM) and a signal generator. Like the VOM, the VTVM measures both volts and ohms. Signal generators, as well as oscilloscopes, have wide application in the servicing of electronic equipment.

10

The Plumbing Center

When you consider all the plumbing jobs that have to be done around the house, you can appreciate the importance of a plumbing center in your workshop. In some instances you can handle a simple job with general-purpose tools, but most often you'll find the work easier and the results better if you have tools designed specifically for plumbing. Read the following descriptions of typical plumbing problems and the tools needed to cure them; then decide what you need for your plumbing center.

CLOGGED DRAINS.   This usually tops the list of plumbing complaints, and the No. 1 tool for the job is the *force cup*. It does just what its name implies: it forces clogging material free so that it can be washed down the drain. You can get force cups (also called plungers and plumber's helpers) designed for sinks or toilets. If you get a two-way variety, you can use it for either. For toilet use it has a flange that folds out.

The second important tool for opening clogged drains is the *auger*, the tool to use when a force cup fails. A closet auger is used for clogged toilets. It is short—usually 5½″—and has a protective rubber guard. For clearing other drains and traps

This plumbing center occupies 4′ of wall space. Tools are hung on perforated hardboard panel. Plastic trays and juice cans hold assorted fittings and small parts.

Three-inch force cup is a handy tool for clearing clogged drains. Folded washcloth is used to seal off overflow drain. Petroleum jelly applied to the rim of the cup gives it a better grip (right).

Closet auger is used on clogged toilets when force cup fails. Power auger fits chuck of an electric drill and handles tough cleaning jobs.

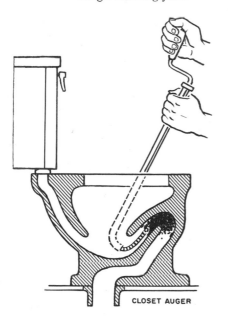

CLOSET AUGER

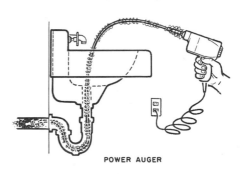

POWER AUGER

there are hook-end or corkscrew-tipped augers ranging from 15′ to 50′ in length. Some are "self-storing." These are a great convenience, and the container into which the snake coil fits prolongs its life and makes it easier to use. For average use, the 15′ auger is the one to buy. If the rare occasion arises when you need a longer one, you can always rent it. There are flat "sewer rods," which come in lengths up to 100′ with blades ¾″ wide. Some augers are of thin clockspring steel. Others, of coiled spring steel, are flexible in every direction.

Power augers are available which fit ¼″ or ⅜″ electric drills. These electric snakes, 6′ and 12′ long, are designed for home use. They work best in drills with variable speeds and a forward-reverse switch.

Opening or removing sink traps is one of the most commonplace solutions for clogging. It is sometimes necessary to remove the trap to insert an auger. Any smooth-jawed wrench can do an acceptable job of removing the nuts without marring

Slip-and-lock wrench and hex wrenches are best tools for getting a nonslip grip on multisided nuts and fittings.

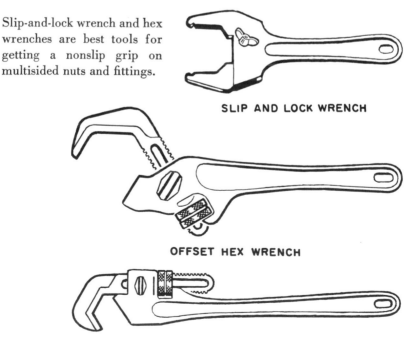

SLIP AND LOCK WRENCH

OFFSET HEX WRENCH

HEX WRENCH

chrome-plating, but an adjustable *slip-and-lock nut wrench* is made specially for the purpose. So is a *hex wrench*, without question the best tool for getting a nonslip grip on multisided nuts and fittings. Its jaws are smooth, so they won't mar plated finishes, and they are narrow, so they fit in close quarters. A hex wrench looks like a pipe wrench, except that its jaws have an elbow crook to fit the hex shape. It comes in sizes with nut capacities up to 3 inches, but the size that handles $1\frac{1}{2}''$ sink and tub drain nuts is all you're ever likely to need. Besides the standard straight hex wrench, you can also get offset designs especially made for working in tight places.

WATER SUPPLY PROBLEMS.   Faucets are the biggest troublemakers. They drip, chatter, or leak at the spindle. Replacing washers calls only for a smooth-jawed wrench and a screwdriver, but if washers wear out faster than they should, and it takes extra-heavy twisting to completely shut off the

Pump pliers with smooth jaws also handle hex nuts when a trap must be removed during a drain-cleaning operation. Bucket to catch water is a necessity.

Replacing a worn washer in a faucet is only half the job if the seat onto which it fits is rough or pitted. A faucet seat dresser can frequently restore seats so they work properly.

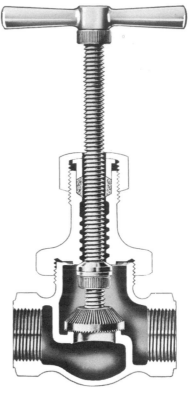

Basin wrench is needed to remove inaccessible nuts when installing a new faucet.

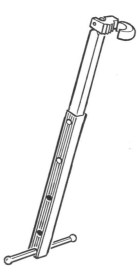

BASIN WRENCH

flow, there may be trouble in the faucet seat. That requires a *faucet seat dresser* or *reamer*. It will smooth the unevenness that is the cause of the trouble.

These drip-stoppers come in seven sizes. Standard faucets have a ⅝″ bevel, utility faucets ¾″, and small faucets ⁹⁄₁₆″ or ½″. Get a kit with three cutters and you'll be able to handle almost any faucet.

When a seat is in hopeless condition, you can use a *new-seating tool* to tap threads in the seat and then screw in a new seat with a screwdriver.

Sometimes an ailing faucet can be saved by replacing its spindle or its entire inner workings. At other times, commonsense dictates replacing the entire faucet, especially if it's an obsolete variety. To remove a faucet and install a new one means getting up behind the basin, and the only way to do it is with a *basin wrench*. You'll find this tool useful in getting at other inaccessible nuts. It belongs in every well-equipped plumbing center.

Internal pipe wrench is used for removing broken pipe, closed nipples, or other fittings when it's impossible to get an external grip. Turning the mandrel forces gripping dogs against inside of fitting; then it is turned with a wrench or, in some models (photo), with a handle that is integral with the tool.

INTERNAL PIPE WRENCH

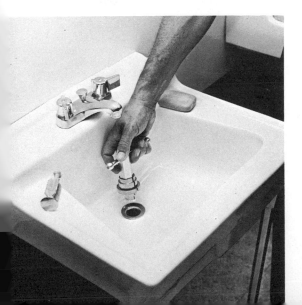
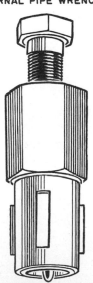

Lack of water pressure may be caused by a well pump whose pressure switch is set too low, by supply pipes that are too small, or by pipes whose capacity has been reduced by scale-like deposits of minerals. These deposits are usually most severe in hot water lines. They may also create an insulating lining in the water tank so that it is impossible to get enough hot water. Scale clogging also makes pipes whistle, bang, and shudder. The easiest way to solve the entire problem is to install a water softener. The softened water will gradually reabsorb the deposits and restore pipes and water heater to near original condition. The tools needed for this job are enumerated in the section that follows.

INSTALLING NEW PLUMBING.   Your project may be as simple as installing an outside hosecock, or as ambitious as putting in an entirely new bathroom. In either case, you will have to work with pipe. You will have to work with pipe if you install a new fixture to replace an old one, install a dishwasher, a clotheswasher, a water softener, a new water heater, a swimming pool, an underground sprinkler system, all or part of a heating system, or new pipes to supplant those that have burst or deteriorated. The tools you need depend on whether it is galvanized steel pipe, or copper or brass tubing.

Copper tubing is the easiest to work, and requires the fewest and least expensive tools. In many cases, you can use copper tubing even though the rest of the plumbing is something else. The transition from steel to copper is made with adapters.

Copper tubing may be cut with a *hacksaw* or a *tubing cutter*. Choose the tubing cutter. It is less work, and it unfailingly produces a square cut. If a cut isn't square, tubing won't recess all the way into fitting sockets and leaks will result. You can get an inexpensive tubing cutter that will handle up to 1″ or 1½″ outside diameter tubing, and a considerably more expensive cutter that will handle 1″ to 3⅛″ outside diameter tubing. You need this large cutter only if you are working on drain and vent pipes.

Tubing cutter always produces a square cut. This one contains a reamer for removing burrs which can cause leaks or clogging.

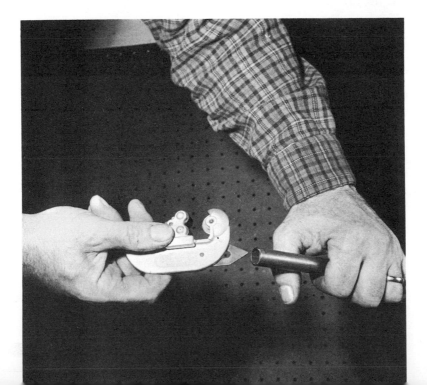

There will be some situations in which you can't use a cutter. That's when you need the hacksaw. The blade is most important. Select one with twenty-four teeth to the inch.

Tubing is either rigid or flexible. Rigid tubing makes a neater installation. You'll use flexible tubing only when you have to snake pipe into existing walls or it is desirable to reduce the number of fittings. For short-radius bending of tubing with ¼″ to ⅝″ outside diameter, get a set of *spring steel bending tubes*. They help prevent kinking tubing. Alternately, you can fill the section to be bent with damp sand. Clean thoroughly afterwards.

Copper tubing is usually assembled by "sweating" or soldering. For soldering either rigid or flexible copper tubing, get a 1 pound spool of 50/50 solid wire solder (half tin, half lead) and either a 2-ounce or a 1-pound can of soldering paste.

Tubing sockets and pipe ends must be thoroughly clean before soldering. For cleaning the tubing ends get a "plumber roll" of *emery cloth*. The cloth is only 1½″ wide and you tear off a strip 4″ or 5″ long for use. If you don't use it all for plumbing, you'll find it has a myriad other applications. For the fittings, get a *copper-fitting brush* for ½″ or ¾″, whichever you are using. You can also get outside copper-fitting brushes in the same sizes. Less satisfactory for cleaning tubing and fittings, but usable, is steel wool.

A standard *propane torch* does an acceptable job in soldering. The only job for which it is undersized is 3″ copper drainage systems. It takes too long to heat up the joints. If you're doing a complete bathroom installation, you may wish to rent a professional plumber's torch or get a gasoline torch. The latter requires unleaded gas and is a nuisance to start, but it does have a big, hot flame.

When joints in copper tubing are ones that may have to be disassembled (like an oil-burner filter, for example), flare joints may be used. Typical *flaring tools* for copper, aluminum, brass, and thin-wall tubing can handle sizes from ⅛″ to 1″. Kits are available that include a flaring tool, a bender set, and

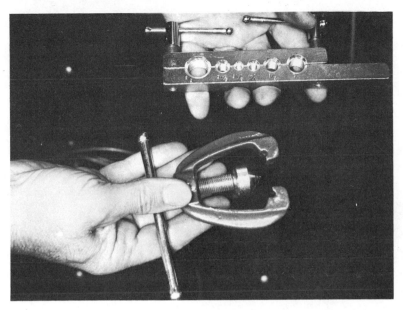

Flaring tool for making connections in copper tubing.

a tubing cutter—all compactly housed in a metal storage box.

Tools for working with steel and iron pipe are considerably more expensive than those for working with copper. You'll need a *pipe vise* or a *machinist's vise* that has pipe jaws. You'll need a *pipe cutter,* a *pipe threader set,* and a *burring reamer.* You can get most of what you need in a kit. If you have only a limited amount of work to do, you can buy pipe in various lengths already threaded. Short lengths of pipe already threaded are known as nipples, and having a few of these on hand never does any harm.

Other supplies you'll need are *pipe-joint compound* and a small stiff brush for spreading it, *plumber's wicking* for wrapping around joints, and *plumber's putty* for setting strainers, faucets, sink rims, etc.

Cast-iron pipe generally requires lead joints. Lead is applied on top of oakum—5 pounds of lead for a 4″ pipe. To pack oakum and lead into joints requires *calking irons,* which come in a variety of shapes to match different situations. At one time only molten lead was used for such joints and a special

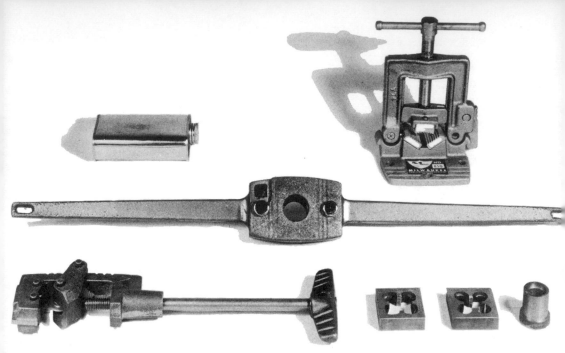

Complete kit for cutting and threading steel pipe.

Dies for threading steel pipe come in several sizes, all fit the same handle.

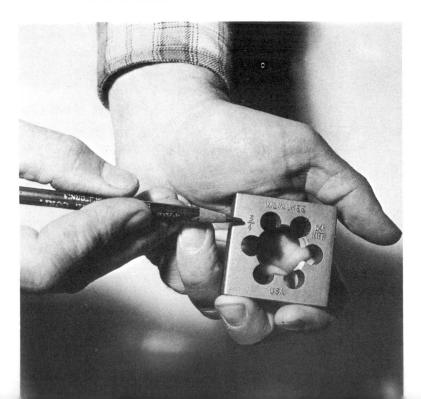

Steel pipe is held in special vise (right) which works by latch action. Cutter requires considerable room to revolve around pipe (below), but vise is detachable and need not monopolize bench space.

asbestos joint runner was needed to contain the lead. Also involved were a cast-iron melting pot and some means of heating the lead, usually a gasoline furnace. Alternately, cold shredded lead, or lead wool, might be used instead of molten metal. Now, codes permitting, there is a lead seal that can be applied over oakum and no heating is required. A pint seals four 4″ joints. Cast-iron pipe is cut with a hammer and cold chisel, sometimes with a hacksaw and hammer.

Flexible plastic pipe is used for pumps, sprinkler systems, and swimming pools. Rigid plastic pipe has similar uses. It is standard pipe for built-in central vacuum systems. Such pipe may be cut with a hacksaw or tubing cutter, though a special wheel for plastic tubing is available. Joining is made with solvent.

For doing major plumbing installations, a ½″ *electric drill* and at least three large self-feed bits are almost a necessity. These bits are expensive, but in time and work saved and the workmanship produced, they are a good investment. A ⅞″ power auger will provide passageway for ½″ pipe, a 1⅛″ for ¾″ pipe. A 2⅛″ will accommodate 1″ and 1½″ pipe. A 2⁹⁄₁₆″ is for 2″ pipe.

The plumber's favorite tool for notching studs and joists and cutting through floors is a *reciprocating saw*. A *saber saw* is best for making counter cutouts for installing sinks. To do the cutting necessary in running some pipes, a *keyhole saw*, a *ripping chisel*, and a *star drill* or *masonry bits* may be needed.

11

Concrete / Masonry Center

What are the jobs around the house requiring concrete, brick, flagstone, and mortar?

There are repair jobs—cracks in sidewalks, broken steps, chimneys that lean, walls that need new mortar, stains of all kinds, basements that leak.

There are building jobs—a new patio, paving around a pool, a barbecue, fireplace, steps, garden wall, a foundation for a new addition, a block garage.

There are enough of both kinds of jobs to require a sizable collection of tools and supplies, and a special place to keep them. Your own collection will depend on the jobs you tackle. Let's consider repairs first.

STAINS. Efflorescence, soot, grease, mortar—these are only a few of the stains that make concrete and masonry unsightly. To remove them you'll need rubber gloves, an eye shield, a stiff-fibered scrub brush, and a variety of stain-removing agents. Muriatic acid is the classic masonry cleaner. If you get mortar stains on brick, flagstone, or tile, it does a great job of removing them. But there are many other equally good, sometimes better cleaners that you'll find at your masonry or build-

Here is one homeowner's concrete/masonry center with
tools and supplies for handling building jobs. The 20-
gallon refuse can contains sand.

Stiff-fibered scrub brush and
a masonry cleaner are often
all that's needed to remove
efflorescence stains caused by
moisture bringing salts to the
surface and depositing them
during evaporation.

ing dealer. Many cleaners are formulated especially for removing oil and grease stains from garage floors and driveways. Trisodium phosphate is the prime ingredient in many of them.

To prevent stains, there are clear, transparent silicone sealers which are applied with a paintbrush. They help keep water from penetrating masonry, and stains from sticking. They are recommended for preserving the cleanliness of grout in tile walls, particularly in showers. Clear sealers can control concrete "dusting." Sealers for brick, flagstone, and marble are important in your arsenal. You'll be collecting various kinds, and for convenience you'll want to stock them all in one place—your concrete/masonry center.

CRACKS, HOLES, CRUMBLING MORTAR.   The first step in almost any concrete or masonry repair is to chisel out cracks and pick away all loose material. A *hammer* and a ⅜"-cut or ½"-cut *cold chisel,* a *bricklayer's hammer,* a 2- or 3-pound *mash* or *drilling hammer,* a *pointed chisel,* and a *small fiber brush* or *whisk broom* will all be useful. You'll need a

Chisel end of a brick hammer (left) is a good tool for removing loose concrete when making repairs. Cold chisel (right) is also an aid in repairing cracks in concrete.

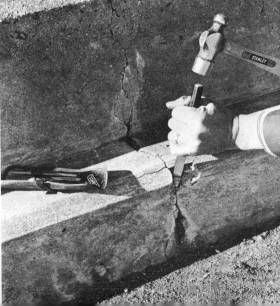

sledge for breaking up old paving, a *railroad pick* for lifting and resetting sections of walk that have settled or buckled.

For digging mortar out of brick joints, a handy tool is a *tuck pointer's rake.* As an aid in holding and feeding new mortar into a joint, you can improvise a *hawk,* which is nothing more than an 8″-by-8″ square of board with a dowel or other handle attached to its underside. You can also use a *steel finishing trowel* as a hawk.

For compacting mortar in joints, you'll need a *jointer* like those used for new bricklaying work. It can have V-shaped or rounded ends to make the style of joint required. If joints are to be filled flat and flush, get a *caulking trowel.* These are available with blade widths from ¼″ to 1″ to match joint requirements. If joints in either brick or stone are to be deeply recessed, you can improvise a *raker* from a scrap of wood with a nailhead projecting as far as the desired jointing depth.

You can mix your own patching material, but you'll find better ones already prepared. Latex patchers are especially good because they can be feather-edged. Epoxy patchers are expensive, but none is more durable. You can buy prepackaged

Homemade hawk (left) is used when jointing brickwork to hold and catch mortar. Steel finishing trowel can also serve as a hawk (right).

If you mix your own patching material, it's a good idea to include a bonding agent and an antishrink agent.

If joints in brick or stone are to be deeply recessed, improvise a raker from a scrap of wood and a nail that projects the depth of the joint.

mixes in bags that contain cement, sand, lime, and other additives. You merely add water. For extensive work you'll find it cheaper to mix your own. Store sand, cement, and lime in refuse cans or other containers that will protect them against moisture. Moisture will quickly cause sand to break through a paper bag.

LEVELING TOOLS. Whatever your building project, you will need one or more levels to keep construction plumb, hori-

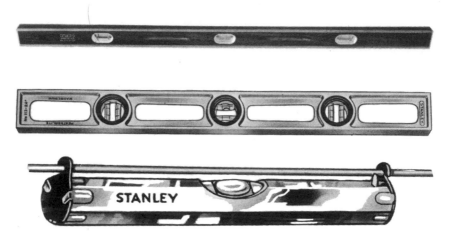

Three useful levels for concrete/masonry work (from top):
48″ wood mason's level; 2′ aluminum level; and line level.

zontal, or at any desired pitch. The mason's favorite is a 4′ brass-bound *mahogany level*. The 4′ length is a good one because it provides a more accurate reading over long spans. The wood is recommended because it is comfortable to touch in any weather.

Walls, walks, and other construction are kept in alignment by means of *lines*. Cotton line is cheapest. Nylon outlasts it many times, but is costs more than twice as much. You can get cotton or nylon lines in green, white, or yellow.

The best way to insure that lines are perfectly horizontal is by means of a lightweight line level which hooks right on the line. *Corner blocks, lineholders,* and *line pins* are devices to which line ends are fastened. For block, an *aluminum stretcher* is a favorite. You can easily make your own line holder out of a 4″ scrap of 2-by-4 cut into an L-shaped piece.

When exacting accuracy is essential, such as for a foundation wall, a *transit* insures that it will be dead level. Rent or borrow one. For less demanding work, you can get a sighting device that thumb-screws to a level.

A 50′ *steel tape* is almost a necessity when building walks,

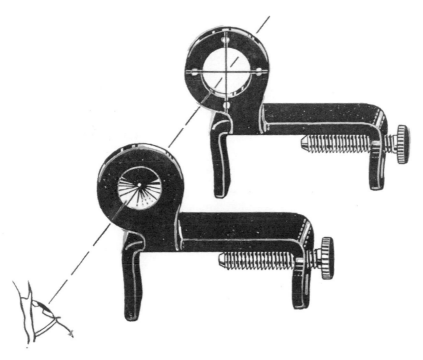

This sighting device attaches to the ends of a level and offers a quick means of getting a reading over a fairly long distance. For more demanding work, use a transit.

Aluminum line holder (left) adjusts to the width of concrete blocks. Homemade holder (right) is simply an L-shaped block with a hole in the corner and a groove along the top to hold the line.

walls, and patios. Just attempt to do it with a 6' folding ruler.

For a firm, level base for slabs and paving, you can use a *garden roller*. You'll also need a *tamper*. You can buy one, or you can quickly knock one together. Make its head of heavy stock, nail a 5' handle to it, and you're ready for business.

CONCRETE WORK.   A *cement boat* or *mortar box* is a necessity for mixing any sizable amount of mortar. Make the sides out of 2-by-8s tapered at each end, the bottom and ends of tongue-and-groove boards. Make it at least 2' wide and 5' long and you'll have plenty of space in which to operate. It may leak a little when you start, but the cement will soon plug it up. You will need a *mortar hoe*. A garden hoe won't do. It's too small. A mortar hoe has a 10" blade with two holes that expedite the mixing process.

For mixing and holding small batches of mortar, you can use a *mortarboard*. It is simply a platform 30" by 30" of tongue-and-groove boards nailed to a pair of 2-by-4 runners.

For building forms to hold concrete, you'll need the

To get a firm, level base for slabs and paving you need a garden roller (left) and a tamper (right). The latter can be homemade of heavy wood.

Rent a power-driven mixer if you have a moderate amount of concrete to prepare. For over a yard, it's advisable to have it delivered.

Two important tools for finishing concrete are shown here: a wood float, in worker's left hand, for rough finishing; and a steel trowel for smooth finishing.

Groover is a special tool for creating patterns or joints on an unsightly plain slab of concrete. Run it back and forth along a straight board.

Power trowel does a fast job in hot weather when concrete may set too quickly if troweled by hand.

following tools: *saw, hammer, level, rafter square, 50' tape, rule, line, hacksaw, pliers* and a *wrecking bar* for disassembly.

You can mix concrete on the sidewalk or driveway or on the basement or garage floor, but be prepared to do a good hosing down afterwards to prevent staining.

The hardest thing about concrete and masonry work is the mixing. Rent a small *electric-* or *gasoline-powered mixer* and you'll cut the work to a fraction.

If you have a yard or more of concrete to mix, you'll be much better off having it delivered. Be prepared with *barrows, shovels,* and *rakes* to spread it as required. The usual home wheelbarrow holds only 3 to 3½ cubic feet. A contractor's wheelbarrow holds 4½ to 5 cubic feet, but before you get one remember that each cubic foot of concrete weighs about 150 pounds.

Troweling is a lot of work too. For a rough finish, you'll use a *wood float.* For a smooth finish, you'll use a *steel trowel.* Rent a *power trowel* and you'll again save yourself a lot of work.

TOOLS FOR BRICKLAYING. For laying mortar when building with brick, you'll need a *brick trowel.* This tool comes in blade sizes from 8½" to 12" long. A 10½" blade is a popular choice.

You'll also need a *pointing trowel* with a blade 5½" to 6" long. It's handy for all kinds of small jobs.

Three indispensable tools for bricklaying (top to bottom): set for cutting brick; brick hammer for chipping brick; trowel for applying mortar.

Mirrored image of mason's ruler shows standard inch markings on one side. Other side has ten different brick-spacing scales.

Brick hammers range in weight from 10 to 32 ounces. Most men are comfortable with one weighing between 20 and 26 ounces.

For cutting brick, you'll want a *bricklayer's set* or *chisel*. These come with blades 2½″ to 4″ wide. The 4″ bit is most popular.

The *mash* or *drilling hammer* is used with star drills for cutting holes. Hammers come in 2-, 3-, and 4-pound weights. Get one that's right for your own size and strength. Masonry bits for your electric drill cut down on the effort of drilling holes.

You may want a special *brick-mason's rule*. It will help you calculate where courses fall.

12

The Metal Shop

You don't need a machine shop to work with metal. This is fortunate, for every home handyman has to work with sheet, angle, and tubular metals. He has to work with heating, ventilating, and air-conditioning ducts, appliances, gutters, and leaders, vehicles, metal furniture. He needs the basic tools for drilling, cutting, and joining metal.

You may want more than the bare essentials. You may want to set aside a corner of your shop for working with metal and include a welder and a metal lathe. If you have a drill press and a grinder in your woodworking shop, these should be located near the metal center. They are as important in metalworking as in woodworking.

The simple bench shown in the drawing is designed for welding, brazing, and casting. The top of the casting area of the bench is covered with asbestos and is 6" lower. The brick-top area, used for brazing, can also accommodate a small smelting furnace. The welding area of the bench is copper-topped. To complete the metal shop, there might also be a bending brake and metal roll, and a power hacksaw.

METALWORKING LATHE. This is the toolmaker's tool, and the heart of any full-fledged metal shop. It is the tool for

COPPER
TOP

BRICK TOP

WELDER   BIN FOR RODS   BRAZING
TANKS

CASTING BENCH

SAND BIN

Bench for a metal shop has three kinds of surfaces: copper for welding; brick for braising; and asbestos for pouring metal into molds. Space beneath the bench is divided into compartments for storing equipment.

gunsmiths, auto mechanics, modelmakers, and inventors. Besides turning metal, it can drill, mill and cut threads. It's a precision tool, and thus one of the most expensive.

In operation and appearance it resembles a wood lathe. Both have a fixed headstock and a movable tailstock. But there the resemblance ends. The metal lathe is designed to endure the most rugged demands and work to the closest tolerances. It has a massive, precisely controlled carriage. The carriage offers provision for feeding the work along the tool bed, squarely across the bed, or at a compound angle to it.

On a metalworking lathe, spindle revolution may be geared to carriage travel, making precision thread-cutting possible. By varying the gears, you can vary the ratio of carriage travel to spindle speed. Cross speed may be automatically controlled.

Lathe size is determined by the diameter of the largest piece of work the machine will turn. This is called its "swing." Typical swings are 6", 9", 10", and 12".

Popular for home use is the midget lathe that will swing diameters up to $2\frac{15}{64}''$. Called the Unimat, it will also function as a miller, borer, drill press, and grinder.

THE DRILL PRESS.   In a machine shop, a drill press ranks second to a lathe. In a home-oriented shop, a drill press comes out on top in usefulness because it works wood as well as metal and is handy for grinding, wire brushing, even shaping.

Drilling metal usually requires greater precision and control than drilling wood. That's why you need a drill-press vise for holding work. Some adjust to holding work at any angle from 0 to 90 degrees. (See Chapter 28 for full details on the drill press.)

A portable electric drill can do some of the same jobs as a drill press, but it lacks precision and control. You can improve these qualities by providing a drill stand for it.

CUTTING AND BENDING METAL.   A hacksaw, snips, and chisels are the standard assortment of hand tools for cutting metal. Among power tools, a table saw, radial saw, saber saw and band saw are all adaptable to the purpose. (See chapters on these tools.)

To cut soft aluminum, copper, and brass with a table or radial saw, you need a small-toothed, taper-ground, nonferrous blade—or a carbide-tipped slotted blade with eight or twelve teeth. Steel-cutting "cut-off wheels" should never be used on a bench or radial saw. Whenever you cut metal, always wear protective goggles.

You can cut light metal with a saber saw fitted with a 32-tooth tungsten blade. Reciprocal-type power hacksaws cut at 90- to 45-degree angles, but this is not a tool for the average home shop.

With special blades, band saws adjustable to slow speeds can be used for cutting metal. You can buy slow-speed convertors for reducing blade speed on some band saws at a 10:1 ratio.

A brake is the professional's tool for bending metal. For the homeowner, a machinist's vise often suffices. You can extend its jaws with a pair of angle irons. Soft metals, like aluminum, can be bent in a straight line with a simple jig. The jig is no more than a saw kerf in a length of wood. The edge to be bent is inserted in the kerf.

A steel pounding block will spare your bench top from a lot of abuse when there is metal to be hammered into shape. The ball-peen hammer is most used in metal work. One with a 12-ounce head is about right for average duty, but you can get heads from 4 to 32 ounces. Polished metal surfaces are damaged by steel hammers so for some operations you will want a plastic-tipped hammer, a rubber-tipped mallet or equivalent.

JOINING AND FINISHING.   Simplest joining is often by means of sheet-metal screws or rivets. Galvanized metal, copper, and aluminum can be soldered. You may use solder to join copper flashing, gutters, copper liners and planters. Solder and a torch are the classic way for joining or repairing joints in galvanized rainware.

There is a special solder and flux for stainless steel. For copper, nickel alloys, and soldering aluminum to dissimilar metals, there is an aluminum brazing alloy and flux.

You can buy inexpensive welders to do your joining jobs, but they are adequate for only the lightest duty. Electric welders require special power supplies. The minimum for even the smallest welder is a 30 ampere line. Most welders require 40 to 60 ampere circuits.

Among other tools needed in finishing are files for dressing metal to size, removing burrs, fins, and ragged edges. A small portable electric sander-polisher is also useful. With an aluminum-oxide disc, it can perform many metal grinding and finishing operations. It is good for grinding down welded joints.

13

The Craft Shop

Carpentry, masonry, plumbing, electrical work—they are essential in running a house, but they don't tell the whole shop story. A vast array of other activities may command your interest and require shop facilities. These interests may include pottery, photography (still or movie), modelmaking, weaving, wood carving, upholstery. If you bind books, carve soap, tie flies, make guns, or work with silver, leather, or plastics, you will want a place to pursue these hobbies.

In many cases, a special bench, and storage facilities for its special tools and equipment will handle a hobby interest within the shop. Shop tools can then be shared, as required, with the hobby. That can be a great convenience and asset.

In most cases, handicrafts and hobbies do not involve the use of noisy machinery, nor do they produce large volumes of debris. That means they can be separated from the main shop and be included within living areas without running into problems. Spare bedrooms, attics, and other space not ideal for woodworking shops can beautifully accommodate handicrafts. These places usually have better natural light. Many hobbies integrate nicely into playrooms or family rooms. When a hobby is the special interest of a younger family member, the shop can often be located in the child's bedroom.

This shop, devoted exclusively to crafts and hobbies, includes work areas and equipment for ceramics, painting, modelmaking, and moviemaking.

Corner of craft shop (right) contains modelmaking bench equipped with a jigsaw, vise, and a 12″-high drill press. The saw can be adapted for sanding, grinding, and buffing. Behind is a movie-editing center with splicing equipment.

Design is often the key to success in many crafts. In this shop a corner is set aside for a desk and drawing board lit by an overhead fluorescent fixture.

A HOBBY CABINET.   Often half the work of pursuing a hobby is getting materials out and putting them away. A good cabinet can enclose everything needed for many hobbies. When not in use, with its top shut, a cabinet can present a good appearance regardless of how disreputable things may look inside.

The cabinet shown, designed by A.M. Warcaske for Rockwell Manufacturing Company, incorporates some of the best ideas found in industrial benches and results from years of experience in varied handicrafts. It has such a variety of facilities that it is adaptable to practically any type of hobby. Closed, the bench lid is a stand-up work surface for such jobs as cutting leather, upholstery, cloth, stencils. With the top set at an angle, it becomes a drafting board, with an instrument drawer conveniently located at its right. At the bottom of each drawer section is a file for catalogs, plans, instructions, letters.

With the top folded back, the sit-down work surface is ready for business. It faces the folded-back top, which is a good place to tack wiring diagrams or other plans or instructions. The work surface itself is hardboard and has a cutout with mortises for bench pins of various sizes. Just below the cutout is a trash drawer. You can do wood carvings right at the edge of the cutout and have most of the waste fall directly into the drawer.

The trash drawer is lined with sheet metal so it can be easily cleaned. A vise can be mounted right over it. Insert a bench pin in one of the mortises and you have a handy surface for working on small parts.

Below the trash drawer is a "jeweler's apron." It's a shallow drawer with a canvas bottom and is a lifesaver when working with small parts. Whatever you drop gets caught by the apron, and doesn't fall on the floor and roll out of sight.

Most of the hobby bench is made of ¾″ plywood. Fir may be the least expensive, but if the bench will be located in a living area you may want to use a cabinet-grade hardwood plywood. It will give the cabinet a real "furniture" look. Assemble all parts of the bench with glue and finishing nails. Set

This craft bench has storage space and work surfaces to accommodate a variety of hobbies—modelmaking, handicrafts, electronics. Chair has high and low seats for different working conditions.

Swinging out hinged end-pieces lets the top slope forward to become a drafting board. Bottom drawer is size to hold file folders. Shallow drawer is designed to hold drawing instruments.

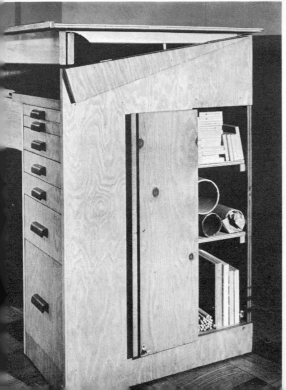

Space between the two work surfaces of the bench permits leaving out work in process. Storage at the back is for long items like lumber and tubing.

Plans for Building the Craft Bench.

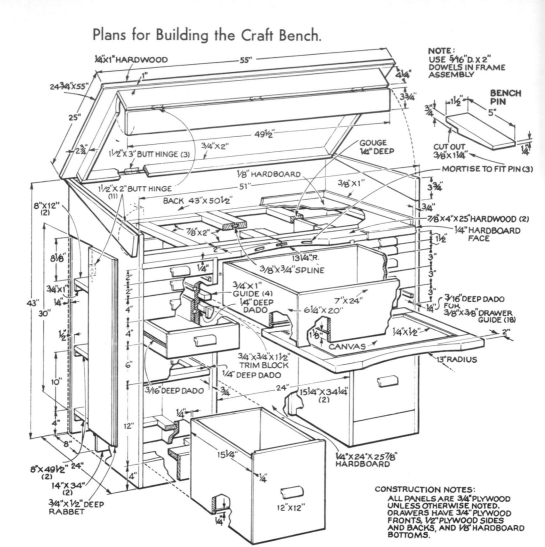

CONSTRUCTION NOTES:
ALL PANELS ARE 3/4" PLYWOOD UNLESS OTHERWISE NOTED. DRAWERS HAVE 3/4" PLYWOOD FRONTS, 1/2" PLYWOOD SIDES AND BACKS, AND 1/8" HARDBOARD BOTTOMS.

the nails just below the surface and fill the holes with wood dough or putty.

Shown with the bench is a high-low stool. It is designed for either bench level. Make it of a fine hardwood, like walnut, equip it with a velvet pad, and it will be a piece worthy of any man's castle.

Here is an orderly procedure for building the bench:

1. Make the drawers and the two drawer compartments.
2. Dado end panels and glue drawer slides in place.
3. Build the frame for the bench top in two sections and join them with a hardwood spline.
4. Screw the hardboard surface to the top, so it can be replaced when worn.
5. Use a ⅜" mortising bit to cut holes for bench pins.
6. Attach shelf cleats for back compartment.
7. Use screws to attach bench top, back panel, and knee-hole panel. The bench can then be easily disassembled for moving.

DARKROOM.   Photo processing ranks high among hobbies. If your shop is in a basement, you may have enough space to wall off one corner of it for a darkroom. But photo work has little relationship to shop activities, so it's just as well to put the darkroom elsewhere if it's more convenient.

You can set a darkroom up in a bathroom or a closet, but if you can find an area about 6' by 10' elsewhere, take it. A 5'-by-5' space is generally regarded as the minimum for a complete one-man facility. A spare room in a living area of the house is good, but it must not be too large. A sprawling darkroom is inefficient, wasting motion and energy.

At first consideration in establishing a darkroom is the availability of running water, preferably both hot and cold. A basement is usually more desirable than an attic merely because water is more likely to be available. If you're in a basement and the location is below sewer level, you can probably provide a pump, codes permitting, to take care of drainage. In a basement, put down a duckboard floor so you won't have the discomfort of standing on concrete for long periods.

You'll need working surface and storage. The working

If darkroom is located below sewer level, a pump arrangement like this one can handle disposal of waste water.

surface should be large enough to accommodate your enlarger and three trays. The best height for the working surface depends on how tall you are and which height you find most comfortable. It will probably range somewhere between 30″ and 36″. You'll need storage for paper, film, and chemicals. Keep the paper and film away from hot-water pipes and heating ducts. Heat and humidity spoil them.

Next comes the problem of darkness. It's easier to make a room dark than to bring water to it. If there is a window, you can buy a lighttight shade or a blackout blind, or equip it with a fitted sheet of plywood. To stop light leaks, entrance doors may require weatherstripping.

Lightproof darkroom fan, made especially for photographic use, exhausts stale air into basement area.

The room should be lighttight, but the walls do not necessarily have to be painted flat black. In fact, it is preferable to enamel the walls a light color so they reflect a maximum amount of safelight.

As for arrangment of facilities, if you are right-handed, you'll find that your work will progress most conveniently from right to left, and the reverse if you are left-handed.

For ventilation, you'll need one or two lightproof fans designed for photographic use. If you have two fans, use one to bring in fresh air, the other to exhaust stale air. That will make a positive continuous flow. You can get by with only one fan that exhausts air if you provide a lightproof intake.

POTTERY.   This is a craft that can be carried on in a garage or basement, or in a spare room in a living area. It can share space with other creative activities such as painting and weaving.

Pottery requires running water, or easy access to it. There may be need for a high-amperage circuit if you have an electric kiln, or gas supply if yours is fired by that fuel.

Potters wheel and kiln are basic equipment for the craft of pottery. Special heavy-duty cable has been run to service electric kiln, which needs a high-amperage circuit.

The principle item of equipment, beside the kiln, is a wheel, either kick- or power-driven. It is unlikely that you will acquire either a kiln or a wheel without previous experience in working with clay, so by the time you are ready for them you'll know what you want. Storage is needed for clay, glazes, completed work, and work in process.

Working with clay is messier than some other crafts. The floor should be durable and easily maintained. Concrete or resilient sheet material are satisfactory.

THE INFORMATION CENTER.   Everyone who engages in a craft knows how many books, magazines, and articles he collects on the subject. Keeping them all in one place is a big help in tracking down a particular bit of data or a design idea. The unit shown makes organizing such material easier.

Every craft shop needs an information center. This wall-hung chest can accommodate books, clippings, catalogs, and plans.

Plans for Building
the Information Center

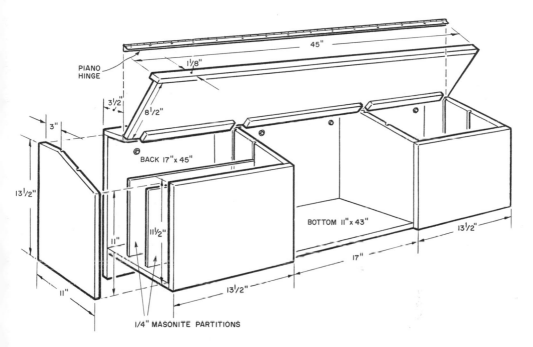

With its lid down, it's a stand-up desk that hangs on the wall and occupies no floor space. A convenient shelf holds books, magazines, catalogs.

Lift the lid, and you find two file compartments that can hold clippings, instruction sheets, correspondence, and other data.

All parts of the information center can be cut from a 4'-by-6' panel of ½" plywood. Masonite partitions slip into slots cut halfway back in the file compartments to keep material vertical when the files are only partially filled. Butt joints fastened with screws and glue are used throughout.

14 | The Portable Shop

Many maintenance jobs have to be done on location. This means carrying tools, nails, other supplies and equipment to where you are working. In some cases, it means transporting them in a car. You'll find it highly convenient to provide easy portability.

HOLSTERS.   The simplest kind of carriers are strong leather tool holders that attach to your belt. A simple loop with two belt slots will accommodate a hammer. You'll find it espe-

Leather holsters enable you to carry small tools on your person when working on jobs outside the shop.

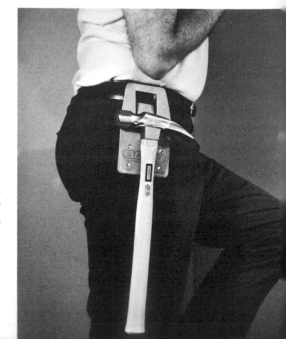

cially useful when climbing a ladder. Another type of single-tool holder is a pocket about 4″ wide and 6″ high, into which you can slip a pair of pliers, a folding ruler, etc.

Other holders may have from three to five pockets of various sizes. In addition, some may have one or more side loops and a T chain to hold a roll of electrician's tape. Some are fitted with harness snaps for holding small tools.

Everyone is familiar with canvas carpenter's aprons, often given away as promotional items by lumberyards. You can buy strong, tough carpenter's aprons made of heavyweight leather. Instead of just one or two nail pockets, they may have four, and in addition a variety of tool pockets, slots, and loops. Instead of tying them around the waist with a string, you have an adjustable web belt which quickly hooks together.

SIMPLE TOTEBOXES.   Carriers for supplies can be made of scrap wood, plywood, and hardboard. You can design these carriers to fit in a drawer or hang on a wall. Attach a strap to a carrier instead of a handle and you can sling it from a shoulder for occasions when you need both hands free.

You can put compartments in a totebox so that tools and supplies fit individually. A saw, a hammer, a torch, chisels—each can have a special place.

Here are two good tricks:

Slot an extra leg on one side of your totebox so it can be tightened by a wing nut in any position. Then you can set the box level on any roof regardless of its pitch.

Bothered by the wood chips and sawdust that collect in your totebox tray? Make its bottom of hardware cloth and the debris will sift through instead of piling on your tools.

There are portable tool caddies you can buy. Unlike the usual toolbox in which you have to rummage to find what you want, these are organized so that tools are easily accessible.

Different kinds of nails are kept separately in this 8-compartment carrier. It is sized to fit into a workshop drawer when not traveling.

Small totebox built of scrap wood holds hammer and oil can in clips at each end, screwdrivers in holes drilled in inside brace. The tray has room for a variety of tools.

Commercial totebox has thirty-nine tool-holding slots, two storage wells for large items, and four small drawers for nails, screws, etc. *Courtesy Acro-Mils Corp.*

Large metal totebox has cantilever tray which swings up for access to tool-storage compartment below. *Courtesy Simonsen Corp.*

Tools can be stored in a strategic place in the house in kit which attaches to back of closet door. When minor repairs must be done, you don't have to tote tools from the shop to the job.

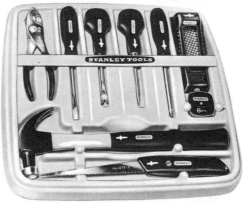

Plans for Building
the Mini-Bench

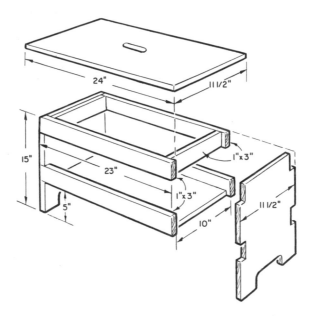

THE MINI-BENCH. For many on-location jobs, you need a sawhorse, a step stool, and a work surface. You can build a "mini-bench" which can perform all these functions.

It's really an old-fashioned carpenter's bench which you can quickly knock together out of 1"-by-12" stock. A good height is 16"; a good length, 24". Brace the bench with a shelf-tray about halfway up and you'll have a convenient place for carrying tools and supplies. Apply glue to all joints before driving screws or nailing and you'll have a miniature work-bench sturdy enough to take all the sawing, hammering, and drilling you do. The mini-bench's 16" height will let you reach an 8' ceiling. Cut an oval slot in the center of its top to accommodate your four fingers and carrying it will be no problem.

CARRY-ALL.   This open-style chest, designed by Masonite, offers the advantage of a perforated hardboard tool rack so that everything is accessible. You can build the carry-all in the size shown, or in a smaller model, with tray dimensions reduced to 12″ by 24″ and hardboard to 24″ by 24″. The cutout for a hand-hold means you'll always pick up the carrier at a point where it balances.

Carry-all holds a large number of tools in side compartments and on perforated hardboard rack. Hand-hold should be cut in the exact center so the totebox balances when picked up.

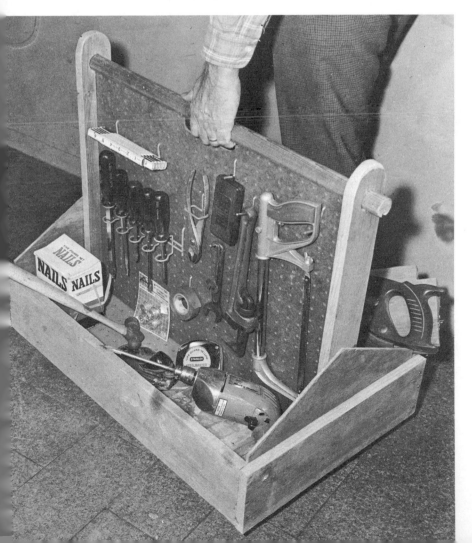

Build the basic box first, joining the ends to the sides with nails and glue. Hardboard bottom fits in saw kerfs cut in the sides. Uprights and plywood end panels are nailed and glued from the inside to the end pieces.

TRAVELING ASSISTANT.   You can travel in style with a 7-in-1 assistant like that shown in the photograph. It has special holders for tools. A plane fits into a holster at one end. At the other end, two springs support a propane torch. Chisels and bits can be kept in the removable tool tray. A handsaw slides into a slot behind a small-parts bin.

Plans for Building
the Carry-All Totebox

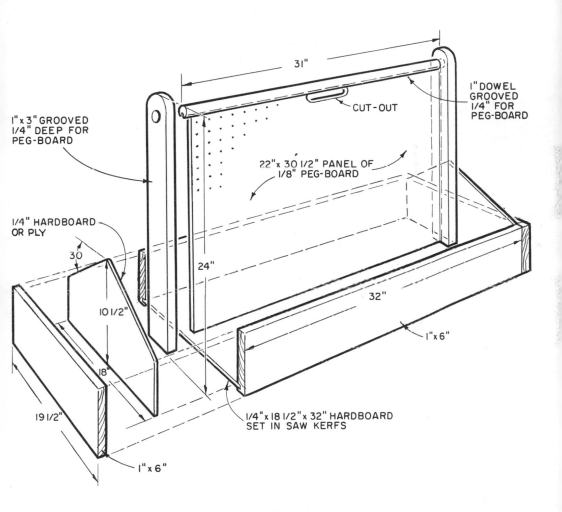

31"

I" DOWEL
GROOVED
1/4" FOR
PEG-BOARD

CUT-OUT

I"x3" GROOVED
1/4" DEEP FOR
PEG-BOARD

22"x 30 1/2" PANEL OF
1/8" PEG-BOARD

1/4" HARDBOARD
OR PLY

30

24"

10 1/2"

32"

I"x 6"

18"

19 1/2"

1/4"x 18 1/2"x 32" HARDBOARD
SET IN SAW KERFS

I"x 6"

The top of the traveling assistant is adjustable. At its lowest position, it serves as a step stool. Raised all the way, it's at sawhorse height. Swung to one side, the top is a support for work that must be held vertically. The box includes a duplex grounded receptacle. Its cord winds up on a built-in spool when not in use.

Traveling assistant is a self-contained workshop that not only carries tools to the job but functions as a sawhorse, miter box, and step stool once there. Here the adjustable top is raised to its full height and used as a sawhorse.

Swung sideways, the top acts as a clamping surface to hold boards for planing or routing. Duplex grounded receptacle on the extension outlet lets you plug in power tools at your feet. Cord winds up on built-in spool.

Tilting the top to form a V with the side creates a handy holder for working on tubing and other round stock.

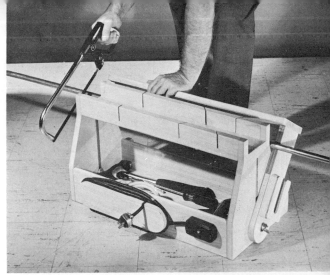

With top out of the way, the miter box is free to handle angle cuts. Box should be made of hardwood.

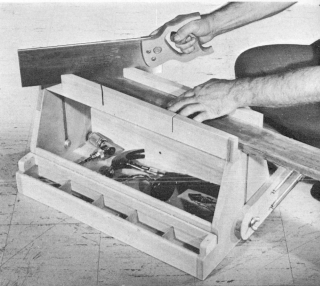

When top is adjusted to this position, the springs on one end hold a propane torch in place. Braze bolt heads and pin washers, as shown in the plans, to keep them from turning when wing nuts are tightened or loosened.

Plans for Building the Traveling Assistant

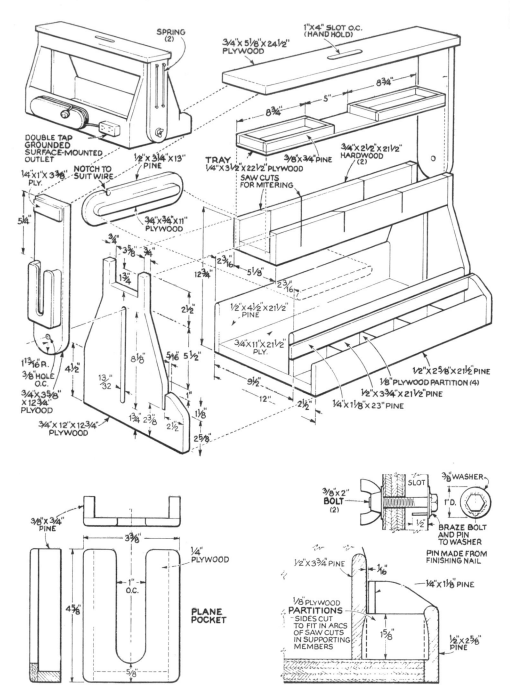

SPRING (2)

1"X4" SLOT O.C. (HAND HOLD)

3/4"X 5 1/8"X 24 1/2" PLYWOOD

8 3/4"

8 3/4"

5"

DOUBLE TAP GROUNDED SURFACE-MOUNTED OUTLET

1/2"X 3/4"X13" PINE

NOTCH TO SUIT WIRE

TRAY 1/4"X3 1/2"X 22 1/2" PLYWOOD

3/8"X 3/4" PINE

3/4"X 2 1/2"X 21 1/2" HARDWOOD (2)

SAW CUTS FOR MITERING

1/4"X1"X 3 3/8" PLY.

5 1/4"

3/4"X 3/4"X 11" PLYWOOD

3/4"

3 7/8"   3/4"

1 3/4"

2 3/16"

12 3/4"

5 1/8"

2 3/16"

1/2"X 4 1/2"X 21 1/2" PINE

2 1/2"

8 1/8"

5/16   5 1/2"

4 1/2"

13/32

3/4"X 11"X 21 1/2" PLY.

1 13/16 R.
3/8 HOLE O.C.

3/4"X 3 5/8" X 12 3/4" PLYWOOD

1 3/4   2 3/8   2 1/2

1"

1 1/8

3/4"X 12"X 12 3/4" PLYWOOD

9 1/2"

12"

2 1/2"

2 5/8"

1/2"X 2 5/8"X 21 1/2" PINE

1/8" PLYWOOD PARTITION (4)

1/2"X 3 3/4"X 21 1/2" PINE

1/4"X 1 1/8"X 23" PINE

3/8"X 3/4" PINE

3 7/8"

1/4" PLYWOOD

1" O.C.

4 5/8"

5/8"

PLANE POCKET

3/8 WASHER

SLOT

1" D.

3/8"X 2" **BOLT** (2)

1/2"

BRAZE BOLT AND PIN TO WASHER

PIN MADE FROM FINISHING NAIL

1/2"X 3 3/4" PINE

1 1/16"

1/4"X 1 1/8" PINE

1/8 PLYWOOD **PARTITIONS** - SIDES CUT TO FIT IN ARCS OF SAW CUTS IN SUPPORTING MEMBERS

1 5/8"

1/2"X 2 5/8" PINE

Most of the traveling assistant is built of plywood and pine. Its miter box, however, should be made of a solid hardwood lumber like maple. Assemble with nails and glue. After assembly, round all sharp edges and sand smooth. Then finish the box with several coats of shellac.

ROLLING TOTEBOX.   This portable tool box, designed by the American Plywood Association, can be carried like a suitcase. It holds a complete carpentry kit. If you wish, you can attach ¾″ wheel casters to the bottom to make handling easier.

Because of the weight of the tools it will carry, this chest should be assembled with rabbet joints, and nailed and glued. Use 4D and 6D finishing nails and a waterproof glue.

Rolling totebox has rack for two saws, drawers for small tools, and larger compartments for bulkier items. It is built entirely of ¼″, ½″, and ¾″ plywood.

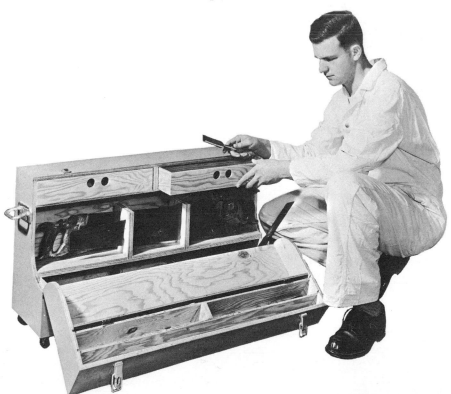

Plans for Rolling Totebox

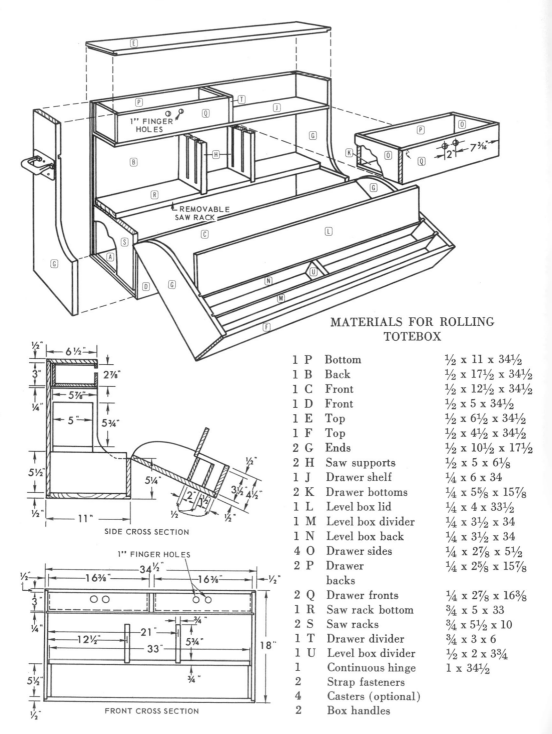

1'' FINGER HOLES

← REMOVABLE SAW RACK

1'' FINGER HOLES

SIDE CROSS SECTION

FRONT CROSS SECTION

MATERIALS FOR ROLLING TOTEBOX

1	P	Bottom	$\frac{1}{2}$ x 11 x $34\frac{1}{2}$
1	B	Back	$\frac{1}{2}$ x $17\frac{1}{2}$ x $34\frac{1}{2}$
1	C	Front	$\frac{1}{2}$ x $12\frac{1}{2}$ x $34\frac{1}{2}$
1	D	Front	$\frac{1}{2}$ x 5 x $34\frac{1}{2}$
1	E	Top	$\frac{1}{2}$ x $6\frac{1}{2}$ x $34\frac{1}{2}$
1	F	Top	$\frac{1}{2}$ x $4\frac{1}{2}$ x $34\frac{1}{2}$
2	G	Ends	$\frac{1}{2}$ x $10\frac{1}{2}$ x $17\frac{1}{2}$
2	H	Saw supports	$\frac{1}{2}$ x 5 x $6\frac{1}{8}$
1	J	Drawer shelf	$\frac{1}{4}$ x 6 x 34
2	K	Drawer bottoms	$\frac{1}{4}$ x $5\frac{5}{8}$ x $15\frac{7}{8}$
1	L	Level box lid	$\frac{1}{4}$ x 4 x $33\frac{1}{2}$
1	M	Level box divider	$\frac{1}{4}$ x $3\frac{1}{2}$ x 34
1	N	Level box back	$\frac{1}{4}$ x $3\frac{1}{2}$ x 34
4	O	Drawer sides	$\frac{1}{4}$ x $2\frac{7}{8}$ x $5\frac{1}{2}$
2	P	Drawer backs	$\frac{1}{4}$ x $2\frac{5}{8}$ x $15\frac{7}{8}$
2	Q	Drawer fronts	$\frac{1}{4}$ x $2\frac{7}{8}$ x $16\frac{3}{8}$
1	R	Saw rack bottom	$\frac{3}{4}$ x 5 x 33
2	S	Saw racks	$\frac{3}{4}$ x $5\frac{1}{2}$ x 10
1	T	Drawer divider	$\frac{3}{4}$ x 3 x 6
1	U	Level box divider	$\frac{1}{2}$ x 2 x $3\frac{3}{4}$
1		Continuous hinge	1 x $34\frac{1}{2}$
2		Strap fasteners	
4		Casters (optional)	
2		Box handles	

3-COMPARTMENT TOOLBOX.   This big box is just the thing when an extensive tool collection must be moved on location. Its large panels are of ⅜″ exterior plywood, and its top, bottom, and sides are of 1″ lumber. Piano hinges are used for the three tool sections and a pair of 2″-by-3″ hinges for the plywood cover. Canvas straps, broom clips, wood latches, wood brackets, and metal L braces may be used to hold tools securely. The plywood cover may be lined with foam rubber to keep smaller items from rattling.

When the plywood cover is closed on its compartment, the unit can be swung shut on the middle compartment. These two compartments together match the thickness of the remaining compartment upon which they close and are latched. The toolbox may now be carried like a suitcase.

This 3-compartment toolbox was designed by the American Plywood Company after study showed that carpenters often spend more time hunting for a tool than using it. The compartments open up to display every tool in its own place, instantly visible and within easy reach.

Plans for Building
3-Compartment Toolbox

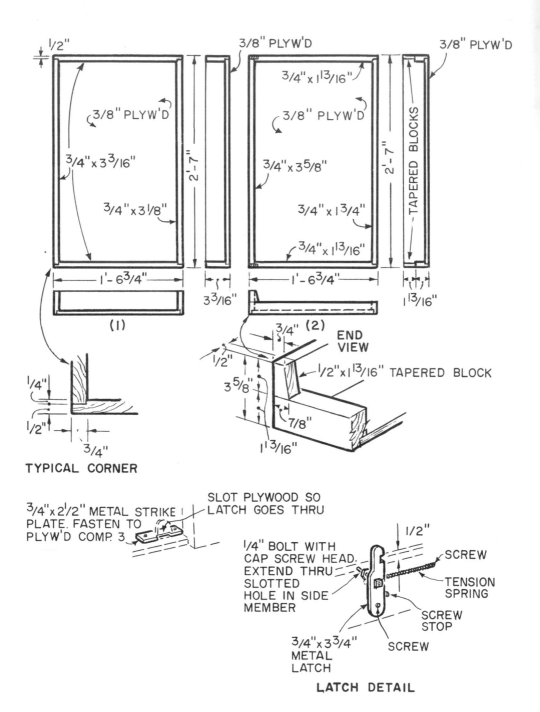

1/2"

3/8" PLYW'D

3/8" PLYW'D

3/8" PLYW'D

3/4" x 1¹³/₁₆"

3/8" PLYW'D

3/4" x 3³/₁₆"

3/4" x 3⅛"

2'-7"

2'-7"

3/4" x 3⅝"

3/4" x 1³/₄"

3/4" x 1¹³/₁₆"

TAPERED BLOCKS

1'-6³/₄"

1'-6³/₄"

3³/₁₆"

1¹³/₁₆"

(1)

(2)

3/4"

END VIEW

1/2"

3⅝"

1/2" x 1¹³/₁₆" TAPERED BLOCK

7/8"

1¹³/₁₆"

1/4"

1/2"

3/4"

TYPICAL CORNER

3/4" x 2½" METAL STRIKE PLATE. FASTEN TO PLYW'D COMP. 3

SLOT PLYWOOD SO LATCH GOES THRU

1/2"

1/4" BOLT WITH CAP SCREW HEAD. EXTEND THRU SLOTTED HOLE IN SIDE MEMBER

SCREW

TENSION SPRING

SCREW STOP

3/4" x 3³/₄" METAL LATCH

SCREW

LATCH DETAIL

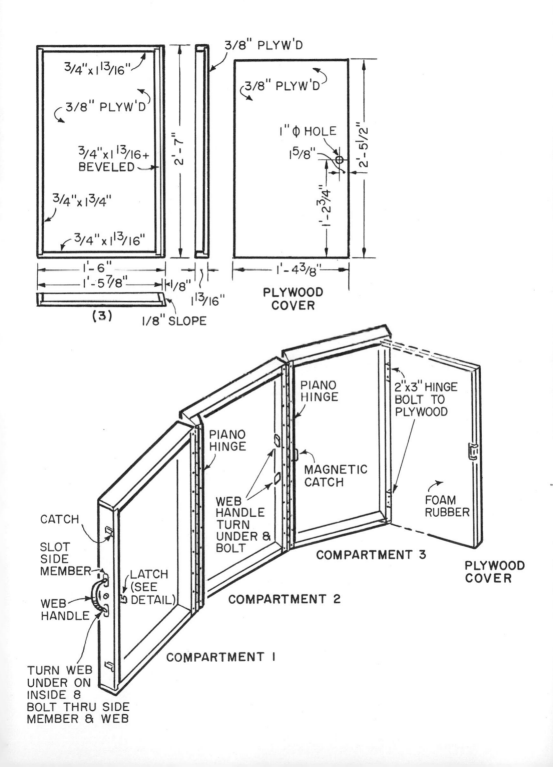

3/8" PLYW'D

3/4"x1 13/16"

3/8" PLYW'D

3/4"x1 13/16+
BEVELED

3/4"x1 3/4"

3/4"x1 13/16"

2'-7"

3/8" PLYW'D

1" φ HOLE

1 5/8"

2'-5 1/2"

1'-2 3/4"

1'-6"

1'-5 7/8"

1/8"

1 13/16"

1/8" SLOPE

(3)

PLYWOOD
COVER

1'-4 3/8"

PIANO
HINGE

2"x3" HINGE
BOLT TO
PLYWOOD

PIANO
HINGE

MAGNETIC
CATCH

FOAM
RUBBER

CATCH

WEB
HANDLE
TURN
UNDER &
BOLT

COMPARTMENT 3

PLYWOOD
COVER

SLOT
SIDE
MEMBER

LATCH
(SEE
DETAIL)

WEB
HANDLE

COMPARTMENT 2

COMPARTMENT 1

TURN WEB
UNDER ON
INSIDE 8
BOLT THRU SIDE
MEMBER & WEB

With each compartment approximately 31″ high and averaging over 18″ wide, it can hold enough tools to build a house. It was designed by the American Plywood Association, who call it the Tamap tool box. The letters of the word Tamap stand for time and motion American Plywood. The design was originated because a study revealed that carpenters often spent more time hunting for a tool than in actually working with it. This toolbox was organized so that every item is clearly visible and easy to reach.

CASTERS are the important aid to mobility. Using two swivel and two fixed casters is best for most shop purposes. Having fixed casters at front, swivel at rear, makes it easier to follow a straight line. For increased maneuverability, put swivels at front and the fixed ones at the rear. But don't use four swivel casters unless maneuverability is more important than straight-line travel. They are uncontrollable if you have to push for any distance.

For heavy-duty use, you may wish to use six casters. In this case, use four swivels—one at each corner—and two fixed casters in the middle.

For moving table or radial saws, a hand truck or wheelbarrow arrangement works well. For this setup, place fixed casters or wheels at rear of stand only, no wheels at front. To move the saw, lift its front end so the rear wheels are free to roll. Use four casters if you want to make your saw stand into a swinger. It will turn in a tight circle. But make sure the two front casters are equipped with locking levers or brakes. For most situations, 2½″ plate-type casters do the job.

Part 2

HAND TOOLS

15 | Handsaws

Despite the inroads power sawing has made, handsaws still have an important place in any tool collection. They form a large group of more than a dozen varieties.

Leading the group in usefulness are the *crosscut saw* and the *ripsaw*. They come 16″ to 26″ in length and with hardwood or plastic handles. The 26″ length is standard. The 16″ size is good where storage space is limited, as in a toolbox or kitchen drawer. Blades may be of conventional steel, stainless steel, or steel coated to prevent rust, provide easier action, and keep blades gum-free.

If you expect to use your crosscut and ripsaw with any regularity and intensity, get good ones. Poor steel dulls fast, and may even buckle. Some better saws are taper-ground— they are thinner on the back edge than on the cutting edge—for easier action and to prevent binding. Others have a blade crown. Sight along the teeth and you will see they rise to a slight crest at the blade's center. This crown helps speed cutting.

The more teeth (or points) a saw has per inch, the finer its cut and the slower its action. Most crosscut saws have 8, 10, or 12 points per inch. The 8-pointer, the most popular, is an all-purpose saw. The 10-point and 12-point saws are for finishing work. Ripsaws are standard at 5½ points per inch.

Crosscut saw (left) is used for cutting across the grain of wood. Ripsaw is used for cutting with the grain of wood. This one is Teflon coated to prevent binding.

Because ripping, or cutting with the grain, is essentially a chiseling action, the teeth of a ripsaw are filed at the tip, like chisels, and each tooth is lined up directly behind the one in front of it. Crosscut-saw teeth are filed like knives, so that each tooth is a sharp bevel that shears its way. The teeth have "set." This means they point outward, each alternate one in the other direction.

Miter saws are designed for use with a miter box in cutting angles. A good saw and miter box arrangement can be relied on to cut miters more accurately than a power saw. A miter saw may be 24″ to 30″ long and has a thick steel reinforcing spine along its length. Because it is for fine finishing work, it has 11 points per inch, and unlike other saws that are held at an angle, it is held horizontally and cuts with its teeth parallel to the work.

Backsaws are similar to miter saws but shorter (10″ to

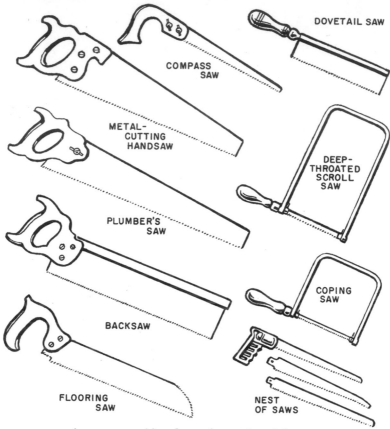

Assortment of handsaws for various jobs.

14″). A backsaw's stiff blade and small teeth adapt it to making precision cuts and close-fitting joints.

Dovetail saws, as the name implies, are for cutting dovetail joints, which they do with extreme precision. A dovetail saw is also useful for cutting tenons and in making models, toys, and other small-scale, finely detailed projects. Typically, it is 10″ long and has 15 points per inch.

Plumber's saws are for the kind of wood-cutting a plumber usually does—flooring, joists, studs and the like, where nails may be a hazard. Hitting an occasional nail doesn't ruin a plumber's saw. It is 16″ long and has 8 points. One type has its handle attached with a wing nut. You can reverse the position of the handle so it's out of the way on awkward cuts.

Flooring saws make their own starting hole. The back edge of the blade tip is curved and has teeth to make a starting slit.

Metal cutters. These are 18″ to 24″ long and may have 13 or 15 points. They're for cutting light-gauge sheet metal.

Cable saws are used by electricians to cut wood and soft metals. Usually 12″ long, they have 8 or 15 points.

Docking saws get their name from their use around docks, but they're also a favorite among farmers, mine workers, etc. They are rugged, skew-backed, 30″ long, and have 4½ points.

Compass saws are the hand-held equivalent of a portable electric saber saw. Usually 12″ to 14″ long and with 9 points, a compass saw is a favorite for making cutouts. To make such a cutout in the middle of a plywood panel, for example, you drill a hole, then insert the compass saw. It is used for making cutouts for electrical boxes. On some types, blades may be reversed for sawing down to a surface, and blades are interchangeable. Among the kinds you can get are carbon steel blades for metal cutting, spring-tempered steel for plywood, and several varieties for woodcutting.

Keyhole saws are smaller versions of the compass saw. Usually they're 10″ long and have 10 points.

Nest-of-saws. This is a handy arrangement, with three saws fitting on one handle. There is almost always a keyhole (10″) and a compass (14″) blade, plus either a nail blade (14″), a plumber's blade (18″), or a pruning blade (16″). Similar are combination saw kits. Usually, they consist of a metal handle and an interchangeable rough-cut blade and a finishing-cut blade.

Coping saws are for making irregular cuts or curves in light stock or softwoods. Their blades have 15 or 16 points. The usual throat opening permits a 4½″ to 5″ cut, but "deep throat" models may give a 6½″ cut. Some coping saws have an adjustable blade angle. Lowest-cost versions have a one-piece frame made of steel rod.

Pruning saws, for trimming trees and vines, come with either curved or straight blades. The latter may have either a single or double edge. The double-edged saws usually have fine peg teeth on one edge for small branches, and twin-pointed teeth on the other edge for large branches. For trimming high branches, there are pruners that have a socket into which fit standard clothes-pole or garden-tool handles. A straight pruner 20″ long is popular for cutting firewood. Another good one: a folding fine-toothed pruner whose 10″ blade folds into a protective handle for easy carrying or toolbox storage. When the saw is folded, the blade exposes a convenient hang-up hole.

Bow saws have a tubular steel frame shaped like a bow. The blade of a bow saw, usually ¾″ wide, has large teeth designed especially for cutting firewood.

Butcher saws are available in special small size for kitchen use in cutting meat. Typically, they are 14″ long and have 13 points to the inch.

Hacksaws. Every shop needs one of these. Get a good one for you'll be using it for cutting pipe, tubing, BX cable, sheet metal, plastics, asbestos board, and many other uncooperative materials. A hacksaw consists of two parts—a frame and a blade. You will use the same frame to accommodate several different types of blades.

Hacksaw is used for cutting metal.

The frame may be flat or tubular. Some are adjustable to accommodate either a 10″ or a 12″ blade. Some take a 12″ blade only. A tubular frame may store extra blades within it. Frames differ in throat size, but the distance between blade and frame usually will be 2¾″ to 3½″. Some frames permit horizontal as well as vertical mounting of blades.

The most important feature of a frame is that it be rigid,

and that it hold blades tight and in accurate alignment. You don't want blades to twist or wobble when the going gets rough, and with a hacksaw it frequently does.

For working in tight quarters, you won't use a regular frame. You'll use special hacksaw blade holders. One can get in a hole no larger than ⅝″. Another, called a "stab saw," needs only enough clearance for the blade to get at the work. It will hold an entire blade or the broken end of a blade.

A hacksaw blade may be of standard steel, molybdenum, or tungsten. It may be flexible or hard-tempered. Flexible blades help reduce breakage. All-hard blades are recommended only when work can be firmly positioned and when cuts are straight. Sometimes only the teeth are hard-tempered and the back is flexible. Standard steel blades, flexible or all-hard, are recommended for nonferrous metals and low-carbon steel. Molybdenum blades are for high-speed sawing. They are extra rugged and can be used for fast sawing under adverse conditions. Tungsten blades command a premium price and are used only for such special jobs as cutting stainless steel, certain bronze materials, etc.

All blade varieties are available in coarse, medium, fine, and very fine. These have 14, 18, 24, and 32 teeth respectively. Choose a blade with enough teeth so that in use at least three

Hacksaw blade holder, called a stab saw, permits cutting flush with a surface or in close quarters where a frame would be blocked.

teeth will be in contact with the work. Otherwise teeth may straddle the work and "shell" off.

Coarse blades are for cutting soft metals, like aluminum, brass, bronze, and copper, in stock $\frac{7}{32}''$ thick or better. The 18-tooth medium blade is best for all-round use. It will handle almost any job acceptably and it can eliminate the nuisance of constantly switching blades to get the one recommended for the exact job.

The 24-tooth blade is especially designed for cross-sections $\frac{1}{16}''$ to $\frac{1}{4}''$, items such as pipe, angles, and small rods.

The 32-tooth blade is especially designed for cutting stock up to $\frac{1}{16}''$, such as sheet metal, light tubing, and BX cable.

Blades with 14 and 18 teeth per inch have teeth set in "raker" pattern. Teeth in 24 and 32 blades have a "wavy" set. Armed with this knowledge you can tell at a glance if a blade has 14–18 or 24–32 teeth.

16

Hammers / Hatchets / Mallets

A shop cannot have too many nail hammers. On many projects it's convenient to have hammers in several locations. It saves carrying one hammer back and forth, and cuts down time wasted in looking for a one-and-only.

Nail hammers are essentially of two types. One is the *claw hammer*, with a curved claw designed for pulling nails. The other is a *ripping hammer*. Its claw is straight, making it easier to get under boards and pry them free or apart. Most hammers come in three weights. The weight is that of the hammer head. The 13-ounce hammer is for light work or for use by someone who can't handle a heavier hammer. The 16-ounce weight is the one most people like. It can tackle almost anything. For driving 16- and 20-ounce spikes, however, the 20-ounce hammer has an advantage. But you won't want to use it ordinarily. On small stuff, it's too heavy for accurate control. Sometimes a 20-ounce hammer is referred to as size No. 1, a 16-ounce as size 1½, and a 13-ounce as size 2.

All-steel hammers are favored by many shopmen. These have tubular or solid handles that are permanently locked to the head. There never is any danger of the head coming loose. Usually they have a perforated, neoprene-rubber grip. This

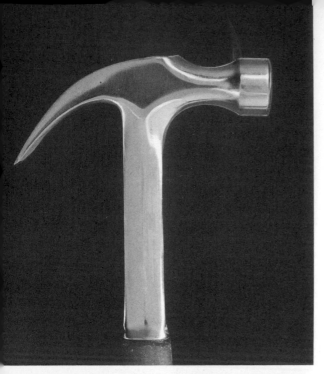

Claw hammer is designed for pulling nails.

Ripping hammer has straight claw for prying.

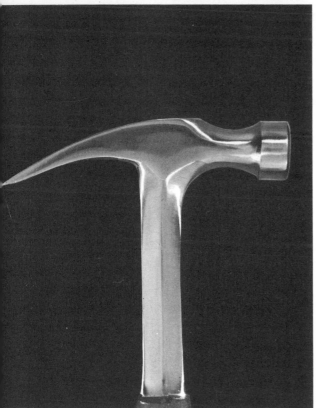

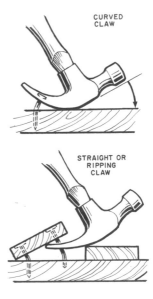

CURVED
CLAW

STRAIGHT OR
RIPPING
CLAW

has a more comfortable feel than a wood handle and is less tiring. It absorbs shock better.

Don't waste money on a bargain hammer. Its head, in most cases, is of cast metal. If you yank too hard on a nail, it will lose a claw. Further, it is seldom balanced properly. It doesn't have a comfortable, authoritative feel. It is only good for driving nails crooked. Cast-iron hammers usually have a painted black finish.

A good hammer has a forged head. Its nailing face is chamfered (beveled) so that the edge won't chip. The striking face has a slight crown to match the arc of a normal striking swing and to provide a square, true blow. The crown also permits driving a nail flush with the surface without damaging the area around the head. A plain-faced hammer leaves marks when nails are driven flush.

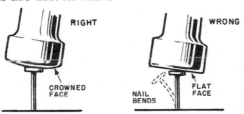

Crowned hammer face matches the arc of the swing and hits a fair blow. Nail doesn't bend. Flat hammer face hits nail at an angle and bends it.

A flying chip from a hammer face may cause injury. Stanley especially tempers its hammer face rims so that they have a lower degree of hardness and won't chip. A rim-tempered hammer may still have a hard-tempered face.

The kind of handle a hammer has affects its balance and the way it feels in your grasp. Rest a hammer across a narrow board and you will find that one with a wood handle balances close to the head. A hammer with a solid steel handle will balance farther back. Those with fiberglass or tubular steel handles balance somewhere in between. It all depends on the weight of the handle as compared with the weight of the head.

Ball peen hammer is used for metalworking.

Ball peen hammer. For working on automotive equipment and machinery a ball peen hammer is the natural choice. Instead of a claw this hammer has a rounded end called a peen. The peen is used mostly for riveting. The three most popular sizes are 6 ounce for light work, 12 ounce for average duty, and 16 ounce for heavy work.

Stone hammer. Handy for concrete and masonry work, and for use with chisels and star drills, is a drilling or stone hammer. These come in 2-, 3- and 4-pound weights. Choice depends on individual preference.

Bricklayer's hammer. If you lay brick or block you will want a bricklayer's hammer. These are available both with hickory and tubular steel handles.

Drilling hammer is used with a star drill for boring concrete. The drill is revolved a partial turn after each blow.

Bricklayer's hammer has a chisel edge at its face and rear. Either one can split a brick, but the face is especially good for nibbling away irregularities.

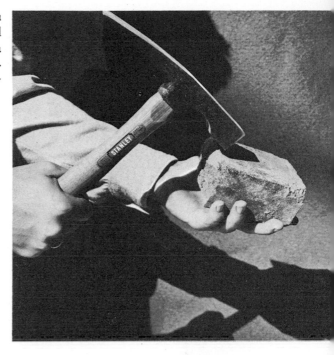

Sledge. For breaking rocks, demolition work, splitting logs, and other heavy hammering jobs, a sledge is a must. Select a sledge you can swing with relative ease. This will probably be a 12-pound weight. It takes extraordinary strength to swing a 20-pound sledge effectively.

Soft hammer. This tool is used on all the materials that might be damaged by ordinary steel hammers. In many cases a pounding block with a regular hammer is a good substitute. This spreads the blow and protects the surface. Among softies, plastic-tip hammers are a favorite. One variety has one tip of vinyl, which won't mar aluminum, wood, or polished surfaces, the other tip of amber plastic for use on iron, steel, etc. Amber plastic tips are replaceable.

Mallet. This wooden hammer is used to drive some wood-handled chisels and gouges. Chisels with tough plastic handles capped by steel take the blows of a conventional hammer and are the best choice for the shop.

Hatchet. To an old-time carpenter, a hatchet was one of the most important tools. In rough carpentry, when a board was to be trimmed, he used a hatchet. It takes off wood faster and easier than a plane or a saw. When a shim, shingle, or board had to be split to size, the hatchet got the call. You will find the hatchet useful for all these purposes and more. Use it wherever a chisel's more accurate cutting is not desired or required. The flat side of a hatchet can be used as a hammering tool.

The most useful hatchet for the home shop is the half hatchet. Its blade is extra thin. Half hatchets come with either a single or double bevel. The single bevel is best for hewing to a line. When hewing to a line, a series of cuts are made against the grain to the depth of the required cut. The board is then reversed and the notched wood removed to the depth of the cuts. For deeper cutting, the process may be repeated. Chopping should be done with the grain whenever possible. The single bevel can be used only with the right hand. The double bevel is an all-purpose hatchet.

17

Planes

A plane is a tool for making wood smooth and flat. It is used for paring a little off the edge of an oversized board, and for taking the sharp edges off a board or panel, an operation known as chamfering.

Out of the wide assortment of planes available, three types figure importantly in the home workshop—the block, the jack, and the jointer plane.

The *block plane* is the smallest variety. Typically about 7″ long, it is held in one hand when in use. This small size makes it easy to handle, and it's the plane most men reach for when just a little has to be trimmed from a board or an edge taken off. It's a champ at end-grain.

The *jack plane* comes in several sizes, but typically it will be 14″ long and have a blade 2″ wide. It's an all-round, all-purpose plane. The smooth plane is similar to the jack plane except that it is smaller and lighter. Typically it's 8″ or 9″ long and has a 1¾″ blade.

The *jointer plane* is the largest variety. Typically 20″ to 24″ long, it's for producing true flat edges on long boards so they fit perfectly together. A prime use around the house would be for planing a door edge. A fore plane is like a jointer except that it's shorter—usually about 18″ long. Remember—

Useful planes for the home workshop (from left): rabbet plane, a specialized type for cutting rabbets; smooth plane, a light-duty plane similar to the jack plane but shorter; rough or scrub plane, with a rounded cutting edge for heavy stock removal; and jack plane, an all-purpose plane for truing boards of moderate length.

Block plane's blade is set at a lower angle than blade in other planes; thus it cuts faster and with less resistance. It will make an edge smooth but, as it is short, not necessarily true.

Jointer plane is designed for truing up long edges, as on a homemade plank door. The longer the plane, the better it is for smoothing and truing a long span of lumber.

the longer a plane, the more readily it bridges low spots, cuts the high ones, and produces the kind of smooth results you want.

Special planes are made for doing specialized jobs such as rabbeting, routing, grooving, etc. Most of these jobs can be done by power tools easier, faster, and more accurately, so they have little application in the home shop. A saw and jointer can do many of the jobs that in other years would have been done with a plane.

PLANE ANATOMY.   The plane iron or blade is what does the cutting. The depth of cut depends on how far it projects through the mouth on the bottom of the plane. This is controlled by a knurled knob. For best results, the iron should project a bare fraction. For an even cut, the blade must be set straight. Set at an angle, it will cut deeper on one side than on the other. There is a lever for making lateral adjustments.

On jack, smooth, fore, and jointer planes there are double plane irons. The top one serves to stiffen the plane iron and curl up the shavings. The distance of the plane-iron cap from the edge of the cutting blade controls the thickness of shavings. After making any adjustment, tighten the cap so it fits very tight. Otherwise, there may be danger of shavings getting between the cap and the blade. The iron cap isn't needed on a block plane because there is no problem of clogging the mouth. A block plane is used only in cutting end-grain, which produces a powder, or in fine shaving.

Some planes have grooved bottoms. The purpose is to make them slide smoothly and with less friction.

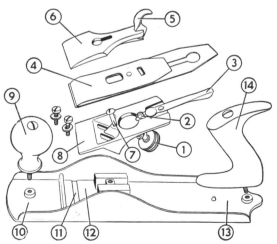

PARTS OF A PLANE
1. Depth-adjustment nut
2. Y-lever
3. Lateral-adjustment lever
4. Double plane iron
5. Cap lever
6. Cap
7. Cap screw
8. Iron support
9. Knob
10. Toe
11. Mouth
12. Bottom
13. Heel
14. Handle

If a plane won't cut, you're trying to make too thick a cut, or the blade is dull. It should be razor sharp. If your cut is rough, it usually means you're cutting against the grain. For a smooth cut, you must go *with* the grain. Don't use a plane on painted or varnished wood. It won't do a good job and you'll dull the blade.

In making a rough cut, slant the plane across the board as you push it. The best technique for a finish cut is to put pressure on the front of the plane when starting the cut and on the rear when finishing it. This prevents breaking end corners. When planing end-grain, avoid breaking corners by planing from each end to the middle. You can use a jack or smooth plane on end-grain, but the block plane is preferred.

Store planes so they are protected from rust and damage to the cutting edge. An enclosed cabinet is best. Stable the planes on a rack made of two ½″ wood strips. The forward strip acts as a stop. The rear strip elevates the plane so it doesn't rest on its blade. For wall mounting, make a shelf with an area routed out into which the plane's blade can project.

18

Chisels/Gouges/Punches/ Nail Sets

There are chisels made especially for cutting wood, metal, and masonry. With the exception that a cold chisel, which is designed for metalworking, can be used on masonry, chisels are not interchangeable. If you expect to work with all three materials, get chisels made for each one.

WOODWORKING CHISELS. The kind of handle on a woodworking chisel determines the use for which it is intended. There are three kinds of handles found on the various chisels available to the woodworker.

For light work, the easy paring away of stock which can be done by hand pressure alone, or by the lightest blows of a mallet, you can use a *tang chisel*. The tang is the rattail end of a chisel, and it is enclosed in a handle of wood, plastic, or other material.

Some chisels have a socket on one end instead of a tang, and a handle of wood or other material fits into this socket. A *socket chisel* is designed for heavier duty than a tang chisel and to be struck with a mallet. The handle comes out rather easily and is replaceable.

The best type of chisel for the home shop, and a favorite

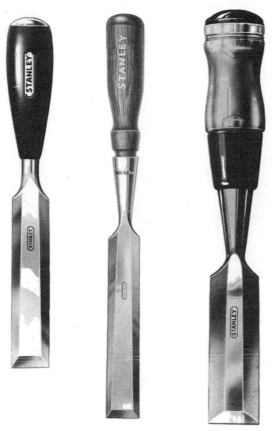

Three types of wood chisels (from left): tang chisel with handle enclosed in plastic; socket-type firmer chisel; heavy-duty chisel with steel cap and amber handle.

with carpenters, is the *heavy-duty chisel.* You can hit it with a steel hammer. The steel of this chisel extends up through the handle and forms a striking face. One type of heavy-duty, or everlasting, chisel is all steel. It has an hexagonal shank and a round head.

There are other words you'll hear used to describe chisels. They relate to differences in the length and thickness of blades and their principal use. There are paring, firmer, butt, and mortise chisels. A pocket chisel is not one you carry around in your pocket. It is just another name for a mortise chisel.

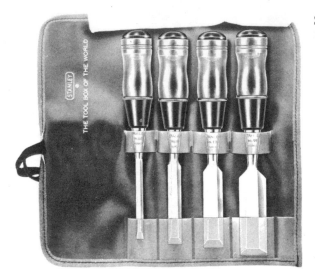

Set of butt chisels in ¼″, ½″, ¾″, and 1″ widths.

Butt chisel being used to cut mortise for hinge on a door.

Paring chisels, which are used without a hammer, usually have tang handles. The blade is short, light, and thin. The short blade makes it possible to maintain excellent control over the chisel and cutting angle when hand paring and carving.

Butt chisels get their name because they are primarily used for cutting the mortise when installing a butt hinge.

Firmer chisels have the longest blades, giving them a wide range of use. They usually have socket handles.

Chisels come in widths starting at ⅛″ and increasing by ⅛″ to 1″. After that, the progression is by ¼″, then jumps to 2″. The ¼″, ½″, ¾″, and 1″ sizes are best for average home needs.

Tips on using a chisel.   Always keep both hands behind the edge of the blade. If it slips, you won't hurt yourself.

When you are hand-powering a chisel, supply the power with one hand, using the other to control the cut.

Chisels have a beveled cutting edge. Rough cut with the bevel down, finish cut with the bevel up.

To get a straight cut when the width of the cut is wider than the chisel, allow each succeeding cut to overlap the previous cut by about one-third.

When you're chiseling along an edge, work from the edge toward the center. If you work in the other direction, you may ruin the edge.

Take out the bulk of the wood with a saw, drill, or plane. Use the chisel for finishing purposes only. Don't rush. Take small cuts. A large cut risks splitting the work.

Observe the direction of the grain where it meets the edge. Cut in the same direction for smooth results. To cut counter to the grain direction means an uncontrolled cut and rough results.

GOUGES.   These are like chisels except that the cutting edge is trough-shaped instead of flat. There are three degrees of blade curvature: flat, medium, regular. Bevels may be on the concave side and such gouges are known as inside-ground. Outside-ground gouges have the bevel on the convex side. An outside-bevel gouge is used in the same way as a chisel with the bevel down. It's a rough-cutting tool. An inside-bevel gouge is used like a flat chisel with the bevel up. If held at a wide angle, it will dig in.

In making any cut, rock the blade slightly as it is advanced so that there is shearing action. In cutting grooves, to avoid damage to edges, start at the edge and work in. In cutting a groove, do it in several stages, getting deeper each time. Don't use the full edge of the gouge, only its inside arc.

Gouges are available with both straight and bent shanks. The bent shank is good for cutting long, shallow grooves. The handle being offset, it permits running the gouge almost parallel to the work.

You can get paring gouges and firmer gouges. Firmer gouges may be outside or inside ground. Paring gouges are inside ground only.

Carving-tool set consists of bent chisel, U tool, skew bevel chisel, veining tool, bent gouge, and carborundum stone. Pocketknife is a useful addition.

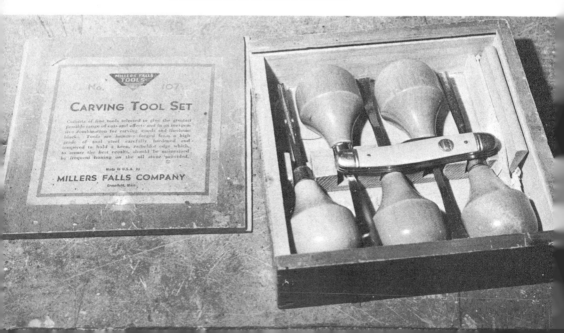

If your project includes carved moldings or panels, don't use carpenter's and cabinetmaker's chisels and gouges like those described. They can be used for rough cutting, but for fine detailing and sculpturing you need a set of carving tools.

A small carving-tool set includes a variety of gouges and a chisel or two. There are deep gouges called fluters and shallow ones called flats. Ones that cut a U-shaped gouge are called veiners. V-shaped gouges are called parting tools. Chisels may have a square cutting edge or an edge at an angle to the blade. There are spoon-bit chisels for digging into right corners and left corners, dog-leg chisels for situations where an offset is needed.

COLD CHISELS.   Essentially metal-cutting tools, cold chisels will cut wire, rods, and sheet metal. They will cut away a rusted nut or rivet that you can't reach with a hacksaw. A cold chisel will cut any metal softer than itself.

A cold chisel is classified by the shape of its point. Besides the classic flat cold chisel with its straight shank and a tip like a screwdriver, there are round-nosed chisels, for chipping rounded corners and cutting trough-shaped grooves; diamond-point chisels, for cutting V-grooves and square inside corners; and cape chisels, for cutting narrow grooves. There are also special "rivet shear" chisels, for rivet cutting.

Cold chisels for cutting metal (from left) : cape chisel, for cutting narrow grooves; diamond-point chisel, for cutting V-grooves and square inside corners; round-nosed chisel, for chipping rounded corners and cutting trough-shaped grooves.

Flat or plain cold chisels and diamond-point chisels are the ones most useful to the homeowner. Special chisels used in masonry work are discussed in Chapter 11, The Concrete and Masonry Center.

The smaller the chisel point, the greater its impact. That is why to cut off a large rivet head, a good mechanic will first cut a slice through the center of the rivet head with a cape chisel, then cut off the head with a flat chisel. The larger the chisel and the chisel point, the heavier the hammer you must use with it.

The size of a chisel is determined by its cut, stock, and length.

Safety with cold chisels.   Wear goggles. Don't allow spectators within line of flying chips.

Always chip away from yourself.

Keep the chisel sharp. Use an emery wheel to maintain the point and keep the original angle. Note that the cutting edge of a flat chisel curves to a high point at the center. Keep a chisel cool as you grind by dipping it in water. If you don't, the chisel edge will lose its temper and become soft.

The cutting angle should be about 60 degrees, not much more or much less.

Smooth away any "mushrooming" on the hammering end. One of those pieces might break off when you're hammering and hit someone in the eye.

When you are chipping work held in a vise, hammer toward the stationary jaw.

Use a diamond-point chisel to extract a broken-off bolt by drilling progressively larger holes into the stub until you have a hole large enough to pound in the chisel point. Then remove the bolt by turning the chisel with a wrench.

PUNCHES.   There are starter, pin, line-up, center, and prick punches. Like chisels, the best way to buy them is in a set. If you can buy a good combination chisel and punch set,

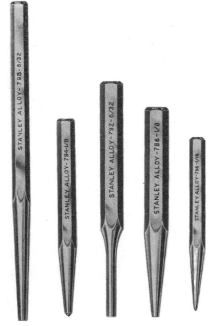

Set of punches for various purposes (from left): lineup punch, for aligning holes when fitting parts; center punches (2), for making a starting point when drilling metal; starter punch, for knocking rivet from hole after cutting off head; pin punch, for finishing the job.

Center punch being used to make a starting hole in metal so that drill won't slip.

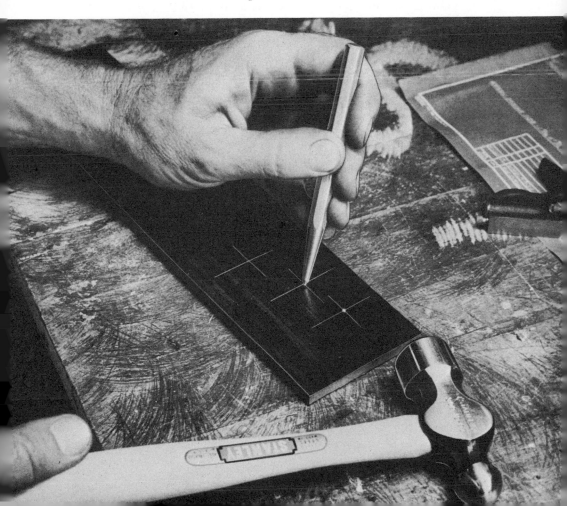

so much the better. A good set will include four chisels rang-ing in size from ¼″ to ¾″ and eight assorted punches. They are not expensive.

Use a starter punch to knock a rivet from a hole after its head has been cut off. You may need the long slender point of a pin punch to complete the job.

Use a lineup punch to line up holes on two parts being fitted together.

Use a center punch to make a starting point when drilling metal. It prevents the drill point from wandering. If you have a variable-speed drill and can start drilling at a very low speed, center punching may not be necessary, but it's still helpful. You can also use a center punch for marking the alignment of metal parts before you disassemble them. By aligning punch marks, there is no guesswork as to their exact positioning.

Prick punches differ from center punches in that they have a longer taper and a sharper point.

NAIL SETS.   Used to drive the heads of brads or finishing nails below the surface, nail sets can also be used for making starting holes for screws. Their size is determined by their point, which may be ¹⁄₃₂″, ¹⁄₁₆″, ³⁄₃₂″, ⅛″.

Use a nail set whose point is a little smaller than the nail you are driving. If you use a larger nail set, you enlarge the hole unnecessarily.

Nail sets may be of round stock their entire length, or they may have square heads. The square head gives a slightly larger striking surface and keeps the tool from rolling when you drop it.

Set a nail head ¹⁄₁₆″ or more below the surface to provide enough of a hole to fill. In some cases you may want to set flat-

Nail set is used to drive the heads of finishing nails below surface of wood or to make starting holes for screws.

Self-centering punch centers screw holes accurately in countersunk hardware. It is also useful in setting finishing nails without marring wood.

head nails—on siding or clapboard for instance.

Use a nail set to prevent marring a surface by accidental hammer blows. Drive the nail close to, but not flush with, the surface. With a single sharp blow on the nail set, drive the nail below the surface. With repeated blows, you have less control. The cupped end of the nail set prevents its slipping off the head of the nail.

19 | Files / Rasps / Scrapers

FILES. There are more than 3,000 kinds, sizes, and cuts of files. Of these you will need about a half dozen for maintenance chores and projects. In both metalworking and woodworking, a file can accomplish things you can't do with other tools, so it pays to have a few of the most versatile ones in your workship.

The terminology used in naming files can be confusing to the novice, so before specifying what files you ought to acquire, it might help to explain the meaning of the most common terms.

The term "bastard" has nothing to do with a file's legitimacy but refers to the coarseness of its teeth. In describing coarseness, file makers use the progression dead-smooth, smooth, bastard, coarse, and rough. A bastard file, then, is one whose coarseness falls in the middle of the spectrum.

The terms "single-cut" and "double-cut" refer to the sharp ridges or teeth on the file surface. A single-cut file has sharp, parallel ridges running diagonally across its surface. A double-cut file has a second set of ridges crossing the first set at an angle, creating a crosshatch. Examine the crosshatch and you'll see it has created a large number of small, pointed teeth. The smoother a double-cut file is, the more and finer teeth it has.

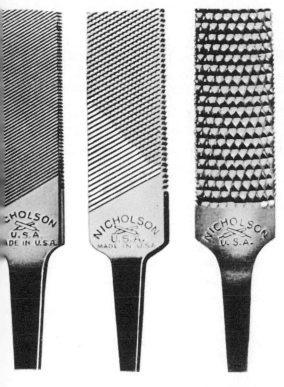

Three types of files (from left): single cut, double cut, rasp. Single- and double-cut files are used in metalworking, a rasp in woodworking.

A double-cut file cuts faster than a single-cut file, but it leaves a rough finish. A rasp has large, individual hooked teeth which slant toward the tip of the tool.

Aside from the differences in teeth, files may be round, triangular, square, flat, half-round, or mill. A mill file tapers in thickness and width in the third of its length near the tip. It gets its name from its original use in sharpening blades in sawmills.

Some files taper, other have a blunt shape. A tapered file is good for enlarging small openings. The blunt shape is good for filing inside corners. A half-round file is good on concave surfaces. A 6″ triangular file is good for filing notches, square holes, and for repairing damaged threads. A 6″ round file, often called a "rattail" file, is useful for enlarging holes and for filing small concave surfaces.

Sometimes one edge of a file is left smooth. This is called a "safe" file. When you are filing into a corner, the safe edge won't rough up the intersecting side. Mill files come with square or round edges or with one safe edge. You can grind the teeth off the side of a file and make your own safe edge.

Selecting files.   Single-cut files are usually used for sharpening cutting edges, such as those on knives, shears, and saws. Use light pressure. Double-cut files are usually used where it is desired to remove metal fast and a rougher finish is acceptable. Use heavy pressure. Rasps cut very roughly and are used principally on wood, leather, and soft metals.

Triangular files are used for sharpening handsaws. They are usually single-cut. A slim-taper triangular file can be used for band-saw blades. Use a 7″ slim taper if the saw has four to six teeth per inch. Use a 6″ slim taper if it has seven to ten teeth per inch.

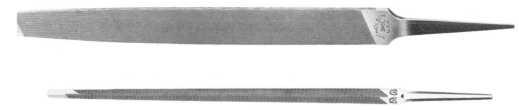

For all-round metalworking, a 10″ single-cut flat bastard file (top) is most favored. Triangular slim-taper file is used for sharpening saw blades.

Mill files are used on circular saws, planer knives, and lawn-mower blades. Use a round-edged mill file for sharpening circular-saw blades' rip and chisel teeth. Use a slim-taper triangular file for crosscut and combination-blade teeth.

Use rifflers, small files with curved ends used in wood carving, for irregular shapes and hard-to-get-at spots. Rifflers have a different shape at each end. Typically there is a rasp end for rough cutting, a file end for finishing.

Use a half-round cabinet file for shaping the cove on a table edge. Use a knife file for cleaning the V's in a scalloped

Two useful woodworking rasps: 8″ flat bastard rasp (top)
and 8″ half-round bastard rasp.

edge. Use a round rasp or file for making flutings. Use a shoe
rasp for filing slots or fitting tenons.

You'll probably use a 10″ mill and a 6″ triangular file
most, so get these first. (The stated length of a file does not
include its tapered end, or tang, which fits into the handle.)
Also handy are a 10″ half-round double-cut bastard, a 10″
round bastard, a 6″ single-cut half-round, and a 6″ round. For
working on wood you'll want a 10″ half-round rasp. If you do
any wood carving you'll want a collection of rifflers, although
these files come in handy for other work.

Using a file. The teeth of all files face toward the tip.
That's why a file cuts on the forward stroke only and why pressure should be applied only on this stroke. On the return stroke,
a file should be lifted slightly off the work. If you don't lift the
file, you dull the teeth. On soft metals, however, allowing the
file to drag lightly on the work as you pull it back tends to free
material that might otherwise clog its teeth.

Chips can be cleared from the file teeth by occasionally
rapping the tool sharply against wood. Really effective cleaning of teeth is done by brushing with short, fine, wire bristles.

In rough filing, stroke across the work at about a 30-
degree angle. For finish filing, keep strokes straight across. For
best results, hold a file so it is exactly parallel to the work on
its forward, cutting stroke. This is necessary to produce a flat

Rasp being used to bring a mortise-and-tenon joint to proper fit. It can also smooth end-grain cuts that have a rough finish.

cut rather than one that is rounded.

To produce a fine finish on a narrow surface, use a single-cut file and draw it sideways over the work, back and forth. It may produce a burred edge, but this can be quickly smoothed up.

If a file slides over hard metal, it's the wrong file for the job. You are dulling the teeth, not cutting the metal.

A file works better after breaking it in. Use wears the teeth down so they are all the same height.

Handles.   Every file needs a handle; it makes the file easier to use and also protects you from getting hurt by the sharp-pointed tang. To attach a handle firmly to a file, insert the tang in the hole of the handle; then, holding the handle with a firm grip, strike its butt end solidly against a wood surface until the tang is all the way in.

Care of files.   Rust ruins files, so store them in a dry

Files should never be thrown loosely into a drawer or piled on top of each other. Here are two types of racks for keeping files apart to protect cutting teeth from damage.

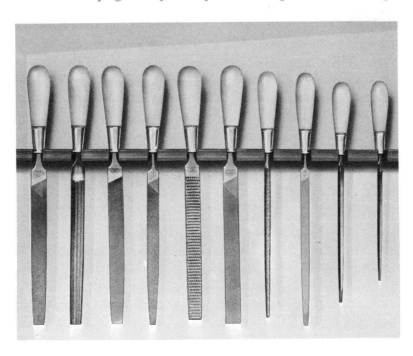

251

File brush at top combines card and brush and is used mostly for cleaning fine-cut files. File card below is for general file cleaning.

place. Don't throw them loosely in a drawer. In contact with one another, they become dull.

If a file card won't clean the teeth, try picking them clean with a sharp point. If sap or paint is the problem, soak the file in an appropriate solvent.

Don't oil files. It may prevent rusting, but it will also collect clogging dirt.

SCRAPERS. A cabinetmaker eliminates the need for much sanding by using a scraper. It takes off finer shavings than a plane. It will produce a smooth cut even against the grain and is a good tool for cleaning up along glue lines.

A cabinet scraper has a blade sharpened to a 45-degree angle, with a hooked edge which is turned over by "burnishing," using a special tool. The hook does the cutting. The blade is held in a frame that has two handles.

The scraper blade is adjusted by tightening a thumbscrew which springs the blade so its hook projects. In use, the tool is pushed away from you.

A hand scraper works like a cabinet scraper except that it has no frame. It is just a blade held in the hand. It may be rectangular or curved steel about $\frac{1}{16}''$ thick. It, too, requires a burnisher to create the burr or hook along its edge.

A rectangular blade may be held in one or both hands and pulled or pushed. On flat surfaces it can reduce sanding

Handscraper is used by cabinetmakers to shape and smooth rough-sawn stock. Scraper is bowed slightly by thumb pressure to provide cutting action.

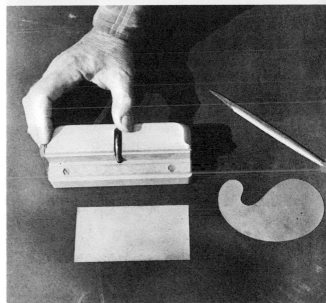

Rectangular and oval cabinet scrapers with burnishing tool used for applying an edge.

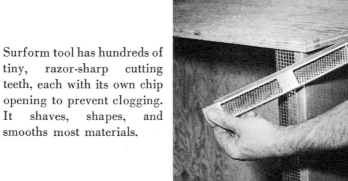

Surform tool has hundreds of tiny, razor-sharp cutting teeth, each with its own chip opening to prevent clogging. It shaves, shapes, and smooths most materials.

and finishing time. In fact, many expert woodworkers scrape instead of sand.

For curved surfaces there is a gooseneck-shaped scraper. It will handle jobs like scraping the inside of a wooden bowl which would be almost impossible otherwise. You can buy a scraper kit which includes a straight scraper, a gooseneck scraper, and burnishers to sharpen both, all for about $6.

A variety of fixed-handle pull scrapers is available for such jobs as removing paint, rust, etc. These have hook-shaped blades which may be single-edged and permanently attached to the handle, or double-edged so they can be reversed. The blade edges of some scrapers are straight, others serrated. The serrated type is especially good for digging into tough paint film, but it leaves groove marks.

20 | Screwdrivers

Screws come in many sizes and varieties, and many sizes and varieties of screwdrivers are needed to fit them. A screwdriver that fits the slot properly does half the job of getting the screw in or out. The blade tip should fill the screw slot exactly, or at least three-quarters of it. If it fills less than that, it is likely to twist out of the slot and chew it up. If it's wider than the slot it will gouge the material into which you are driving.

How well a blade holds in a slot also depends on how good a driver you use, and how its tip is finished. Good blades are cross-ground. Inferior ones are ground lengthwise or made of pressed metal. Good tips are forged.

The most economical way to acquire a screwdriver collection is to buy a matched set. Matched drivers also make a more attractive display in the shop and toolbox. Finding the screwdriver you want is also easier when you have a single image of what to look for.

But a set is only the beginning on which to build the collection of drivers you'll need to satisfy every demand. To drive tiny screws with precision and ease you will need a set of midgets. For portability, you will want a kit with many blades that fit into a single handle. For awkward situations, you will want screw-launching drivers which have gripping sleeves to

Screwdriver should fit the slot of the screw to do the job properly. Standard blade at left it too wide for the screw, will damage the wood. Cabinet blade, right, is too narrow, will twist out and damage the slot.

hold the screw. You will want an offset driver for situations where you can't get in with anything else. Its lever action multiplies torque (twisting force) many times. Also good for multiplying torque is a bit brace. A variety of blades are available to fit it.

A standard screwdriver has a blade that fans out just back of the tip. This extra width is convenient for getting a grip on the blade with a wrench when extra leverage is needed. However, it prevents the tip from following a screw into its hole. You can't recess screws into deep holes in furniture, for example, with a standard blade. For this purpose, as well as for elec-

Types of screwdrivers and the screws they fit.

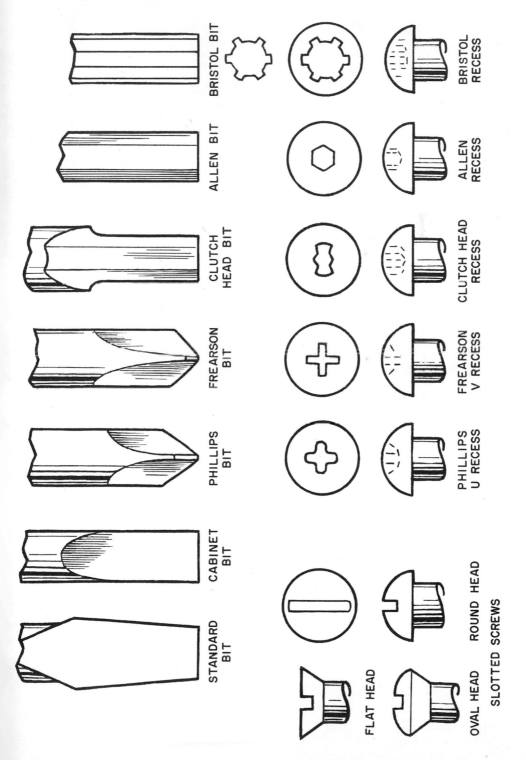

BRISTOL BIT   BRISTOL RECESS

ALLEN BIT   ALLEN RECESS

CLUTCH HEAD BIT   CLUTCH HEAD RECESS

FREARSON BIT   FREARSON V RECESS

PHILLIPS BIT   PHILLIPS U RECESS

CABINET BIT

STANDARD BIT   ROUND HEAD

FLAT HEAD   OVAL HEAD   SLOTTED SCREWS

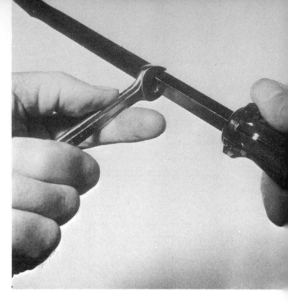

Square-shafted screwdriver is designed for use with a wrench to hold blade in slot and gain maximum torque.

tronic work, there is a "cabinet" blade. It doesn't fan out; its tip is no wider than its shank.

For tough going, get a screwdriver with a square shank. You can grip it with a wrench anywhere along its length. Avoid using pliers on a screwdriver. They will damage it.

A traditional rule is: never hammer on a screwdriver. But, as usual, there are exceptions. One type of screwdriver has a shaft that extends through the handle. You can hammer on it as much as you please. The blows strike steel, not the handle itself.

The best test of a screwdriver handle is how it feels in your grip. Most screwdrivers these days have plastic handles. Will those deep flutes cut into your palm on heavy use? Many plastic handles are covered by rubber grips. These cushion the hand, offer protection against electric shock, and may give extra turning power.

Old-timers say, use a pry bar for prying, not a screwdriver. Once a screwdriver shank is bent, it is difficult to restore. If prying breaks off a corner of the tip, the tool is useless. Blade tips are hardened to make them durable and keep the ends from rounding over. The harder they are, the more brittle. Reworking a broken blade may salvage it, but it will never be the same.

Usually the shank and blade (or tip) of a screwdriver are referred to as the blade. A screwdriver's size is the combined length of its blade and handle.

SPECIAL SCREWDRIVERS.   Phillips screwdrivers fit screws with cross slots. Besides their attractive appearance, these screws have the advantage of preventing the blades from slipping out of the slot and gouging the work. One size of Phillips driver can handle a range of screws, but it may take pressure to seat the driver in the cross slot. Similar to the Phillips screwdriver is the Frearson bit, which fits screws whose cross slots are slightly concave.

Three other types of screw heads require special drivers: clutch head, Allen recess, and Bristol recess. The hex-shaped Allen screw may be removed either with an Allen wrench or an Allen-bladed screwdriver. The Bristol recess is shaped like a rounded six-pointed star. The clutch head recess is shaped, roughly, like an hourglass (or butterfly), or like a flat, blunt-tipped propeller.

A close cousin of the screwdriver is a "turnscrew." This is a screwdriver made especially for wood screws. Handles are eggshaped or oval rather than cylindrical, this giving them unexcelled twisting power. The upper blade is flattened to take a wrench.

For electrical work you may want to get an insulated electrician's screwdriver. This has a blade coated with resistant plastic to protect you against accidental shorts. A good insulated electrician's screwdriver will protect you up to 5,000 volts. Never use an ordinary screwdriver to check an electrical circuit where the amperage is high, as on standard house voltage. If an electrical current is strong enough to arc, it will damage the screwdriver blade. Spark plug current may be high in voltage but it is low in amperage. It may be safely tested with an ordinary screwdriver. Better are screwdrivers made especially for circuit testing. These have fully insulated handles and blades, making them completely safe. The handle lights up to indicate a hot wire or side.

If you work on radio or television receivers, you will have need for a driver made of a nonmetallic material. It is used for the lining of sensitive tuning gear, which cannot be done with a metal driver.

There are a variety of "reversible" screwdrivers. While you are using one blade, the other blade is concealed in the handle. For a different blade, you merely pull out the one you are using and reverse it. A good combination is one that pairs a Phillips with a regular blade. For working with small parts, there is a "mini" reversible with a pocket clip. It has a ⅛" regular bit on one end and a No. 1 Phillips bit on the other. It comes with a special protective pouch that fits in your pocket. One reversible set is three-way. Besides the reversible screwdriver, a ¼" nutdriver is built into the dome of the handle. Another reversible set has a single cushion-grip handle and four double-ended blades.

There are many screwdriver novelties. You can buy magnetized screwdrivers which, as the name implies, will pick up and hold screws. A key-shaped screwdriver is available in the popular ¼" width to fit your key chain.

Nutdriver bits in sizes from ³⁄₁₆" to ½" are commonly available. These can be used in screwdriver handles made for interchangeable bits and are especially effective in ratchet-type handles.

Screw-holding driver is essential in tight quarters. It grips screw firmly while starting and holds it as it is removed.

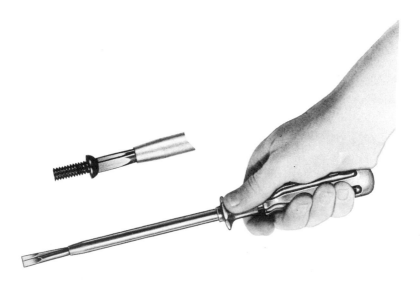

RATCHET SCREWDRIVERS. Spiral ratchet screwdrivers are time- and labor-savers. One push on the handle turns a screw almost three times. The direction of drive can be reversed, or it can be locked. It is then a rigid screwdriver. A quick-return spring in the handle permits one-hand operation. Some have three-way ratchet action without the spring-return.

Most ratchet drivers come with three screwdriver bits. For

Spiral ratchet screwdriver speeds up work and reduces effort. One push on the handle turns a screw three times.

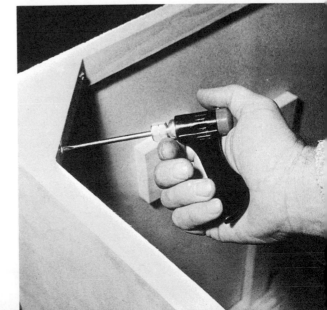

Pistol-grip ratchet driver with interchangeable blades is useful for light work. The pistol grip gives added turning power.

some, you can get an accessory set that includes cabinet bits, drill points, and a countersink. There are offset ratchet screwdrivers for both slotted and Phillips head screws.

Oxwall distributes a pistol-grip ratchet screwdriver with an aluminum chuck. It comes in a kit with three blades. The pistol grip gives it 45 percent greater turning power. There is also a type of ratchet handle that has a brace which fits into it. Any of a number of screwdriver tips then fit into the collet at the end of the brace. The brace provides crank action and multiplies power.

21

Nutdrivers

On many jobs where hex nuts and screws are used, you'll need a nutdriver, a tool that resembles a screwdriver except that in place of a blade it has a socket that fits over the nut or the screw head.

Most nutdrivers fit only one size hex nut, but there are others that are self-adjusting to a variety of sizes. One manufacturer, Vaco, makes a nutdriver that automatically adjusts to sizes from ¼″ to ⁷⁄₁₆″. It has multiple nesting hex sockets and when the driver is pushed down on the nut, the appropriate socket slips over it.

Stanley's Hex-a-Matic accommodates fifteen standard sizes of nuts and screws. These include five sizes of hex nuts from ¼″ to ⁷⁄₁₆″, five sizes of hex-head screws from No. 8 to ⁵⁄₁₆″. It will also fit all metric-sized fasteners up to 11 mm. It works by means of a six-fingered collet chuck which adjusts automatically to the required size and locks into position when the driver is pushed down.

Unlike tools with multiple, nesting hex sockets, the Hex-a-Matic has an infinite range of adjustment. It will fit and hold on even damaged nuts and screws. It is available as an attachment for Stanley's Yankee spiral ratchet screwdriver. Com-

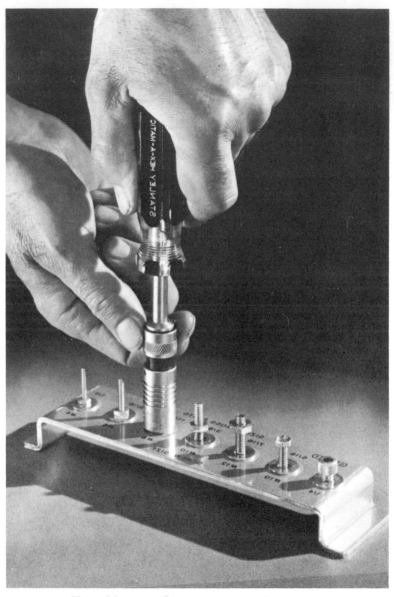

Hex-a-Matic nutdriver automatically adjusts to the size
of nut or screw head. Disassembled collet chuck (below)
shows six fingers that enable tool to fit any hex-head nut
or screw within its range of capacity.

bined with the ratchet screwdriver, it has an extra-long reach, a valuable feature in getting at remote fasteners in large appliances or TV cabinets.

Extensions, commonly 5″ long, are available for many nutdrivers. A good kit to have is one with an interchangeable handle that accommodates hex bits, a variety of screwdriver bits, and a series of nutdriver bits. Vaco offers one kit with thirty blade styles and three handle styles, all interchangeable. You can get pouches with seven, fourteen, or thirty-six sections. This permits starting with a basic kit, and adding pieces later as you require them.

Four types of adjustable wrenches (from top): chain wrench; monkey wrench; heavy-duty pipe wrench; adjustable open-end wrench.

22

Wrenches

A bike, car, lawnmower, plumbing fixture, oil burner, air conditioner—you can't repair any of them without wrenches. Having the right kinds and knowing how to use them can save you time and heartburn.

There are five basic types of wrenches you need and should know about: adjustable, open end, box, socket, and pipe wrenches. This is also the probable order in which you will acquire them. Though all are made for nuts of one kind or another, each wrench has its own special merit and purpose.

ADJUSTABLE WRENCHES. The monkey wrench was the first of the adjustable variety. It has largely been superseded by wrenches that are lighter and handier. The simple adjustable wrench included in most automobile kits resembles the monkey wrench, but in scaled-down form. Obviously, its advantage is that it will fit nuts of many sizes. However, the automobile wrench can't be used unless there is easy accessibility and swing space.

Somewhat more maneuverable is the adjustable-end wrench. Because its jaws are set at a 22½-degree angle to the handle, it can get in places where the ordinary adjustable wrench cannot. By flipping it over, the grip is varied so that a new hold can be taken on a nut with only half a swing.

The limitation of an adjustable wrench is that it doesn't keep its adjustment and is likely to slip and chew up the nut. It also lacks durability. If you don't push it in the direction of the jaws you may break the lower one. If you don't keep the jaws snug on the work, you may break off the teeth in the adjusting mechanism. It is definitely not a wrench to break loose frozen nuts, or to snug nuts excessively tight.

A series of adjustable-end wrenches made by P&C overcomes the tendency of the ordinary adjustable-end wrench to lose its adjustment. By ingenious design, every adjustment clicks and holds.

In buying an adjustable wrench look for the word "forged" or "drop-forged" on the handle. Forged metal is stronger than cast metal. Drop-forged means that the metal was formed by being forced into a die under a drop hammer.

Wrench size indicates overall length. A 6″ wrench has a capacity up to ¾″. A 10″ size has a 1⅛″ capacity. You can buy a three-piece set, which includes the popular 6″, 8″, and 10″ sizes for less than you would pay individually. Adjustable-end sizes generally range from 4″ to 20″. The 20″ has a maximum opening of 2½″.

OPEN-END WRENCHES.   The opening, not the length, determines the size of an open-end wrench. If the jaw opening at one end is ½″ and at the other ¹⁹⁄₃₂″, it is a ½″ by ¹⁹⁄₃₂″ wrench. The length of the wrench, however, determines its leverage, and manufacturers proportion length to opening in accordance with what they feel use demands. Wrench ends are usually at a 15-degree angle. Flopping the wrench permits continuous turning of a hex nut in a 30-degree swing.

A wrench end should fit the nut exactly, so you need a collection of them. A typical six-piece open-end set has wrenches with openings ranging from ⁵⁄₁₆″ to 1″. A set of ten wrenches with openings from ¼″ to 1⅛″ provides every size you are likely to need in the home. Sets usually come with kits in which they can be kept.

For tubing connections of oil burners, air conditioners, and refrigerators, a flare nut wrench is useful. It is a specialized kind of open-ender.

BOX WRENCHES.   These fit over a nut or bolt head and surround it completely. The "box" is a circle of twelve notches, so you may hear it called a twelve-point wrench.

Because the box construction is sturdier than open jaws, this wrench can be thinner, permitting you to get into tight places with it. You can loosen or tighten a nut with a swing of only 15 degrees. In contrast, the open-end wrench requires 30 degrees, even when flopped. If not flopped, it takes 60 degrees.

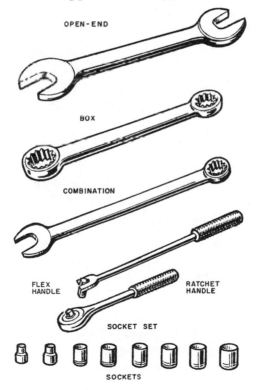

Four different kinds of fixed wrenches.

Another advantage of the box wrench is that it is easier to keep on the nut. It can't slip like an open-end wrench. That's why it is a favorite for breaking loose tight nuts and getting the last quarter turn on a nut that is being snugged down.

In use, a box wrench must be lifted off the nut and re-positioned for each added turn. That makes the open-end wrench just a little faster. For this reason some wrenches are made with a box at one end and an open-end at the other. The box can then be used for the tough jobs, and the open-end the rest of the time. Both ends in a combination wrench fit the same size nut.

As always, the longer the wrench handle, the greater the leverage. That is why a length of pipe is sometimes slipped over a wrench end. This makes it possible to apply a much greater torque, but unless done carefully it can result in a ruined wrench and/or work. The same caution or prohibition applies to striking a wrench with a hammer. There are, however, special heavy-duty industrial wrenches made for use with long extension handles. There are others, called "striking wrenches," that have a square striking surface for use with a sledge or hammer.

Skinned knuckles are a common problem when using wrenches. Some box wrenches have their handles tipped up at a 15-degree angle from the head, providing a clearance to spare your knuckles.

Box wrenches also come in ratcheting style. Turning over the wrench reverses the direction of the action.

SOCKET WRENCHES.   The secret of this tool's success lies in its handle. A single handle will fit all the sockets in the set.

It may be a ratchet handle. This means that the socket doesn't have to be raised off the nut at each swing. By flipping a little lever, the ratchet will either tighten or loosen a nut. By means of a "ratcheter," any nonratcheting handle can be made into a ratcheting tool.

With a hinged offset handle, you can swing the handle

down at right angles to the socket and get tremendous leverage. When the nut has broken loose, the handle can be raised to a vertical position and turned between the fingers.

A sliding offset handle can be positioned so as to make up a T handle. Or it can be set to one side for increased leverage. It can be used in combination with an extension bar to get at hard-to-reach nuts.

A speed handle works like a brace. It makes short work of nut removal once the nut has been broken loose by use of the offset or ratchet handle.

In close quarters and awkward situations, a universal joint makes it possible to use the speed handle at any angle to the socket.

Handles for socket wrench sets come in four sizes, the size being determined by the square peg on the drive end of the handle. The sizes include $\frac{1}{4}''$ drive (or midget) for light-duty work, a $\frac{3}{8}''$ drive is for medium work, and $\frac{1}{2}''$, $\frac{3}{4}''$, and $1''$ for various jobs. The $\frac{1}{2}''$ drive is most popular for working on cars, and a fifteen-piece set will have sockets ranging from $\frac{7}{16}''$ to $1\frac{1}{4}''$. You can buy auxiliary handles and attachments later.

Also useful for the homeowner is the $\frac{1}{4}''$ drive set. At modest cost you can get a twelve-piece set including nine sockets to fit $\frac{3}{16}''$ to $\frac{1}{2}''$ nuts, with a flex handle, crossbar, and metal case.

A handy accessory for your drive handles are screwdriver sockets. These come for regular, Phillips head, and hollow head screws.

Torque-limiting handles are used in working on engines and other equipment where tightening must be done according to specifications supplied by the manufacturer. Unless you are a car buff, they have limited application in the home shop.

Better-made sockets have thin walls for getting into tight places. They are chrome plated to resist rust.

PIPE WRENCHES.   These are for turning and holding pipes, rods, and other things that do not have flat sides. The pipe wrench differs from the ordinary wrench in that it has teeth in its jaws. On other adjustable wrenches, the lower jaw moves. On the pipe wrench, it's the upper jaw.

The Stillson is the most familiar variety of pipe wrench. The toothed arm that moves its jaw up and down is loose within a retaining collar. This collar pivots on a rivet or shaft, which permits the upper jaw to have a rocking motion. When you pull on a Stillson, the hingelike action of the jaw closes it on the work. Relax your pull, and the biting jaw comes free.

Because of its teeth, a pipe wrench should not be used on any finish you don't want to mar. Wrapping a cloth around a chrome pipe helps some, but it is no positive insurance against damage.

You need a pair of pipe wrenches for most jobs. One wrench holds, the other turns. They don't have to be the same size. A 10″ Stillson will take pipe up to 1″. An 18-incher takes pipe up to 2″. They make a good pair.

Similar to the Stillson is the "heavy duty" pipe wrench. It differs from the Stillson in that its collar doesn't pivot. The toothed-jaw arm is loose within its collar and this is what permits its action. It sells for almost twice as much as the Stillson variety.

One kind of pipe wrench has a hex jaw. It is made especially to provide a nonslip grip on hex and square nuts. Its smooth jaws won't harm plated finishes, so plumbers use it for a nonslip grip on sink and tub drain nuts, etc. It is also available in an offset model with the jaws at an angle to the handle. Some straight and offset pipe wrenches come with aluminum handles. These are about 40 percent lighter than standard wrenches.

A chain pipe wrench uses a chain instead of toothed jaws to get its grip. It is especially good for working in tight places. It fits pipe, conduit, or irregularly shaped material. It has a ratcheting action and a big capacity. A chain pipe wrench with a 12″ handle and a 15″ chain can handle pipe from ¼″ to 4″ in diameter.

Allen, or key, wrenches are useful in the shop for adjusting headless setscrews, as on the miter gauge of this table saw. They are available in a set, with sizes to fit every size setscrew (below).

Operating on a similar principle, but using a strap instead of a chain, the strap wrench has the advantage of not chewing up the work. A 12″ strap wrench, typically, has a break strength of 3500 pounds, and has from ⅛″ to 2″ capacity.

SPECIAL WRENCHES.   Indispensable in the installation or removal of faucets and in getting at hard-to-reach nuts, the basin wrench with its foot-long handle and self-adjusting jaws is a valuable tool to have in your shop. Its jaw flips over for reversing direction.

Allen or setscrew wrenches are for headless setscrews. A typical complete set comes in a plastic pouch and includes every size you'll ever want. Because some of the most useful sizes invariably get lost or disappear, you might consider getting a set in which the various keys are inseparable. One kind has them opening up like the blades in a pocket knife. You can also get Allen heads for your socket-wrench set.

To the British, every wrench is a "spanner." In countries where a wrench is a wrench, the name spanner is reserved for devices with hooks or pins. These fit into holes or notches on the nut to be turned. Most of them come in service kits furnished with appliances or other equipment.

23

Pliers / Snips / Nippers

PLIERS.   Wrenches supply their own grip; with pliers you supply the grip. Your grip on the handles of a pair of pliers is multiplied many times by mechanical advantage into a powerful force. An 8-pound pressure on the handles can become a 300-pound pressure on the object between the jaws. Considering that most jaws measure about ⁵⁄₁₆″ by ⁵⁄₁₆″, this is about 2½ tons per square inch.

A well-equipped shop may have a dozen or more different kinds and sizes of pliers. Some grip, some cut and grip, while some only cut.

Slip-joint pliers. Of the six kinds of pliers every shop should have, No. 1 on the list is a pair of slip-joint pliers. You'll use them for everything from pulling out a cotter pin to tightening the Sunday roast on the barbecue spit. The pivot rivet joining these pliers slips into two, sometimes three positions, varying the jaw opening from a slit to over an inch. Plier size is measured by length. Common sizes are 5″, 6″, 8″, and 10″, with the 6″ and 8″ sizes the most popular.

Good slip-joint pliers have joints that work easily, but not sloppily. Their shear-type wire cutter won't work if the joint is sloppy. The wire will slip between the cutters, which

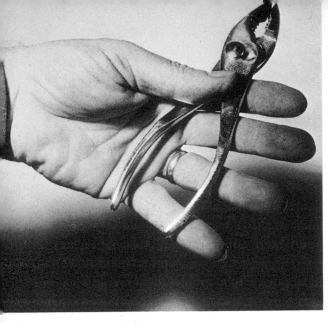

Slip-joint pliers adjust to two or three positions, varying the jaw opening from a slit to over an inch. For shear-type wire cutter to work effectively, joint must work smoothly but not loosely.

will chew it instead of cutting it. One type of slip-joint pliers has a special hard-steel side cutter. Another has thin jaws, extending like a long, slim nose. This slim nose will reach into tight places. Still another, called the "multi-plier," which has a four-position slip-joint, provides compound leverage that multiplies applied pressure ten times. Some slip-joint pliers have double-curved jaws that can grip ³⁄₁₆″ stock or 1″ pipe with equal force.

Engineer's pliers. A very useful type of pliers has jaws which open 1½″ or more with the jaws remaining parallel. They are commonly called engineer's or pump pliers. Typically, they have five channel adjustments, but they may have as many as eleven. They are especially good for plumbing jobs.

Engineer's pliers have great gripping power. Pair at left is best for gripping pipes and other round objects. Pair at center is designed for gripping flat-sided objects like bolts. Smooth-jawed pliers, right, won't damage plated finish on plumbing fixtures.

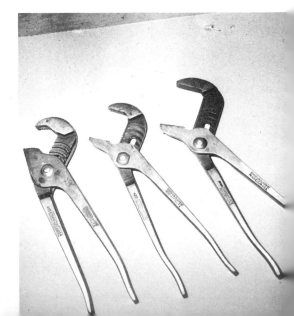

One type has smooth jaws that will not mar chrome fittings. You'll use them for taking off traps or disassembling faucets. Unlike ordinary pliers, engineer's pliers can handle nuts without mangling them or your hand.

Battery pliers. These pliers, with their long handles and tiny jaws, have great gripping power. A 7½" pair has only ½" capacity, but where titan-like force is required, they are the ones you'll use. Their upper jaw is angled and toothed, perfect for wrapping around a recalcitrant hex nut.

Parrot-nose plier wrenches combine the action of pliers and a pipe wrench. They exert a powerful grip and are ideal for pipe and tubing.

Locking-plier wrenches. For loosening rusted nuts and studs, use locking-plier wrenches. They are a clamping tool and vise, as well as pliers, and have many workshop applications. Their powerful jaws, which may be either flat or curved, are quickly adjusted to fit the work; then, with a squeeze, they lock tight. No more than a finger touch is needed to release them. "Vise Grip" and "Grip-Lock" are two popular trade names.

Parallel-jaw pliers. These pliers fit snugly on nuts, and because of their compound-leverage design have unexcelled gripping power. This leverage also helps their wire-cutting action. They'll cut a 10-penny nail. Wire can be fed through an opening between the handles so that a straight, head-on grip

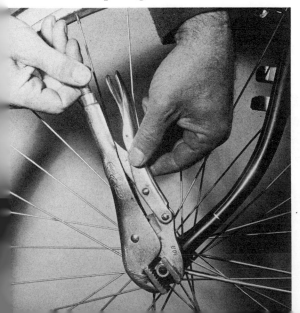

Locking-plier wrench does many of the jobs commonly assigned an adjustable open-end wrench, but it is far less delicate. It has teeth that bite, and because it seldom slips, doesn't mangle the work.

on the wire is possible. This is useful in making splices or in winding springs around a form. The pliers are available with either toothed or smooth jaws. The smooth ones are kind to highly polished finishes and are effective in breaking away narrow cuts of glass.

Five kinds of pliers are especially useful for electrical work.

Lineman's pliers have a fixed pivot which gives them cutting action far superior to that of slip-joint pliers. Their cutting edges run half the length of their jaws. They can cut soft metals, such as copper, brass, and aluminum, but are damaged by hard steel. The flat surfaces on the jaw end are suited for gripping wire and flat metal.

Button's pattern pliers are a special variety of electrical pliers with a curved gripping section in the jaws. Wire cutters are on the outside of the jaws. Their action is a shearing one, similar to that in slip-joint pliers, but because of the tightly-fixed pivot they do a much better job.

Needlenose pliers have a very thin nose. They're good for getting into places with restricted clearance. The thin nose is especially useful in bending and shaping wire, as at terminals. For getting around obstructions, you can get needlenoses with the nose bent at a 79-degree angle. Needlenoses are useful in retrieving nuts or other small parts which fall into inaccessible places.

Diagonal cutting pliers are indispensable in electrical work. They excel at cutting, and their thin, narrow nose can reach into tight spots to nip wires and perform other operations. Their diagonal slant makes it possible to flush-cut without the handles getting in the way. Diagonal pliers are good for spreading cotter pins and for removing them.

Wire strippers are essential in most electrical work. As strippers, they cut the insulation but not the wire. An adjustable stop equips them to handle wire of various sizes, typically from 12 to 26 gauge. They also have a good wire-cutting action.

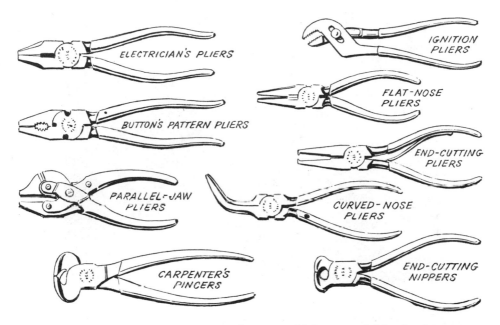

ELECTRICIAN'S PLIERS

IGNITION PLIERS

BUTTON'S PATTERN PLIERS

FLAT-NOSE PLIERS

PARALLEL-JAW PLIERS

END-CUTTING PLIERS

CURVED-NOSE PLIERS

CARPENTER'S PINCERS

END-CUTTING NIPPERS

Pliers and cutters which are useful in the shop.

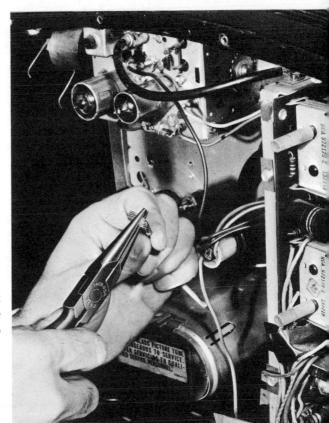

Needlenose pliers can cut wire to length and form the ends in the proper shape to fit a terminal screw.

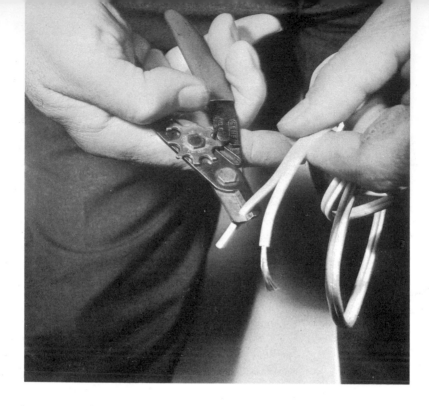

Wirestrippers are adjustable to every size wire commonly found around the house. They neatly cut the insulation, but not a hair of the wire.

Another tool that can be used for cutting and stripping wire is one that can also be used for crimping solderless terminals to wire and for slicing bolts. Typically, there are separate holes in which wire from 10 to 22 gauge can be inserted for stripping. There are also holes for inserting six sizes of bolts. The bolts can be sliced neatly with no burrs remaining to be filed.

SNIPS.   Shears used for cutting thin sheet metal are called snips. Aviation snips are unexcelled for cutting thin sheets of aluminum, copper, or galvanized steel. They have compound-lever action so that cutting is effortless. If you don't ruin them by attempting to cut heavy metal, they will last forever. Never exert more than hand pressure on them. These compound-power snips are of three varieties: one type cuts to the left, another to the right, and the third cuts right or left.

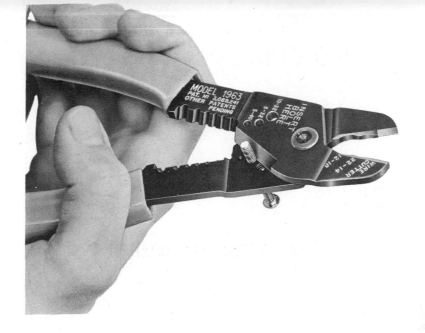

This tool cuts and strips wire, crimps solderless terminals to wire, and slices six sizes of bolts without leaving burrs.

Straight-cut snips demand more muscle power. One way to get it is to insert the lower handle in a special slot in the workbench top. You can then put all your weight on the upper handle for tough cutting jobs. A 12″ size is a good choice.

When cutting with snips, insert the sheet metal all the way into the jaws. Cutting with a "full run" of the blade means a smoother cut. To avoid overrunning a cut, use the tip ends of the snips for complete control.

Wiss manufactures compound-action snips with a piercing tip. This makes starts quicker and easier. Otherwise, in making a hole or opening in sheet metal, use a punch or chisel to create a hole in which the snips can be inserted.

NIPPERS. End-cutting nippers have blunt-nosed jaws which can cut bolts and rivets close to the surface. They will cut heavy wire and nails. They are for heavy cutting and twisting.

A special type of end-cutting nippers is used for cutting tile, especially small ceramic mosaics. When completely closed, the jaws are still about ⅛″ apart and, unlike those of ordinary nippers, are off-center.

24

Prybars / Nailpullers

"Give me a lever and a place to stand, and I will move the world," said Archimedes, the Greek inventor who, over 2,000 years ago, understood the enormous power of this simple device. Today, the homeowner frequently needs the added muscle that leverage can give him. A nail that a hammer can't budge, a wrecking bar with its added leverage can extract with little effort. For prying apart boards, lifting heavy weights, dismantling a brick wall, laying stone, getting under a log, opening a wooden box or crate, and dozens more jobs, leverage tools are indispensable.

How do you pull out a sunken nailhead? With a nail claw. It's a sharp-edged claw at the end of a lever. With a hammer, pound the claw under the nailhead, then rock the lever back to lift the head. The claw end of these tools has varying degrees of curvature or offset. The curve or offset serves as a fulcrum.

Where space won't permit you to get in with an offset design, you can use a puller with an almost straight claw. After you have the nail started, you can slip a block of wood under the bar to act as a fulcrum. Nail pullers like these may be of hexagonal or round stock and 11″ to 14″ in overall length.

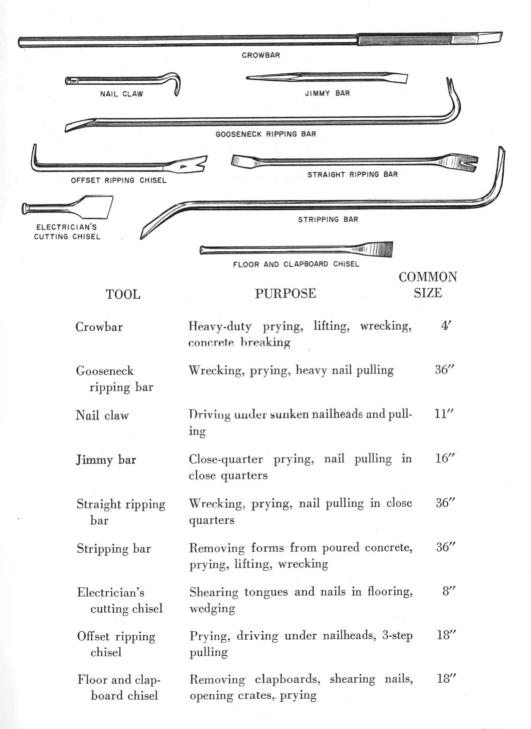

CROWBAR

NAIL CLAW

JIMMY BAR

GOOSENECK RIPPING BAR

OFFSET RIPPING CHISEL

STRAIGHT RIPPING BAR

ELECTRICIAN'S CUTTING CHISEL

STRIPPING BAR

FLOOR AND CLAPBOARD CHISEL

TOOL	PURPOSE	COMMON SIZE
Crowbar	Heavy-duty prying, lifting, wrecking, concrete breaking	4′
Gooseneck ripping bar	Wrecking, prying, heavy nail pulling	36″
Nail claw	Driving under sunken nailheads and pulling	11″
Jimmy bar	Close-quarter prying, nail pulling in close quarters	16″
Straight ripping bar	Wrecking, prying, nail pulling in close quarters	36″
Stripping bar	Removing forms from poured concrete, prying, lifting, wrecking	36″
Electrician's cutting chisel	Shearing tongues and nails in flooring, wedging	8″
Offset ripping chisel	Prying, driving under nailheads, 3-step pulling	18″
Floor and clapboard chisel	Removing clapboards, shearing nails, opening crates, prying	18″

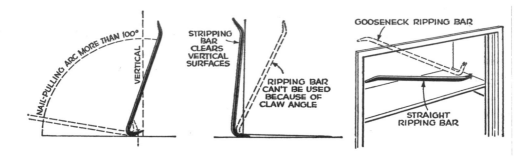

Gooseneck ripping bar (left) has tremendous leverage
but needs a long swing. It's not good for starting nails—for
that you need a nail claw. Because stripping bar (center)
has a shallower hook than a gooseneck, it can get up close
to vertical surfaces. Choose it for lifting a safe, refrigerator, or for prying up anything heavy. The flat claw of a
straight ripping bar (right) lets you get in and pull nails
a hammer couldn't reach. It can also get in where a gooseneck can't.

For pulling up old flooring boards or taking out a partition, a ripping chisel is the tool to use. Usually 18″ long, with
a ¾″ hex shaft, it has dual nail slots. One is at the end, and
is like a claw. The other, just back of it, is a teardrop opening
which can be dropped over a nailhead. It is just the right distance from the end to give excellent leverage. You can pound
with a hammer on the end of a ripping chisel's shaft if you
have to. Millers Falls makes a ripping chisel with an offset at
the pounding end. This provides a larger target for the hammer, as well as an extra claw puller. A bar similar to this one
is made of lighter-weight flat steel.

A wrecking bar has one slightly offset chisel end, for prying. The other end has a gooseneck shape and is specially designed for pulling up tough nails and spikes. Most wrecking
bars are 18″ to 30″ long.

Designed especially for wedging, and for cutting nails
behind flooring or siding, the electrician's cutting chisel has a

broad flat blade. With a somewhat narrower blade and a longer shaft is the floor and clapboard chisel. As its name implies, its specialty is clapboard removal and attendant nail cutting. It's good for prying in depth.

A lining-up bar is designed for prying and aligning jobs. It is sometimes called a jimmy bar. This is a tool especially useful in metal work. The end with the long slim taper is for lining up bolt and rivet holes.

For moving rocks, boulders, and breaking up concrete, choose the crowbar. It is a straight bar, tapered at one end and usually 4' to 6' long. If your object is lifting you must provide your own fulcrum. For prying out a boulder, or wedging into a crack in a brick wall, it is unexcelled. Being straight, it offers better control than an angled bar.

For removing trim, use a molding chisel. Its offset blade is 2" wide and has a beveled nail slot.

Every shop needs at least one cat's-paw type of nail puller. A gooseneck ripping bar comes next in importance. Between these two tools, you can do most jobs. Add the others later as need arises.

25

Tools for Measuring and Marking

A good part of the time on any project is spent measuring and marking. The right measuring equipment will help you to do the job faster and better.

MEASURING TOOLS. Your first choice for most measuring jobs should be a metal tape. There are several points to watch in selecting one. Don't buy a 6′ tape. The first time you try to measure a 4-by-8 sheet of plywood or plasterboard, you'll wish you hadn't. Even an 8-footer is inconvenient for many jobs, but it does have the merit of being light in your pocket.

A 10′ rule is a good choice. Its tape is ½″ wide, and so it's still a compact package. A 12′ rule usually has a ¾″-wide tape, and so becomes considerably bulkier and heavier. If you're involved in a big project, like building an addition or adding a shed dormer, you will find a 12′ tape useful. You may like a 16′ tape even more. There are few measuring jobs it can't handle in a single take.

Whatever you do, get a tape that is marked both in inches and in feet-and-inches. If you get one marked in feet-and-inches only, you'll get involved in translating measurements

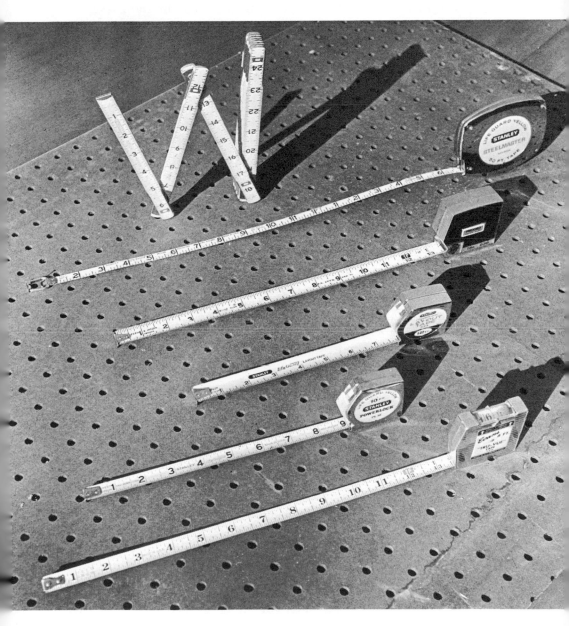

Metal tapes come in a variety of styles. A good choice is a 10′ tape marked in inches and feet-and-inches. Six-foot folding rule at rear still has some adherents.

from inches to feet-and-inches, and who can do that success-fully for very long? Some tapes don't have a power return. You have to push them back into the case. This is a nuisance.

It's convenient to have at least two tapes. Then you can have one at your project site and another at your table saw. Most shops eventually collect a half-dozen tapes, but one or two are favorites and get almost all the use.

Wooden rules. Asked why he used a folding wood ruler when it was so much slower than a tape, a carpenter replied with a grin, *"That's* the idea."

A zigzag or folding rule is no more accurate than a push-pull rule. The push-pull rule is almost universally used in the cabinetmaking industry where accuracy is far more demand-ing than in carpentry. Cabinetmakers like it because it allows the measurement of both regular and irregular shapes as well as the taking of inside and outside measurements. Also popu-lar is the 24″ folding rule. It folds into a 6″ length, easy to tuck into a pocket. Often made of boxwood, it is now also available in white nylon which is impervious to moisture and humidity. Its hardware is stainless steel. Gradations are very distinct and easy to read.

Try square. The try square is a blade set into a handle at a 90-degree angle. It is a tool for marking lines at right angles across a board so you can get a true cut. You can use it to check corners and joints to see if they are exactly right-angled. You can also use it to check boards for warping and cupping. With the blade set across a board, any light visible beneath the blade as it is slid along will show exactly where the board is out of square.

Some try squares have a handle that makes a 45-degree miter where it meets the blade. These are sometimes called miter squares. By placing the handle's angle against the edge of a board, a 45-degree miter cut can be marked. Since a miter square does everything a try square does and marks miters besides, get it if you can.

Try square is essential for marking lumber for true cuts, and for checking right angles of corners and joints.

Steel or rafter square. A book could be written about the many uses of the steel square, and many books have been.

If you are building a roof, this is the square to use. Tables on the square will enable you to make all the rafter cuts and notches that would otherwise be almost impossible. But a steel square has many other uses besides roof-building.

The short, wide blade on a steel square is called the body. The long, narrower blade is called the tongue. Typically, the body measures 24″ by 2″ and the tongue 16″ by 1½″. Because of its large size, the steel square can do many layout jobs that are beyond the capabilities of a try square. Cabinetmakers use a steel square for marking the angles on a supporting brace, as well as determining its length. They use it instead of a protractor for laying out angles of varying degrees. If you're building a planter with sloping sides, a steel square can give the measuring information you need. Because of its size, it's

Steel square being used with screw-on gauges to mark repeated cuts on a stair stringer. Square is also used to measure and mark rafters, angles of braces, etc. Tables on the square give data for measuring rafters.

the best square to use for marking on plywood or other large surfaces.

Combination square. This is like a try square except that its handle can be slid to any point along the length of the blade. Because of the sliding handle, it can be used as a marking gauge and a depth gauge. Its handle or beam may include a level and a removable scriber. It makes a convenient plumb, level, and straightedge. The angle on its handle permits marking off 25-degree as well as 90-degree angles.

Combination square has a handle with 90- and 45-degree angles which slides along blade. Handle contains a bubble level and a metal scriber. Many uses of the tool are shown at right.

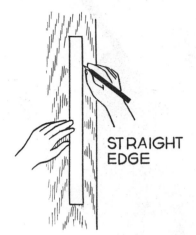

STRAIGHT
EDGE

INSIDE TRY SQUARE

OUTSIDE TRY SQUARE

LEVEL

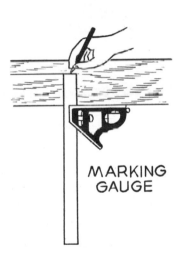

MARKING
GAUGE

PLUMB

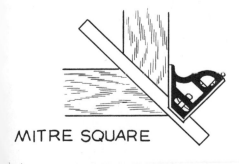

MITRE SQUARE

DEPTH
GAUGE

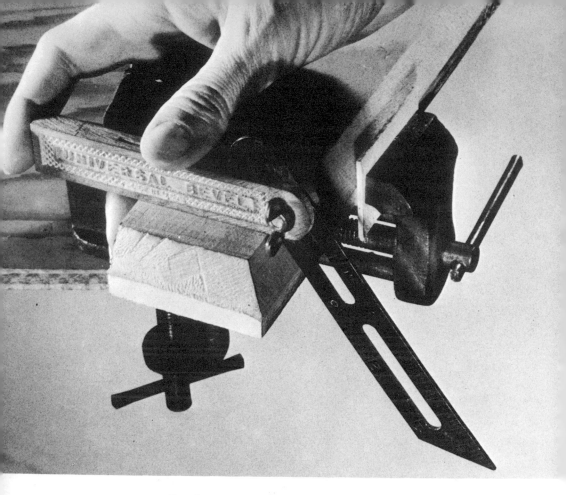

Bevel square can be locked at any angle. Here it is used to check a bevel being planed on both sides of a board.

One variant of the combination square has all the usual features plus these in addition: It can be used as a nail, screw, or dowel gauge. It can be used as a protractor and beam compass. It can be extended to 16″ for use as a stud marker.

Bevel square. The blade on this square can be set at any angle from 1 to 179 degrees and locked there by means of a thumbscrew. You can set it on work and adjust its blade to match the exact angle required for a perfect fit. The bevel square is sometimes called the sliding T bevel because it can be used to lay out and test the angle of a bevel.

ROUGH MEASURING.   Mark off feet or inches on a post or Lally column in your shop. It's both useful and decorative.

Measure your stride. By adjusting your natural stride to make it either shorter or longer, you can learn to pace off distance in 2' intervals with good accuracy.

Measure the span of your hand. If it comes out exactly 9", you have a ready means of estimating whether a board is 8", 9", or 10" wide.

What is your reach with both arms extended? If it's exactly 6', you have it made.

Other good built-in measurements are the breadth of your hand, and the breadth of your hand with thumb extended. Most men find the former to be approximately 3" and the latter 7".

LEVELS.   In this tool, a bubble in a glass tube or vial tells you when work is level or plumb, or how much it is off. You need levels not only for such jobs as setting fence posts vertical, shelves horizontal, and making a drain pipe pitch at exactly the right slope, but for every kind of construction job. Three basic levels belong in every well-equipped shop.

Aluminum level with six vials is used here to check work in progress on a ceiling. Center vials register for horizontal reading, end vials for vertical.

First, you need a 24″ aluminum-frame level. You'll use this for most jobs and it is important that it be accurate. A good level has six vials, so that no matter how you pick it up, it's always in the right position for taking a reading.

Check the accuracy of all vials before you buy. Here's how: Put it on any flat horizontal surface. If it doesn't register level, put some folded paper under one end until you get a level reading. Now reverse the level by swapping ends. The level's bubble should come to dead-center again. Check the plumb vials by the same swapping technique. If a level doesn't read the same in both directions, its calibration is off. Some levels have adjustable vials. This is some help in correcting inaccuracies, but adjustment requires considerable care.

When vials are paired, read the lower vial. If there is just one vial, be sure the vial is turned with its curved side up. When checking the horizontal, a bubble will move toward the high side of the level. In checking a vertical the bubble moves away from the direction in which the vertical tilts. Read the bubble carefully. If you are setting framing, or anything else that's vertical, and you doubt the accuracy of your reading, use a plumb bob as a check. A plumb bob is never wrong. For checking a horizontal, you can also use the plumb bob. Establish the true vertical, then get your horizontal by setting a rafter square blade against it.

You can't get into tight spots with a 2′ level. That's why a 9″ torpedo level is essential. If you think it gets its name from its shape, you're right. A typical torpedo level has three vials—horizontal, vertical, and 45-degree. A torpedo level can be a lifesaver, but don't use it unless you have to. Because of its small size, it's much more difficult to get an accurate reading.

The third level you need is a "line level," a single-vial device which hooks onto a line. It enables you to take a level reading over a considerable distance. For instance, you can use it for establishing the level of a fence, a garden wall, or a foundation. For an accurate reading, your line must be kept very taut. If your eye is sharp, you won't be more than ½″ off in 60′.

That much error isn't bad for many projects, but it isn't good enough for a house foundation. To come within ⅛″ of target in 80′ you can use a pair of inexpensive sights that clamp to a 2′ level. In use, the sight-equipped level is placed on a level table. The target is a 3″-by-5″ file card which an assistant slides up and down on a vertical rod. When the lineup is dead-center on the target, you've established the horizontal you are after. Reverse the level and take additional sightings to verify your accuracy.

If you undertake any masonry construction, you'll need a 4′ mason's level. It will bring an accuracy to your work that a 2′ level can't match.

MAKING YOUR MARK.   The thickness of a pencil line may be all that stands between you and perfect craftsmanship. A carpenter's broad-lead pencil is all right for marking 2-by-4s but for cabinet work you need something more pointed. Use either a very sharp pencil or a marking knife. A scratch-awl can be used for marking, though its main talent is for marking hole locations and for making starting holes for screws and brads.

To avoid measuring mistakes, cut a stick to the length you need. This is especially handy when you have many pieces to cut to the same length. A more elaborate version of a measuring stick is a technique known as "rod layout." Every measurement needed for the construction of a project, such as a cabinet, is made on a length of wood, such as a 1-by-2. This 1″-by-2″ "rod" must be longer than the longest-sized board that is required. Height, width, and depth measurements are each marked on a different side of the rod. You can then forget about using a ruler.

The easiest way to draw the line for a job like trimming 1″ off a board is with a *marking gauge*. This tool, usually of wood, has a head which slides on a beam that's just under 8″

Marking gauge is used to scribe a true line along the edge of a board. It's more accurate than a pencil.

long. By turning a thumbscrew you can fasten the head at any point along the beam. At the end of the beam there's a projecting spur. In use, the head is held firmly against the edge of the board and by pushing it away from you, the spur scores the required line.

Where extreme accuracy is not needed, you can improvise a marking gauge using a ruler, with your clenched hand as the sliding head. For example, if you want to make a mark 1″ from the edge of a board, hold a ruler so that 1″ of it projects onto the board. Place the point of the pencil at the end of the ruler and slide the ruler along the board's edge, making a mark as you go.

A *chalk line* (a length of twine impregnated with chalk dust) is the only means of marking a long line with accuracy. The line, resting on the surface, is pulled taut between the points where the mark is to be made. A few inches from one end, the line is picked up between thumb and forefinger and then released. As it snaps back, it deposits a line of chalk that is easy to follow.

Chalk lines are used in laying floor tile or shingles in a straight line. Some chalk lines come in containers that you can fill with white or blue chalkdust. You can also buy small hemispheres of blue or white carpenter's chalk, and chalk any length of twine for the purpose.

Chalk line makes a straight line on a large surface, useful in laying floor tiles or shingles. Here the line, after being snapped, is raised to show chalk mark.

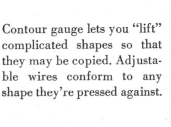

Pair of dividers is used to scribe tiles and paneling to conform to irregularities in the wall line.

Contour gauge lets you "lift" complicated shapes so that they may be copied. Adjustable wires conform to any shape they're pressed against.

Dividers and compasses have more use than just scribing small arcs and circles. They can be used for fitting a shelf, cabinet, or flooring against an uneven wall. With one leg held against the wall and drawn along it, the other leg will record every irregularity on material held against the wall.

Another good device for handling irregularities, especially such problems as fitting around moldings, is a *contour gauge*. Its adjustable wires can be fitted to any irregular surface and pick up its exact conformation.

26

Clamps and Vises

CLAMPS. Clamps are extra hands. Stronger than human hands, they give you the muscle to do many tasks you would otherwise find impossible. There are at least five of the following types that you'll find useful around the shop. Each has its own special purpose. A generous assortment will make many jobs easier and improve the quality of your work.

Adjustable hand screws. These clamps have wide wooden jaws so the chances of marring wood on which they are used are minimized. They can be used without protective pads under their jaws. They can be adjusted to clamp angular or irregular work. By turning only one screw, the jaws close at an angle instead of parallel to each other.

Hand screws are adjusted by holding the right hand on the end screw, and the left on the screw which goes through the middle of the jaws. Revolving the end screw in a clockwise direction closes the jaws. Revolving it in a counterclockwise direction opens them. Place the jaws on the work so that the jaw area near the center screw touches first. Then, when you pull the jaw tips up tight, you'll obtain maximum pressure.

C-clamps. One glance at these clamps and you'll know why they were so named. Primarily designed for metalworking, they have many uses including the clamping of wood.

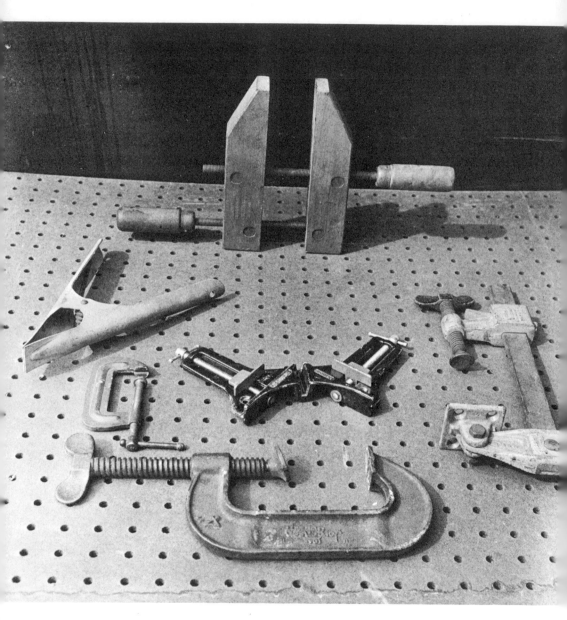

Some of the most useful clamps (from the top, clockwise):
hand screw; bar clamp; large and small C-clamps; spring
clamps. Miter clamp is at center.

When used on wood, it is usually necessary to use pads of scrap wood under their jaws to prevent marring the work.

You can get small, lightweight C-clamps whose maximum opening is 1″ and big, heavy iron ones that open 8″. Throat depth is limited in standard C-clamps, but there is one variety that has a throat depth two or three times that of standard clamps.

Bar clamps. Available in sizes ranging from 2′ to 8′, bar clamps are indispensable in making furniture and built-ins. They adjust by means of a movable jaw at one end and a crank that turns a screw at the other. Scrap wood pads must be used under their jaws to prevent marring. The pressure they exert is tremendous.

Pipe clamps work the same as bar clamps except that the jaws slide on pipe. You buy the set of jaws, supply your own length of ¾″ threaded pipe. Because you can use any length of pipe, this arrangement has great flexibility. It is also an economical way to get large clamps for spanning cabinet-sized dimensions.

Spring clamps. Resembling big clothespins, these handy items come in sizes that open from ½″ to 4″. Some come with plastic-covered tips to minimize marring the work.

Spring clamps do not hold as tightly, or exert as much pressure, as screw-type clamps, but their uses are legion. The larger sizes are generally more useful. It's a good idea to get at least four of each, but if you get a dozen you won't be sorry. They are quick and easy to use.

Corner or miter clamps. You need these for making screens, window sash, picture frames, or whenever you want to get a tight corner joint. Miter clamps will hold any degree of miter joint and prevent it from slipping. You can nail or screw the joint while the clamps are in place.

A typical set of four clamps will hold pieces up to 3″ in width and almost any length. They can be fastened to the workbench, if desired. However, there is one set that substitutes a "miter-box clamp" as the fourth clamp in the set. This accom-

Three methods of storing clamps in the shop. Steel clamp hangers (top), made especially for the purpose, fasten to the walls with screws and support heavy loads. A board bracketed to the wall (center) serves as a storage rack. If joists are within reach, they make a good place to store long bar clamps (bottom).

modates a backsaw or handsaw, adjusting to blade width, and can be used as a guide in cutting a perfect 45-degree angle miter.

Also useful in holding miters firm are "pointed-end" clamps. These are applied by means of a plier-like spreader. They go on quickly and have heavy tension. A set of eight of these spring clamps, four of each of two sizes, along with a spreader, costs less than a set of standard corner clamps. They will handle stock from ⅝" to 1¾" in width. There is also a larger size with a capacity of 1¾" to 3½".

Band clamps. These use a fabric band for clamping around irregular-shaped work, like the four legs of a chair.

Bench holdfast. This is for clamping work firmly to the top of a workbench. It consists of a collar that sets flush into a hole bored in the bench top. The shaft of the holdfast fits into the collar. Turning a screw tightens an arm firmly down on the work. It has the maximum reach of 5⅞". Extra collars are available so that you can use the holdfast in more than one place.

Hinged clamps are available that attach to the underside of the front edge of your bench. In use, they swing up and a sliding head and screw hold the work firmly to the bench top. When not needed, the clamp swings under the bench.

Useful tricks with clamps.   Have you ever had the experience of trying to clamp a series of boards in a bar clamp and have them buckle? You can use a hand screw to keep them in line. Place a board at right angles across the work you are clamping, and fix it in place with a hand screw. Now, no matter how tightly you turn the bar clamp, the work can't buckle.

Have you ever had a board that's too long and heavy to hold in a vise? Give the vise an assist by supporting the board at the other end of the bench with a hand screw clamped to the bench top.

Use two hand screws for holding a door when you are planing its edge. Set the door on 2-by-4s near the front of the bench. Clamp one hand screw near the top edge of the door so that its flat side rests on the bench top. Use the second screw to clamp the first hand screw to the bench top.

When a badly cupped board won't fit into a dado, draw it up flat against a length of 2-by-4 using a clamp at the center of the bulge. The board will give you no further argument.

When you are trying to move something and there's nothing to get a hold on, use a C-clamp as an improvised handle. Just be sure you tighten it enough so that it won't pull loose.

Make a press for flattening records, or anything else that's warped out of shape, by using two sheets of ¾" plywood of appropriate size and a C-clamp on each side to hold the sandwich together.

Who will hold the other end of that heavy board when you have no helper? Clamp a cleat to a post, stud, rafter, or other support, and rest the board's end on it.

Use a clamp to fasten a stop lock or fence to the table of your saw to make a series of cutoffs of equal length.

For clamping two boards at right angles, such as when making a drawer, set a heavy-duty shelf bracket into the angle made by the two boards and use two C-clamps to hold the bracket in place.

When your largest clamp isn't large enough, use two clamps in tandem. Hook the end of one clamp inside the end of the other. You won't get a reach equal to the combined capacities of the two clamps, but you'll come near it.

SELECTING A VISE.   The first choice for any shop is a *utility* or *bench vise*. It mounts on top of the bench and is designed for holding metal.

Big vises bolt to the bench top. Smaller ones may clamp on and have the advantage of portability, but they don't have the strength to handle all the jobs that come up in the average household.

Vises that bolt down may have a fixed base (usually the cheaper ones) or a swivel base. The latter may let the vise

Bench vise is essential in any shop. This one screws to the bench top, has a swivel base, pipe jaws below its main jaws, and anvil in rear.

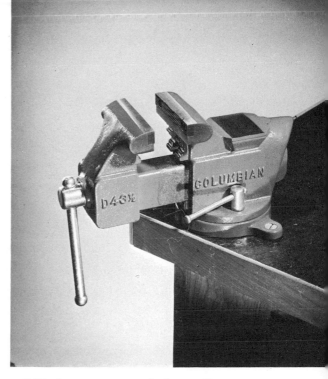

swivel a full 360 degrees, or 165 degrees—enough for ordinary purposes. There are kits available for converting stationary vises into the swivel kind.

Some vise jaws have serrated faces. These give the surest grip. But if you're finicky about preserving the finish of your work, you may be happier with smooth-faced jaws. If you have a vise with serrated jaws, you can get smooth caps to go over them, or you can improvise your own. Jaw faces may become worn after a while. Some vise manufacturers offer replaceable jaws. To prevent marring work, use a protective metal pad that is softer than your work. Brass is softer than steel, copper is softer than brass, and lead is softer than copper. The relatively narrow jaws of a bench vise can exert a pressure of many tons. If you're not careful, they can easily mangle many metals.

Some vises have pipe jaws below the regular jaws. If you don't own a pipe vise, this can be a handy feature. These curved, toothed jaws take a firm bite on many round objects that regular jaws can't handle effectively.

Woodworker's vise. This is the one other vise that every shop needs. The bench vise handles metal jobs, and this one handles wood. Unlike the bench vise, the woodworker's vise

All-angle bench vise mounts on a post and swivels 360 degrees. It can be used upright (left) or on its side (center). With a collar adapter, it can also tilt (right). Vise locks automatically in position as you tighten the jaws.

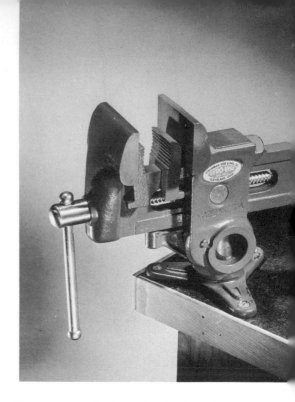

mounts below the bench, with its jaws flush with the bench top.

The best woodworker's vises have these two features: 1. A dog or stop in its outer jaw which can be raised above the bench level. This permits clamping work between it and the back of the bench or a bench stop. 2. Quick-acting jaws that open and close without laboriously screwing every inch of the way. The screwing is only for final adjustments.

There is a small clamp-on woodworker's vise that is handy as an auxiliary, or if you are not ready to make an investment in the kind that fastens on a bench permanently. This portable vise has L-shaped jaws which open to 2¾″. They can hold work either horizontally across the bench or vertically at its end. Each jaw is 5½″ long.

Vise advice.   A vise can easily damage wood or metal. Always protect your work. A scrap block of wood, a sheet of cardboard or plastic, or a piece of sheet metal may be all it takes to save the day.

Apply only enough pressure, no more. Most vises are designed to take only as much pressure as you can apply on the

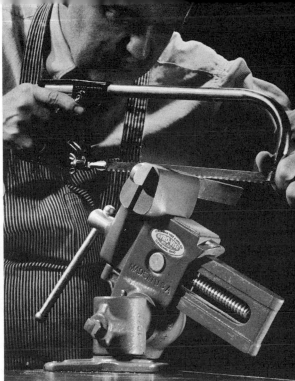

Good woodworker's vise should have at least a 12" capacity. Underbench mounting, an advantage of this model, keeps the top clear and work low for easy sawing and planing. Jaw can be slid in or out for fast setting; the screw engages only for final tightening against work.

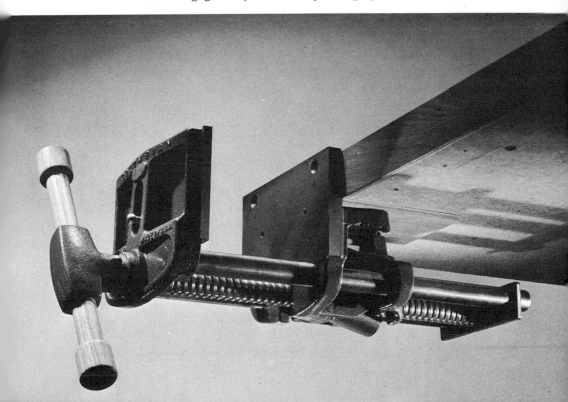

Two-way carpenter's vise holds work either horizontally across the bench or vertically off the end. For portable use, it can be clamp-mounted to a sawhorse.

handle with your own hands. If you slip a length of pipe over the handle for extra leverage, you may break the vise.

Once in a while, oil the moving parts on the vise. Wipe away the excess with a clean rag.

Part 3

POWER
TOOLS

27

Electric Drills

One of the most common operations in a workshop is drilling holes, and thus the first power tool people usually get is an electric drill. It is simple, safe, and inexpensive. In the bargain, with appropriate attachments it can be converted to a circular saw, jigsaw, hedge trimmer, grinder, polisher, and buffer.

For the homeowner, there are ¼″, ⅜″, and ½″ drills. These sizes refer to the capacity of the drill's chuck, the part that holds the bit. If it is a ¼″ drill, its chuck will hold bits with shanks up to ¼″ in diameter. If it is a ½″ drill, it will hold bits with shanks up to ½″.

But it is speed rather than chuck size that determines what a drill does best. Typically, the larger chuck sizes have more power and less speed. This is because their motors are geared down, usually in two or three stages. Just as a car has more power in lower gear, so does a drill.

The standard ¼″ drill is fast, 1500 to 2400 rpm, and is designed for drilling small holes in metal and up to ½″ holes in wood. If required, it will drill a 1″ hole in wood occasionally without protest, but it won't be happy about it. A drill is being used beyond its capacity if it labors or stalls. The ¼″ drill should not be used regularly for large holes in wood or

Three standard-sized electric drills (from top): ¼″, ⅜″, and ½″. Fractional designation refers to size of bit shank that will fit chuck. Generally, the larger the drill, the slower and more powerful it is.

metal, or for drilling in concrete. But it does so many jobs so well that no home shop should be without one.

A ¼″ drill may be had with a two-speed switch which enables it to operate at 1600 or 2250 rpm. Other ¼″ drills have completely variable speed from 0 to 2250 rpm at the squeeze of the trigger. This makes it possible to choose the exact speed that is best for each job.

Infinite speed control of electric drills is accomplished with a silicon rectifier circuit. One type has a setting adjustment so that you can get any selected speed at full-pull on the trigger. It makes for better control. The ability to start at extremely slow speeds ends the problem of bits skittering or jumping on hard surfaces like tile or steel. It is no longer necessary to center-punch to drill metal. Variable speed also makes it possible to use the drill without attachments for driving screws or nuts.

In using the drill as a screwdriver, start slow until the screw is set, then speed up to drive it home. A reversing switch found on some drills is not only handy for backing out screws, but also for removing jammed twist drills. The reversing feature is also handy when using a circular sanding attachment. Speed is also variable in reverse.

The Skil variable-speed drill has an adjusting knob for presetting the maximum speed at which you wish the drill to run. Regardless of the pressure you apply on the trigger, the

311

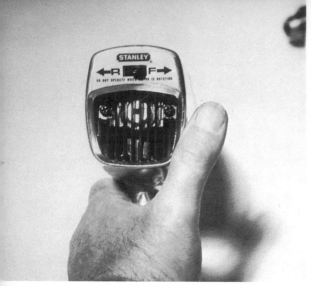

Reversible drive aids in removing drill from material when it gets stuck.

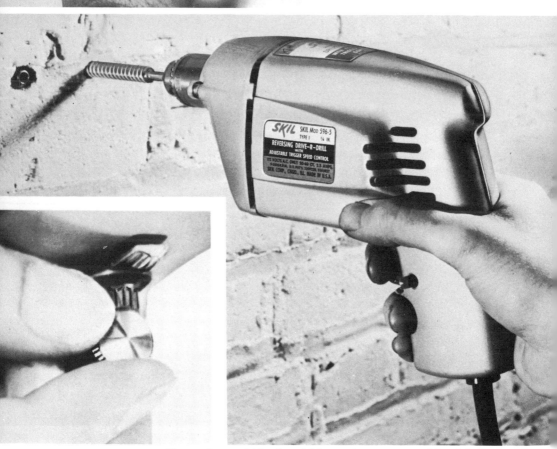

Expensive carbide-tipped bit can burn out quickly if drill is run at standard speed. In addition to its variable-speed trigger control, this drill has a control knob which prevents it from exceeding desired speed.

drill will not run faster than the maximum speed at which you've preset it. This control is especially valuable for driving and removing screws, drilling into ceramic tile, or in other applications where accuracy and control are critical. There is little danger of cracking ceramic tile at slow speed. The drill can be used to thread or rethread screw holes in metal and plastic.

For the average homeowner with a limited budget, a ¼″ drill is the unquestionable choice as it is the most versatile. For somewhat heavier duty the ⅜″ is a good bet. If you do big construction projects and require a ½″ drill, you will find you also need the ¼″ one for lighter, simpler jobs.

If you plan to do plumbing, you need a ½″ drill. You will be using power augers and self-feed bits in sizes up to 2½″.

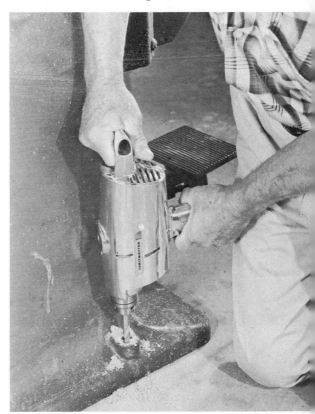

Husky ½″ drill is needed for tackling such jobs as drilling into concrete, installing plumbing, or doing heavy construction work.

If you install locksets, you'll be using large-sized hole saws. For drilling any hole ¼″ or larger into concrete a ½″ drill is recommended.

Halfway between the ox-strong ½″ and the rabbit ¼″ drill lies the ⅜″ variety. Drill speeds are rated without load. A typical ¼″ drill will have a no-load speed of 2000 rpm. A heavy-duty ¼″ drill may have a no-load speed of 2500 rpm. A ⅜″ drill will run at 1000 rpm. A ½″ drill, 500 to 600 rpm.

A motor's power is sometimes indicated by its ampere rating, sometimes by its horsepower. Because manufacturers have different methods of arriving at these ratings, they are usually useful only in comparing tools of the same brand. For example, a manufacturer may offer four different ¼″ drills. The cheapest will be rated ⅐ horsepower and 1.9 amps. Next up the line is one rated ¼ hp and 3.2 amps. A still higher quality ¼″ drill will be ¼ hp and 3.5 amps. The best of the line, usually tagged as "professional quality," may be ¼ hp *and only 2.2 amps*, proving perhaps that amperes after all are no absolute key to a drill's performance.

Other important factors are a drill's general design, its bearings, its lubrication, and its cooling system. Drills that carry an Underwriters Laboratory "Industrial Rating" will usually deliver their power for longer periods without overheating. Their amperage rating is also a more accurate indication of their power.

A motor's ampere rating indicates the amount of current it will draw when working under "normal" load. A drill will operate under these circumstances without overheating. Under more than normal load, the current draw in amperes will be greater than the rating, and the drill will deliver up to its maximum power. But at maximum power, it will overheat. If you push it beyond this limit it will draw even more amperage, but its power will decline until the point is reached where the drill stalls. When a drill stalls, the motor still draws a maximum of current, but since the current can't be converted into work it becomes heat. A motor can take only so much heat without burning out.

Horsepower ratings are sometimes confusing. Do not be misled into thinking that a drill that "develops ¼ hp" is a ¼-hp drill. The initial current surge when the motor starts and is developing its maximum torque or turning power may reach ¼ hp, but under operating conditions it is far below the ¼ hp rating.

The relative capabilities of different-sized drills can be defined as follows: A ¼″ drill can cut ¼″ holes in steel, ½″ in hardwood. A ⅜″ drill can cut ⅜″ holes in steel, ¾″ in hardwood. A ½″ drill can cut ½″ holes in steel, 1″ in hardwood. The larger the drill, the bigger the job it can handle. There is little weight difference between the ¼″, ⅜″, and compact ½″ drill. The ¼″ and ⅜″ weigh about 3 pounds, the ½″ about 3¾ pounds. The standard ½″ drill, however, weighs close to 10 pounds.

A drill's case or housing may be of metal, plastic, or a combination of both. A "shockproof" drill with a plastic housing is lighter in weight than an all-metal drill. Its plug is two-pronged, eliminating the nuisance of having to use a three-hole grounded outlet or an adapter. All parts you touch, including the chuck, are insulated. It gives complete shock protection when working in wet areas or around plumbing pipes. The plastic is also pleasanter to touch than metal. Plastic handles feel warmer in freezing weather, cooler out in the

Tools labeled "double insulated" have two separate insulations, both of which would have to fail in order to present a shock hazard. Double-insulated drills have a convenient two-prong plug instead of a three-prong plug.

broiling sun. The typical fiberglass plastic housing is of fiber-glass-reinforced polyester. Other plastic housings are of nylon.

The pistol-grip drill is most popular. Some heavy-duty drills have end or spade handles. These permit maximum pressure to be applied. In addition to the spade handle, there may be a side handle which can be shifted to the top of the drill or used at either side. If a pistol-grip drill feels heavy and out-of-balance in your hand, try gripping it higher on the handle or partially around the barrel. You may find it easier to handle and less tiring.

Two types of battery-operated drills are available. One type has its battery built-in and is cordless. The other operates from a battery-pack clipped to your belt.

Battery drills are recommended only for situations where no electricity is available, or where use of regular equipment might be a hazard. A battery power-pack recharges in about ten hours. Another kind of battery charger offers two charging rates—fast charges in fourteen hours, slow in thirty.

ACCESSORIES.   The most economical way to buy accessories for a drill is in a kit. Drills are often sold in combination with a kit. Such kits may include a wheel arbor, wire-wheel brush, drill bits, buffing wheel, chuck-key holder, rubber backing-pad, etc. The wheel arbor is for attaching grinding wheels, wire brushes, and buffing wheels.

A drill stand is a useful accessory. The horizontal type frees both hands for grinding, polishing, and sanding. Another good accessory is a flexible shaft that lets you perform operations in tight places.

A bench drill stand, more expensive than a horizontal stand, converts a portable drill to a drill press, permitting greater control and accuracy in drilling operations. The handle leverage on this setup multiplies pressure smoothly and easily. Some drill stands adjust to any angle by tilting the table. Some work in two positions—vertical or horizontal.

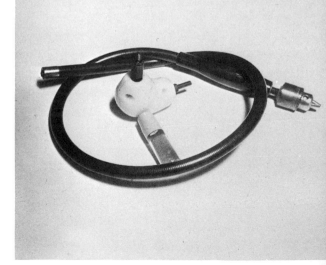

Horizontal drill stand frees both hands for grinding, polishing, or sanding. With flexible shaft and right-angle drive (right), you can get into tight places.

Bench drill-stand converts a portable drill to a drill press.
Handle levers drill up and down, multiplying pressure and
providing control and accuracy.

A rasp is another useful accessory for an electric drill. One type is a rotary drum which can be used for cutting or shaping wood, wallboard, light metals, and plastics. Another is a ¼″ rod rasp, especially useful for rough contour forming.

Somewhat less in favor today than formerly are paint mixer attachments for the drill. Under some circumstances their use has proved hazardous.

To use a drill for hole sawing, you need buy only one high-speed mandrel. Various-sized saws fit on this same mandrel.

Circular-saw attachments will fit most ¼″ and ⅜″ drills and will cut up to 2″-by-4″ lumber. A hedge trimmer attachment, typically, has about a 10½″ cutting width.

A "right angle" attachment extends a drill's capabilities, permitting work in otherwise inaccessible places. Depending on which end of the attachment is connected to the drill, its rpm is increased 1½ times or reduced to ⅔ of its regular speed.

Drills seldom require maintenance. One of the most common causes of trouble is blockage of air holes. Manufacturers like Black & Decker offer inexpensive tool maintenance kits. These contain replacement brushes, brush springs, brush caps, and gear lubricant.

The low-cost electric drill has all but made obsolete the brace and bit. Manufacturers still make them, but mostly for sale abroad or in depressed areas of the U.S. The brace and bit and other hand drills still have application where a power drill cannot be used, such as where use of electric power is not practical or safe. With a screwdriver bit in its chuck, a brace becomes a powerful screwdriver.

The hand drill that works like an eggbeater can do little that an electric drill cannot do more easily. The automatic push drill remains as the most popular of nonpower drills. Its appeal is its small size and ease of handling. When many small holes are to be drilled, it can do them quickly and with little effort.

28

The Drill Press

The drill press was originally used for making holes in metal. Now it is a versatile home workshop tool with many woodworking applications.

Drilling holes, rectangular as well as round, is only one of the jobs it can do. A drill press is also a planer, sander, and shaper. It can be used for cutting dovetails, routing, tapping, surfacing, finishing, and polishing. It can cut dowels and plugs from the wood you are using for a project, so that you have an exact match. It can even be used for wire-brushing, honing, and paint mixing. If you've admired Damaskeening, the overlapping spotpolish marks on metal that give a hammered effect, you can duplicate it with a drill press.

The heart of a drill press is a steel rod (called the spindle) which rotates inside a hollow sleeve (the quill). A feed handle moves the rotating rod up and down. At the end of the rod is a chuck which can grip a wide variety of twist drills and other tools.

The table of a drill press can be moved up and down on a column to adjust the distance of the chuck from the work. The size of a drill press is determined by the distance from the center of the chuck to this column. If this distance is 7″, it

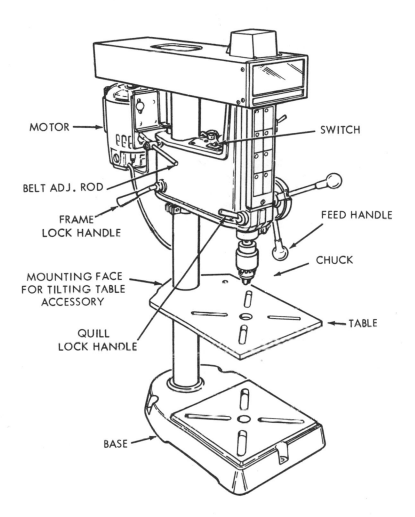

Parts of a typical drill press. Table can be moved up and down on column to adjust distance of chuck from work. Turning the feed handle lowers and raises the chuck during actual drilling. *Courtesy Sears, Roebuck Co.*

is called a 14″ drill press because it can drill to the center of a 14″ circle.

Two other measurements that determine the size of a drill press are the maximum distance between the chuck and the table, and the maximum depth you can drill with one

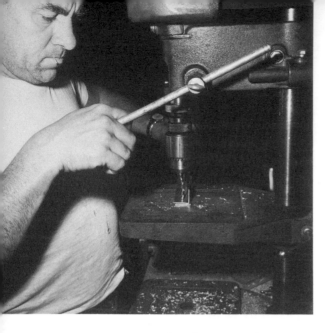

Drill press being used for drilling holes in metal. Operator is lowering the bit into work with the feed handle.

Grinding is another of many tasks a drill press performs. Here the operator inserts a grinding wheel into the chuck and is about to tighten it in place with the key. Failure to remove chuck key before starting machine can be dangerous; this one is kept on a chain to prevent it from being hurled across the shop.

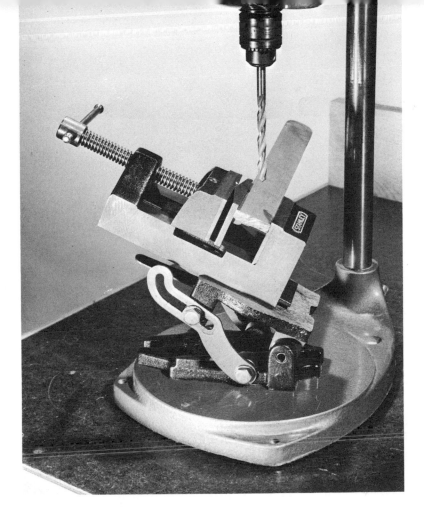

Special tilting vise bolts to drill-press table and holds work securely at any angle.

stroke of the feed lever. A typical 14″ drill press has a 4″ stroke, or "spindle travel." Larger presses may have a 6″ stroke. Though a 4″ drill press can only bore 4″ deep in a single operation, deeper holes can be bored with the proper bit by first drilling a 4″ hole, then resetting the table until the bit touches the bottom of the hole and drilling another 4″. You can also work from opposite sides of the material with a guide block clamped to the table to help you line up the holes accurately.

Speeds on most drill presses range from about 600 to 5000 revolutions per minute. The very slow speeds are needed for drilling metal and large holes in wood. Speeds in the 4000 to 5000 range are best for routing, shaping, and carving.

A tilting table permits angle-drilling. If you have a table that doesn't tilt, you can make a simple jig to hold your work at the required angle. When drilling on an angled table, it is very important that work be securely clamped to the table. Otherwise it is likely to slide as the drill pushes into the wood.

BITS AND ACCESSORIES.   Spur bits in a drill press make the cleanest holes in wood, but you can also use twist drills, auger bits, hole saws, expansive bits, and fly cutters.

The best wood-boring auger bits have a brad point rather than a screw point. When using a bit with a screw point, you have to match the rate of feed to the rate the screw pulls into the wood or the work will be lifted from the table. If your bits have screw points, it's easy enough to file off the threads.

Routing on a drill press may require replacing the chuck with a special holder for the router bit. Work must be done at the fastest possible speed and a fence used to support the work and keep it from being pulled out of your hands. The fence may be a board bolted or clamped to the table or a special shaper-fence attachment available for drill presses. These come equipped with a special hold-down. With this setup, you can make picture frames, moldings, trimmings, etc.

Other important drill-press accessories are a rotary planer, a buffing wheel, a dovetail attachment, a mortising attachment, and a flexible shaft for powering grinding wheels and drill chucks. Special vises are available for holding work. Also, you can buy adjustable hold-downs and guides of cast iron which fit almost any drill press.

29

Twist Drills and Bits

To drill that hole, you have a choice of seven basic types of bits.

Twist drills. These are essentially for making holes in metal and other tough material. Use them for drilling holes up to ¼″ in wood. If you use them for larger holes their flutes pack with wood, hampering the cutting action and causing overheating.

The twist drill's blunt point tends to move off course. If you're drilling close to an edge, the point is likely to break through the edge, where a bit with a brad or screw point would be tied in place. There is, however, one type of sharp-pointed twist drill especially designed for wood, including boring into end-grain. For drilling in metal, the point of a twist drill is usually ground to an angle of 59 degrees with the center line. For drilling in wood, this angle is usually 30 degrees, a much sharper point.

Twist drills are made either of carbon or high-speed steel. Carbon drills have a shorter life, particularly when used for drilling metal. It's best to restrict them to drilling wood. High-speed drills may have a black oxide coating. This acts as a lubricant and lengthens drill life. Larger twist drills may come with turned-down or reduced shanks. With a reduced shank, a ½″ shank can be used in a ¼″ drill or a 1″ shank in a ½″ drill.

Spade bits. Adaptable to either a portable drill or a drill press, these flat-bladed bits have shanks ¼″ in diameter but will cut holes up to 1½″ in diameter. They are also called wing, flat, or zip bits. Contrary to the usual rule, "the larger the hole the slower the speed," these bits work well at high speed.

SEVEN BASIC BITS

1. Twist drill: Most widely used type for boring holes in wood and metal up to ½″ diameter.

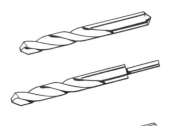

2. Small-shank bits: Twist drills with ¼″ shanks that permit the use of larger bit sizes in ¼″ drill chucks.

3. Spade bits: Broad, flat wood bits with ¼″ shanks for drilling big holes up to 1¼″.

4. Auger bits: More expensive than spade bits, but make especially smooth holes in wood up to 1″ in diameter.

5. Screw bits: Combine pilot hole, clearance hole, and countersink in one for fast drilling of screw holes. For Nos. 6, 8, 10, and 12 screws.

6. Masonry bits: Carbide-tipped for drilling brick and concrete. Common sizes: ¼″ to ½″ with ¼″-diameter shanks.

7. Hole saws: Circular cutters for large holes up to about 3″. Some are adjustable to several hole sizes; others provide one fixed size.

You can buy spade bits in sets with sizes from ¼″ to 1⅛″. For economy, some sets have only one shank to which any of the various-sized cutters can be attached, reducing cost about one-third. Some sets have two shanks, somewhat reducing the nuisance of changing cutters. Cutters are replaceable; when one is damaged, you buy another instead of a whole bit. On some spade bits, the outer blade edges form points which cut the wood fibers at the perimeter of the hole and produce cleaner work. The blade itself performs a chiseling or scraping action.

Because a spade bit has a point instead of a screw, it is your pressure that pushes it ahead into the work. This makes it more likely that it may splinter wood as it breaks through. For this reason, where a clean break-out is wanted, back up the work with a piece of scrap wood. A spade bit doesn't push the sawdust out of the hole as it drills; to clean the hole, you must pull the bit back.

You can get spade bits of high-speed steel which can run into an occasional nail without serious damage. Spade bits, because of their simple design, are easy to resharpen.

Auger bits. Essentially these are for use in a hand brace only. The chuck end of their shank has a square taper. The business end has a screw point. The point pulls the bit into the work, minimizing the pressure you have to apply. Hand-drilling is largely obsolete, so you aren't likely to have much use for this type of bit.

However, there are auger bits made for use in electric drills. Often used by plumbers and other professionals, they come in sizes from ¾″ to 1½″, are available at mill supply houses, and are expensive. They are made for use in ½″ chucks. Power auger bits pull into wood with amazing speed, and are not easy for the inexperienced to control.

You can modify a hand-brace auger bit for use in an electric drill. First, cut off the square shank. Second, file off most of the threads on the screw point to reduce the speed of its self-feed and make drilling more controllable.

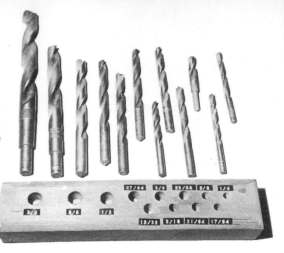

Piece of scrap wood makes a good holder for twist drills. Tags showing drill sizes were stamped with a labeler.

Combination screw bits. Special drill points are available for setting screws. One type drills the pilot hole and countersinks in a single operation. It can be used for screws ranging in size from #6 to #12. It comes in twelve sizes ranging from ¾″ by #6 to 2″ by #12. The bit's ¼″ shank fits both power and hand drills. Another type drills pilot holes, cuts a circle to accommodate the screw head, and counterbores for a plug or filling compound. It comes in the same range of sizes. Still another type of countersink attaches to a drill by means of two set-screws. The screws set into the

Large number of twist drills and auger bits are stored in drawer in drilled wood blocks hinged to the sides.

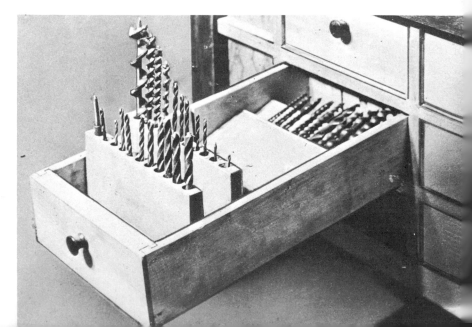

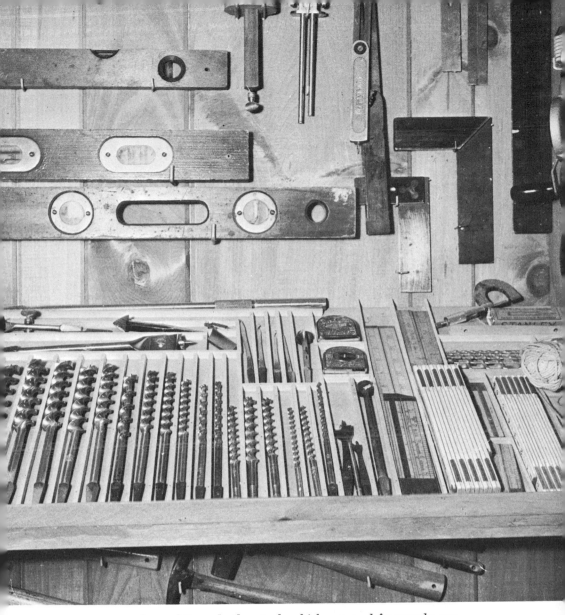

Auger bits and other tools which are used frequently can be conveniently stored on slanting, partitioned shelf.

flute of the twist drill and the countersink can be spaced at any desired distance from the drill point.

The best way to buy screw bits is in a kit. A typical kit includes five popular sizes. For accurate control of drilling, get a depth-stop set. For plugs to fit in the holes made by screw drills there are plug cutters in matching sizes to fit counterbores. A good cutter produces satin-smooth plugs.

Masonry bits. These have a carbide tip and will drill into concrete, brick, stone, mortar, plaster, slate, ceramics. You can get sizes up to ½″ that will fit in a ¼″ chuck, and up to ¾″ that will fit a ½″ chuck.

Tungsten-carbide, used on the tips of masonry bits, is one of the hardest of all man-made metals. But if you run a bit at high speed, you can burn it out in no time. It is happiest at 600 rpm.

Most masonry bits have an overall length of 4″ or 6″, but you can get them 12″ long. The extra-long ones are designed for drilling through 11″ foundation walls.

For masonry bits larger than ¾″, go to a mill supply house, which generally stocks them up to 1½″. Bits in sizes from 1″ through 1½″ are of two-piece design. The shank fits a ½″ chuck. For these large-sized bits, you can also get extension shanks from 6″ to 36″ in length.

Carbide tips are tough, but they will get dull. They can be resharpened on a bench grinder using a silicone-carbide grinding wheel.

Hole saws. These are for drilling holes from ¾″ to 2½″ in diameter. Most come in two parts—a mandrel and a blade. The mandrel goes into the drill chuck; the desired size of hole-saw blade is attached to the mandrel. You can buy very cheap seven-blade hole-saw-mandrel combinations, designed to drill

Hole saw being used to install a lock set in a new door. Blades from ¾″ to 2½″ are available, attach to a special mandrel held in the chuck.

holes from 1″ to 2½″, but they aren't very durable. They are recommended only for very light duty.

A good hole saw will cut metal, wood, plastics, wallboard, even plumbing fixtures. Use a hole saw for drilling doors for lock sets, though if you have many locks to install you may wish to get a somewhat more expensive "lock set bit" which drills holes from 1¾″ to 2⅛″ and is recommended for ½″ drills.

You can get an adjustable hole-saw attachment for cutting holes 1⅛″ to 2½″ in wood or plastic which mounts in a ¼″ or larger drill chuck. It cuts holes slightly more than 1″ deep, or more than 2″ if you drill from both sides.

Circle cutters. Commonly known as a "fly" cutter, this tool has a center pilot drill with a single cutter that revolves at the end of an adjustable arm. In an electric drill it will cut diameters from ½″ to 11½″. It's the tool you need for cutting large holes such as those for hi-fi speaker enclosures. The secret of its operation is a special side-cutting drill bit. It's like scribing a hole with a compass, except that this tool cuts. Since the bit used is ⁵⁄₃₂″, it has a cutting line much wider than that of a saw blade and allowance must be made for it.

Special bits. If you are doing electrical work, you may wish to invest in an electrician's bit. It comes in ¾″ size and is specially designed for boring holes for BX and Romex cable, or in conduit. Its ⁵⁄₁₆″ shank will fit a ⅜″ or larger chuck. Its overall length is 6⅜″.

Countersinking screws? You can get high-speed countersinks for metal or wood. They fit ¼″ and larger drills.

Doing plumbing? There are special self-feed bits to drill holes for all regular pipe sizes. Most sizes are in the range of 1⅛″ to 2⁹⁄₁₆″, but if you have money to spend you can even get 3⅜″ and 4⅜″ sizes. All the bits mentioned require a ½″ chuck.

Square holes? Get a "drill saw." It drills round or square holes in wood and plastic. This bit cuts all along its shank as well as at its tip. You can use it for cutting designs and scrolls.

30

Saber Saws

This compact, inexpensive power tool is the answer for the man who has little space for a shop or many power tools. It can do the work of a handsaw, circular saw, band saw, keyhole saw, jigsaw, coping saw, hacksaw, and knife. For the man with a well-equipped shop, it does things other power tools can't do, or does them better. It will cut wood, plywood, hardboard, fiberglass, plexiglas, steel, copper, brass, bronze, aluminum, zinc, lead, tubing, pipe, wallboard, acoustical tile, and corrugated sheet materials.

The development of small motors during World War II made this tool possible. The first ones, made in Switzerland, were good but expensive. Now, they are mass produced by a dozen manufacturers in this country and you have your choice of many models at modest prices.

In all of them, the rotary motion of the motor is converted into a back-and-forth sawing motion. Some have a single speed, usually about 3000 strokes per minute. Others have two, multiple, or infinite speed variation. Having at least two speeds is a decided advantage. Cutting metal at high speed dulls and breaks blades quickly. A two-speed saw permits low speed for metals and other hard materials, high speed for soft wood and easier going.

Saber saw is unexcelled for making intricate cuts. Two-speed switch on this model lets you saw metals at low speed, wood at high speed.

The length of stroke is usually about ⅝″ and typical wood-cutting blades are just long enough to cut through a 2-by-4. A few saws have a 1″ stroke and can use blades long enough to cut through a 6-by-6 at 90 degrees, or a 4-by-4 at 45 degrees.

Most saber saws have a base that can be tilted right or left for angle cutting, as well as a removable guide that can be used for accurate ripping without measuring or marking, or for cutting circles up to 12″ in diameter.

One of the most unusual and useful features of the saber saw is its ability to make cutouts in the middle of a board or wall, without drilling a hole. By tilting the saw up on the front

Tilting base, a feature of most saws, allows you to cut bevels; adjustable guide eliminates need for measuring and marking work to be sawed.

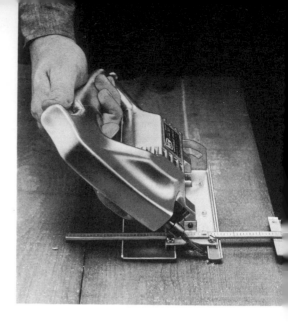

Latest improvement in saber saws is the handle-controlled blade on this model. Extremely fine work can be done by turning blade itself as it cuts sharp curves.

Plunge cuts are saber saw's specialty and make it easy to cut openings for sinks, outlet boxes, etc. Simply rest the saw on the edge of its base, then lower the blade into the work to start the cut.

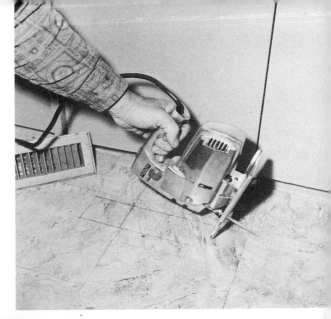

More powerful saber saws, with longer strokes, can cut through 4-by-4s, slice up small logs for firewood.

edge of its base and gradually lowering its blade to touch the work, you can cut its own slot. The saw can make cutouts for sinks, electrical outlet boxes, floor registers, fan openings, loudspeakers, etc.

Another outstanding feature is its ability to make flush cuts. You can cut right up to a vertical board, wall, or other obstruction. These plumb cuts are made possible by a special blade whose saw tooth edge projects beyond the front face of the tool, or by a tilting base which angles the saw blade forward of the tool.

The saber saw doesn't cut as fast as a circular saw, but its light weight permits your taking it places where it would be difficult or dangerous to take the latter. It's easy and safe to work with on a ladder, or for making overhead cuts.

Several manufacturers make tables to which you can attach their saws, turning the portable saber saw into a stationary jigsaw. A table frees both hands and permits accurate control for such jobs as scroll cutting.

Saber saws have certain basic design differences. They may have a metal or plastic housing or a combination of both. The plastic housing usually indicates a shockproof tool. These have a two-prong plug and can be connected to any outlet. Other saws have a three-prong plug and can be connected only to grounded outlets or used in regular outlets with a special grounding-plug adapter.

In selecting a saber saw, you will find a great variation in "feel." Of special importance is the location of the switch and whether it fits naturally with your way of working. Some saws have slide-type switches, others have trigger-type switches. Some saws have special inserts to prevent splintering, especially of plywood and veneers.

Most saber saws come with two or three blades, but there are at least a half dozen you can use to advantage. Basically, blades are of three types—wood-cutting, metal-cutting, and toothless knife blades. The knife blade is for cutting soft materials such as rubber, vinyl, cork, and insulation board.

Wood-cutting blades usually have from 6 to 10 teeth per inch. The blades with 6 or 7 teeth are for rough ripping in softwood. Those with ten teeth are for crosscutting in hardwood.

Metal-cutting blades have 14 to 24 teeth per inch. The ones with fewer teeth are for thicker, softer metals. The ones with many teeth are for hard metals and thin stock such as sheets. A metal-cutting blade with fewer teeth is good for cutting wood when there's danger of running into nails. Some blades have teeth that splay out. This "set" gives a rougher cut than blades without set.

Saw can be mounted on a special table (above), freeing
the hands for guiding intricate scrollwork, or clamped in
a vise for convenience in cutting BX cable (below) and
similar jobs.

If the saw jumps when you are cutting metal, it is because the work is not firmly clamped or the blade is too coarse. At least two teeth of a blade must contact the work, or the teeth will straddle the work and catch. When sawing sheet metal, avoid tearing by sandwiching the sheet between ¼″ plywood, held with clamps. Cut through the entire sandwich.

31

Circular Saws
Table / Radial / Portable

Most woodworking involves sawing. In the shop it's usually done with a table or a radial saw. On location, and even sometimes in the shop, the portable saw is the only power tool that can do the job.

The table and radial saw do essentially the same jobs, but they work differently and their capabilities are different. There is general agreement that a radial saw is better for crosscutting and a table saw better for ripping. For this reason, some men have both. An additional advantage of having both is that you don't have to shift setups for either operation.

TABLE SAWS usually cost less than radial saws. Generally a table saw has a blade 7¼″ to 12″ in diameter, which can be tilted for angle cuts and raised or lowered to conform to thickness of stock. It is located below the table and work is pushed through it both for ripping and crosscutting.

The table saw's regular blade may be replaced with a dado blade for operations requiring a greater width of cut, with a molding head for special shaping operations, or with a sanding disc.

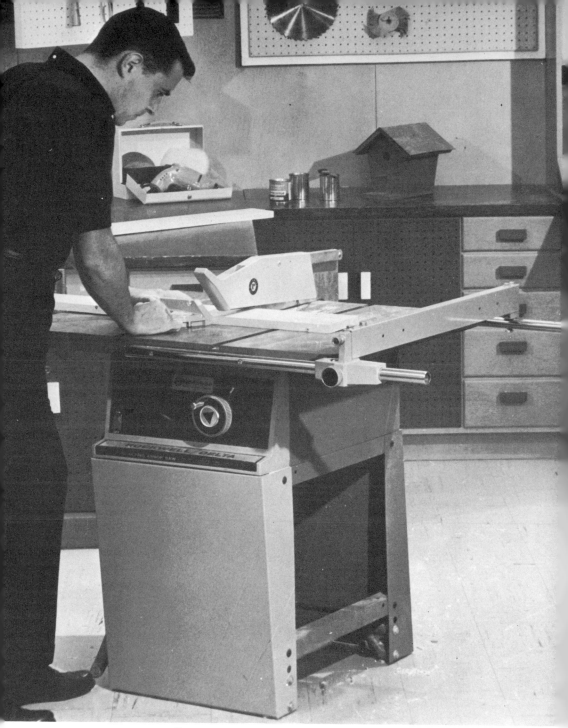

Best position for a table saw is in the center of a shop. This model has a 10″ blade, a built-in motor, and an ample extension table. Stand has provision for adding a shelf to hold a box for sawdust and scraps.

This saw rests on a homemade stand which stores under
the workbench, rolls out on casters when needed, and has
space for keeping lumber and accessories. *Courtesy Western Wood Products.*

Box attached to front of saw
stand provides place for storing tenoning jig, wrench, and
other accessories.

The usual location for a table saw is in the center of the shop. Sometimes it is combined with a jointer, and both tools are run by the same motor.

RADIAL SAWS are generally considered somewhat safer to operate, more accurate, and more versatile than table saws. A radial saw is above the work, and on crosscutting operations is pulled across the work. This permits better control, and hands may be kept safely out of the way.

In ripping, work must be pushed past the stationary rotating blade. There are "dogs" to help prevent kickback (sometimes carelessly ignored) and the blade cover can be tipped down to hold work.

Radial saw performs a wide variety of woodworking jobs. Since it is pulled across the work, which remains stationary (except when ripping), it is extremely accurate. Fingertip controls give precise depth and miter measurements.

For miter and bevel cuts, the arm of the saw is swung to the required angle and locked in place.

The radial saw is really a multipurpose tool. In addition to sawing, it can sand, grind, wire-brush, drill, rout, and shape.

Owing to the design of the radial saw, it is best located against a wall, with sufficient clearance at either side to permit ripping long stock.

In choosing either a table or radial saw, consider that its depth of cut is sharply reduced when a blade is tilted. Though an 8" blade may cut a 2-by-4 at a 45-degree angle, it won't do it as quickly or easily as a 10" blade. Smaller saws are also less powerful, less durable, usually harder to control.

Best position for a radial saw is against one wall, but in attic shop, with its low eaves, this was impractical. Instead saw was stationed in the center, in front of plywood sawdust box which hangs on 2"-by-4" uprights. Large cardboard tray for sawdust and scraps rests on bottom shelf.

Just looking at several models will give you a good idea as to their relative quality. Which will rust more easily? Are calibration scales easy to read? Does the fence slide and lock readily? Does it lock at both ends? How about the action on the miter gauge? What is the size of the table? A small table makes it difficult to handle large work. Are there table extensions? How about the saw stand or cabinet? Is it sturdy and wobble-free? How about mobility? Will the saw do the kind of work you will be doing, or is its capacity beyond your needs and its special abilities ones you will rarely if ever call upon? What are minimum motor requirements? Some 8″ saw manufacturers suggest you can get by with ¼ hp, but most specify ½ hp. A 10″ saw invariably demands ¾ to 1 hp.

PORTABLE CIRCULAR SAW.   As good as your table or radial saw may be, you'll find many occasions when it can't do the job. You may want to cut into a wall, floor, or ceiling. You may be up on the roof with 2-by-4s to cut, or the roof edge to trim. You may want to cut a plywood panel that's too big to wrestle onto a saw table. You may want to make a sink cut-out in a counter.

For some of these jobs, you may find a portable saber saw satisfactory, but there are many occasions when it falls far short of the rugged bull-strength required. That's when you need a portable circular saw.

Portable saws aren't meant for precision work. They're essentially for rough sawing. With a special abrasive blade, you can cut concrete blocks, brick, stone, but it's slow work. You'll probably reach for a hammer and chisel instead.

Saw size is determined by the size blade the tool takes, and the usual range is from 6¼″ to 8¼″. The 6¼″ size is the smallest that will cut 2″ stock at a 45-degree angle. The prime advantage of the larger saws is more power and greater capacity for work. They won't slow down, overheat, and stall if you push them a little, and you are sure to.

Bigger saws are heavier, however, and there is a handi-

Portable circular saw is at its best on outside construction jobs where speed and mobility are needed. It'll buzz through a 2-by-4 in seconds, and with adjustable baseplate (below) will cut fairly accurate miters and bevels.

Adjustable guide, a feature on many portable saws, aids in ripping long boards without measuring and marking.

cap when using the saw overhead, on a ladder, etc. At other times, it means easier guiding and straighter cutting. A cutting guide comes with most saws, or is available from the manufacturer, but chances are you'll be cutting by eye and following lines or score marks.

Introduction of a clutch made the portable circular saw safer. Formerly, when it hit a knot or started binding it would kick back. Now the clutch lets the blade stop while the motor continues turning.

A portable saw may have an aluminum or a plastic housing. Plastic makes a saw lighter in weight, and also shockproof. It doesn't require a three-prong grounding plug.

CIRCULAR-SAW BLADES. The most versatile blade is the *combination* blade. It will both rip and crosscut softwood satisfactorily. But it is a compromise, and it doesn't perform either operation as efficiently or smoothly as a blade made specifically for ripping or crosscutting. Still, it's the blade you'll probably get first and use most.

Combination blades may be "all purpose," for general cabinet work, or "chisel tooth." The latter is for rougher cutting and is designed especially for portable saws. It's a fav-

By raising saw so it rests on its baseplate edge, then lowering blade into work, you can make internal cutouts as with a saber saw.

With special nonferrous or carbide-tipped blades, saw can cut plastic laminates, aluminum, copper, and lead.

orite of contractors for framing operations and can be used on construction-gauge plywood.

A *rip blade* is for cutting along the grain of both hard- and softwoods. Its deep gullets clear sawdust fast, so each tooth has a free path in which to move ahead.

A *cutoff blade* cuts against the grain of hard- and softwoods. It can also rip hardwoods.

347

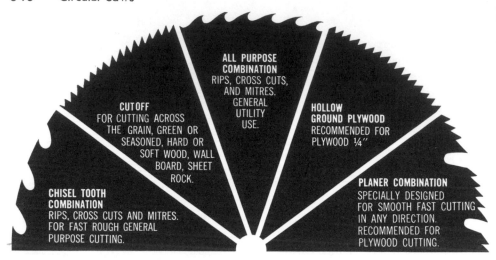

Five types of circular-saw blades. *Courtesy Nicholson File Co.*

A *planer blade* is a combination blade that's hollow-ground. It cuts smoothly in any direction. You'll want one for all of your finest work. You can't afford to use it for general rough cutting or for plywood. It dulls too fast. Some planer blades are flat-ground.

A *plywood blade* has small teeth and is designed for splinterless cutting of laminated stock. Glue is hard on saw teeth, but a plywood blade can take it.

A *flooring blade* is handy in remodeling work, for cutting through gritty boards, knots, or when an occasional nail may be encountered. It also can take plywood.

A *nonferrous blade* is the one to use for cutting aluminum, bronze, copper, lead—any metal but iron or steel.

A *carbide-tipped blade* is for plastics and plastic laminates, asbestos, aluminum, brass, hardboard, plywood, and other tough or abrasive materials. It crosscuts or miters hard- and softwoods. It is expensive, but long-lasting—some say up to twenty times as long as ordinary steel. It is also available in an 8-tooth "safe" version for portable, bench, and radial-arm saws.

Dado blades and dado blade sets are available for both hand and stationary saws. Some are carbide-tipped. One of the best varieties combines precision-ground blades and matched chippers. If your saw has an arbor approximately $1\frac{1}{2}''$ long, an 8″ dado set can make a $1\frac{1}{8}''$ cut in a single pass. A $^{13}\!/_{16}''$ cut is especially important to the homecraftsman. This is the slot needed for $\frac{3}{4}''$ shelving.

A *tenoning blade* is thicker than the average all-purpose blade. It cuts square-bottom grooves $\frac{1}{8}''$ wide, and is useful in cutting mortises, tenons, splines, box joints. On a bench saw, use it with a tenoning jig.

A *cordwood blade* is for fast, free cutting of brush, stove wood, logs, or heavy timbers. Its teeth are stronger than those on most regular blades.

Many circular-saw blades are available coated with special friction-reducing plastic to make them run smoother, cooler, and cleaner. The coating may not stand up in cutting some kiln-dried hardwoods—they're too abrasive—but blade life between sharpenings is generally improved.

32

Band Saw / Jigsaw

Superficially, a band saw and a jigsaw appear to do the same thing. Both cut curves. But there are major differences. The band saw is for big jobs. The jigsaw is for delicate or intricate work.

THE BAND SAW consists of a blade in the form of a continuous loop traveling on the rims of two, sometimes three, flangeless wheels. One of the wheels is adjustable. Moving it up or down controls the tension of the blade.

The width a band saw can cut depends on the clearance between its blade and the rear column or post. On most home-shop saws, this throat depth will be 10″, 12″, or 14″. It is this dimension that gives a band saw its size designation. A 10″ saw has a 10″ throat depth. Typically, the thickness of stock you can cut on a band saw is 6″ or more, but on some small models it may be as little as 3″.

Because of the band saw's ability to cut thick stock (a cylinder from a 6″-by-6″ block for example), it's the ideal tool for cutting blanks to be turned on a lathe. Pros especially like a band saw because it can mass-produce identical shapes. You can make a pad of six 1″ boards and cut them all at the same

Typical band saw consists of a continuous blade mounted on two wheels. Upper wheel is adjustable to control tension of blade. Here a craftsman cuts a chair arm freehand from walnut stock.

time in the same pattern. Or you can achieve the same result by cutting a 6"-by-6" timber in the desired pattern, then slice it into a number of thin sections. Each section, of course, will have the same pattern. It's the quick and easy way to cut out identical boat ribs, furniture parts, fancy valances, etc.

The tightness of the curves you can cut on a band saw depends on blade width. Small saws use blades with widths up to ³⁄₈". Bigger ones may accommodate widths up to ½" or even ¾". If you're not cutting curves, it's best to use as wide a blade as possible. The wider the blade, the less likely it is to break. Some blades are plastic-coated. The plastic acts like a lubricant, allowing the blade to glide easily through the work and protecting it against rust.

351

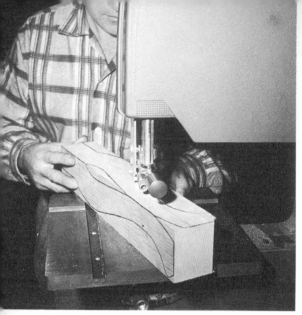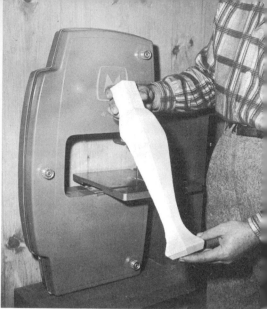

Compounds cuts—sawing from two or more sides—are the band saw's specialty. Cabriole leg shown here is typical of intricate shapes which can be created in this manner.

For woodworking, a band-saw blade is usually run at 2000 to 3000 blade feet per minute. For cutting nonferrous materials a speed of 250 to 350 fpm is recommended, for iron and for steel, 75 to 150 fpm. If your saw doesn't come with variable speed, you can get a device to provide it.

As power tools go, a band saw is relatively safe. This is because its teeth face down and it won't throw work at you. But like any power tool it must be handled with respect. Things to look for when you buy a band saw are a tilting table, a rip fence, and a miter gauge. The last two are often available as accessories.

THE JIGSAW. Unlike the rotating blade of a band saw, the blade of a jigsaw travels up and down, activated by a mechanism similar to the crankshaft in a car. The blade fits in a lower chuck. An upper chuck, connected to a spring, maintains tension on the blade. This upper chuck, and the entire upper arm that holds it, are removable to provide greater clearance. Then a heavier (saber) blade is used. About twenty-five different kinds of blades are available for the jigsaw.

A jigsaw permits turns with a much smaller radius than

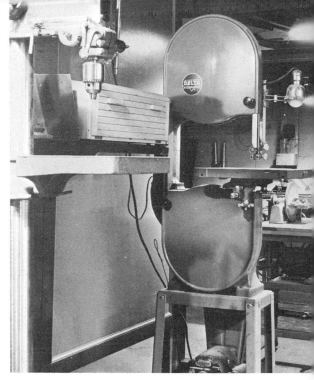

Band saw is often placed near the drill press along one wall of the shop. Both are vertical tools with similar space requirements. This saw is mounted on a steel stand which contains the motor and brings the saw table to elbow height—usually 42″ to 44″.

does a band saw. It also removes less stock. Though it can't slice big, heavy timbers like a band saw can, it can cut metal, nonferrous and hard, and intricate patterns.

Fitted with an abrasive sleeve, a jigsaw can smooth concave and convex surfaces. With a file in its chuck, it can shape and smooth metal. Inlaying, jigsaw puzzles, cut-out letters and signs are popular jigsaw projects.

Because the jigsaw is generally rated as the safest power tool in the shop, it is usually the first one a child is permitted to use. Attractive results are easy to achieve.

Perhaps the most important talent of the jigsaw is its ability to make interior cuts. After drilling a hole in the work, you slip the work over the blade, which has temporarily been disconnected at its top. No lead-in cut is necessary, as it is on a band saw.

One useful internal cut, or series of cuts, made in this manner is the "drinking cup." In this cutting operation, concentric rings are sawed with the table tilted at a slight angle (about 5 degrees). You can then open the rings to produce a reasonable facsimile of the familiar fold-open drinking cup. Glue these rings in place (no clamps needed) and you have a bowl blank ready for turning on the lathe. Or you can create

planters, lamp bases, etc. By varying the contour of multiple
cuts, you can make model boat-hull shapes. With a single cut
on the outside, you can make trays or plates with a raised edge.

When you remove the upper arm on a jigsaw, it becomes
a saber saw. If you have a portable saber saw, you can give it
some of the same benefits as this stationary kind of saber saw
by buying or building an auxiliary table to hold it. With the
tool held by a table, both your hands are then free to guide the
work. It gives you much better control.

A typical jigsaw is an 18″ model, though 24″ is also

Especially popular with modelmakers, this 15″ jigsaw has
a flexible shaft which runs off the same motor and can be
fitted with sanding, grinding, and buffing attachments.

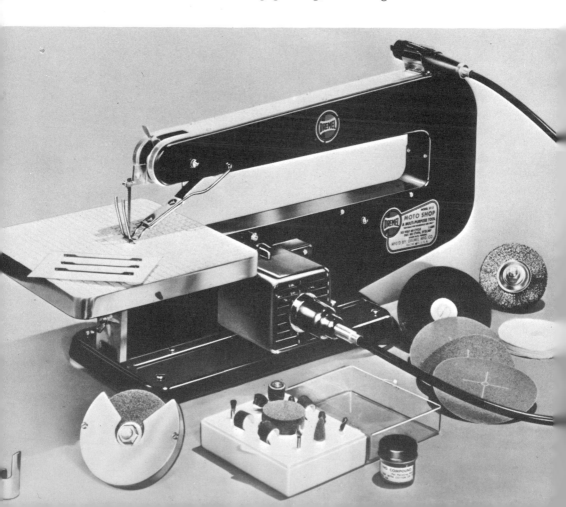

popular. As in the case of a band saw, the size designates the clearance from blade to back support. One smaller 15″ jigsaw has a variety of slip-on attachments which fit a flexible-shaft unit and convert the saw to a sander, grinder, and buffer for light modelmaking. It will cut up to 1¾″-thick wood, light metal and plastics.

Small hand-held jig or scroll saws may have no motor but work by magnetic impulse like a doorbell. One variety produces 7200 strokes per minute, has a finger-control trigger switch. Its throat is 9½″ deep, which means it can cut to the center of a 19″ circle. It will cut both wood and light metals.

Hand-held jigsaw will cut ¾″ stock, as well as plastic and light metals. It is especially suited to sawing intricate scrollwork in very thin material.

33

Power Sanders

The difference between turning out an amateur or a professional job in your shop is often a matter of proper sanding before applying the finish. Whether you intend to stain, varnish, or enamel the work, thorough sanding is necessary to get the maximum beauty from the finish. With a power sander you not only save considerable time and effort, but you are able to produce that fine sanded surface on all parts of the work which is impossible to achieve by hand sanding alone. In addition, a power sander enables you to do accurate fitting and joining (often necessary after saw cutting), to remove paint and varnish on refinishing jobs, and much more.

There are three basic types of sanders available for the home workshop. Let's look at each one in turn.

FINISHING SANDERS.   These cost the least and are the most important in getting a fine surface. A finishing sander is the one to get first.

Lowest in cost is the type driven by magnetic impulse. It has a vibrator rather than a motor and its action adds up to 14,400 strokes per minute. For very light duty, one of its best applications is the sanding of enamel or varnish between coats. Typically, the sanding area of its pad is around 14 square inches, so you don't get a lot of work done in a hurry, but you

Dual-motion sander, controlled by thumb switch on handle, has orbital action for rough sanding, straight-line action for fine finishing work.

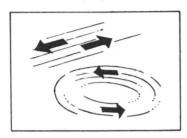

can get in fairly tight spots. Some magnetic-impulse finishing sanders may have a pad size of around 25 square inches. These are good for large, straightaway surfaces. With a lamb's-wool pad a finishing sander can also be used as a polisher.

A motor-driven sander may be straight-line, orbital, or dual-action. As its name implies, a straight-line sander has a back-and-forth motion. Action can thus be confined completely with the grain. Straight-line sanding is best for final smoothing. It can take your project to the point where only the last few finishing touches must be done by hand. Its 9000 strokes a minute, each ¾₁₆″ long, surpass anything you can do by muscle alone.

An orbital sander is best for relatively rough work because at least half of each cycle is movement against the grain. It removes wood at a faster clip. Though it does technically violate the precept never to sand against the grain, its strokes are so short it can produce a highly acceptable finish.

In a dual-motion sander, motion can be changed from orbital to straight-line by flicking a lever. You use the orbital action for preliminary sanding, then switch to straight-line for finish and flush sanding.

You can test the relative power of two finishing sanders by bearing down on them. See which one is the easiest to stall. In actual use, of course, you won't exert pressure. The weight of the tool is all the pressure that is needed or should be used.

BELT SANDERS.   These make short work of the toughest sanding job. In one hour, its 3″ or 4″ wide belt travels 9 miles. It goes 14 feet in just one second. With a rough-grit (60 grit) belt, it takes wood down incredibly fast. It can trim stock for an exact fit with ease. It will strip off old paint and varnish, smooth irregular floors, remove rust and corrosion. With a special nylon mesh belt, impregnated with silicon-carbide abrasive, it will remove scuff marks from plastic floor tiles, clean and renew stainless steel, give a satin finish to plastic panels, and even polish furniture. These belts are used with a special lubricant. Some belt sanders have two speeds—low for polishing, high for sanding.

Belt sanders kick up a lot of dust. Some models have a dust-pickup bag attached. Others can be connected by means of an attachment to almost any tank-type vacuum cleaner.

DRILL SANDERS.   With a disc attachment you can do power sanding with a ¼″ electric drill. It is satisfactory for rough sanding, shaping, taking off paint. It is not for finish sanding as it is too inclined to skip, gouge, and leave swirl marks.

The standard sanding attachment is a flexible rubber disc mounted on a shaft. In use, it is tilted slightly so only the outer third of the disc touches the work. On narrow boards, only the edge of the disc is applied, not the center.

A special variety of ball-joint disc-sanding attachment is available. It is designed to lie flat against the work and is "self-leveling." This helps somewhat in eliminating scratches, but it is still not a finishing sander. With a lambswool polishing bonnet, a drill sanding attachment can be used for buffing wax or chemical polishing agents.

Belt sander, the workhorse of the group, is best for heavy stock removal, paint and varnish removal. With a silicone-carbide belt, it can be used for polishing. Some models have two speeds—low for polishing, high for sanding.

Disc sander used with electric drill does adequate job of sanding small surfaces. Here it is attached to a right-angle drive to get into a tight spot.

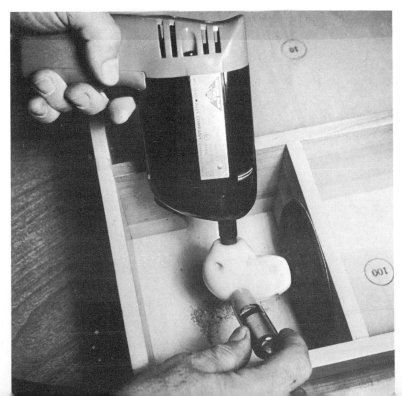

Belt-disc sander, a stationary tool, is unexcelled for finishing work, for shaping stock when making accurate joints, as well as for metalworking with aluminum-oxide belts and discs. Above, a miter gauge is used with the disc sander to square the end of a board; below, belt sander at work on the surface.

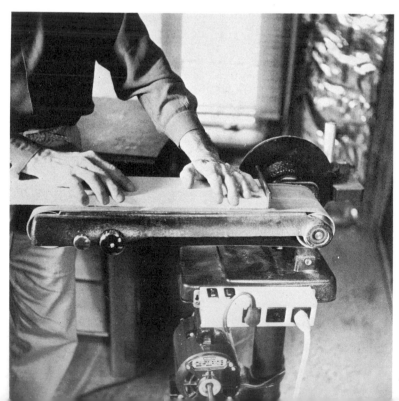

BENCH-TYPE SANDERS.   A belt-disc sander is one of the most useful tools in the shop. The answer to problems of accurate fitting and joining, it's a shaper that produces perfect inside and outside curves, bevels, and chamfers.

Often overlooked is that a belt-disc sander is a metalworking as well as a woodworking tool. Its aluminum-oxide belts and discs use the same abrasives from which grinding wheels are formed. You can use them to sharpen power-mower blades, precision-grind lathe tool bits and hollow-grind plane blades and chisels. They are much safer than solid wheels because they can't shatter. They also cut cooler as their large surface dissipates heat.

You can get separate disc and belt sanders, but the combination tool has the features most wanted in a home shop. By tilting, the belt can cut any bevel angle from flat to vertical. The disc can give you glass-flat surfaces on either wood or metal. A miter gauge slides in the slot of the tilting work table so you can get any angle desired as you slide work across the disc. The work table can also be used with the belt.

A 6″ belt and 9″ disc are best for the average home shop. Belt width doesn't limit the size of the boards you can sand. To sand wide boards, you merely make repeated passes. The tool can be bought with or without a motor, for mounting on a bench or with a separate pedestal stand.

SELECTING AN ABRASIVE.   In addition to the *type* of abrasive, there are four other items to consider in making a selection. Read the print on the back of the sanding paper and you will find a grit number, a grade number, a word description of how fine the grit is, and a letter designation of the weight or stiffness of the backing.

There are seven kinds of minerals used as abrasives or grit: flint, garnet, emery, crocus, aluminum oxide, silicon carbide, and tungsten carbide.

Flint is cheap and wears out fast. It's good for hand sanding softwood and for removing paint.

Garnet is a natural abrasive. Aluminum oxide is man-made. Both have similar characteristics, though garnet runs a little finer. Both are good for the final sanding of fine cabinet work. Aluminum oxide is also good on many metals. It's very hard and very tough.

Emery is for polishing unplated metals and removing rust. Crocus is for polishing metals to a bright gloss. Both come with cloth backing.

Silicon carbide is the hardest abrasive, about as hard as diamond, but it fractures under pressure. Use it for materials it cuts without heavy pressure: nonferrous metals, ceramics, plastics, glass, fibrous wood, enamel.

Tungsten carbide is very tough and long lasting. It's also expensive.

Grit number or size may range from 12 to 600. The bigger the number, the finer the grit. Numbers on the backs of abrasives, most commonly ones like 80, 100, 120, refer to the mesh openings in a 1"-square piece of screening through which the abrasive grits pass. An abrasive designated as 100 means that its grits can pass through a screen with 100 divisions per inch.

Grit size may also be designated by an older system in which numbers range from $4\frac{1}{2}$ to 10/0. In this system, $4\frac{1}{2}$ is 12 grain, 1 is 50 grain, 0 is 80 grain, 2/0 is 100, and 10/0 is 400 grain.

Sometimes, numbers are not used and the grit is merely described as "extra coarse," "coarse," "medium," "fine," "very fine," "extra fine." Coarse paper is 2 to 1, medium is 1/2 to 2/0, fine is 3/0 to 5/0. Extra-fine garnet paper may run as high as 10/0.

Papers with lightweight backing are graded as "finishing." Stiffer, heavier papers are graded as "cabinet." Weights are also designated by letters. A is light, C, D, and E are progressively heavier. There is no B. Cloth weight is indicated by J, H, and X.

Abrasive coating may be open or closed. A closed coat has grains over the entire surface of the backing. An open coat covers only 50 to 70 percent of the surface. Usually, the coarser the grit, the more open it is.

34

The Router

Most men don't get a router until they first acquire a ¼″ drill, a finishing sander, a portable saber saw, and a portable circular saw. Then they discover what they've been missing. A router, they suddenly realize, is the secret of achieving those sophisticated professional touches that are almost impossible to duplicate by any other means, and they wish they'd known about it sooner.

A router is a high-speed motor (18,000 to 30,000 rpm) mounted nose down in a frame in which it can be raised or lowered. Into its nose, or chuck, fit a variety of cutting bits. Raising or lowering the motor controls the depth to which the bits cut. The shape of the cutter blades determines the configuration of the cut produced.

Most routers you see will probably range from about ¼ to ½ horsepower. Professional models may be ¾ to 1 horsepower. The smaller and lighter a router is, the less its capacity for heavy-duty work.

Here's what a router does: It cuts smooth dadoes for attaching shelves in cabinets, bookcases, and built-ins. It makes perfect grooves for sliding doors, or for recessing panels and drawer bottoms.

Smoother than a saw, it cuts rabbets with or across grain

WOODWORKING CUTS
YOU CAN MAKE
WITH A ROUTER

Dadoes

Rabbets

End Dovetails

Decorative Edges

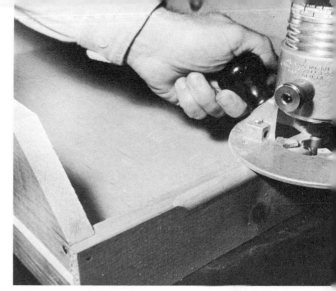

Inlaid Letters

Trimming Plastic Laminate

365

for making lap joints. It machines recesses for receiving glass, screening, or cabinet backs.

You don't have to be a skilled cabinetmaker to cut dovetail joints. With a router and a dovetail jig, you can turn out dovetail drawers with machine precision and factory speed (thirty seconds per joint). Both parts of a joint are cut simultaneously, so they fit exactly.

With a rounding-over bit, a router takes the sharp edges off drawers, table tops, and furniture. Besides being useful for carving decorative edging, rounding-over and cove bits are just the thing for drop-leaf table joints.

With a veining bit, a router tools signs with raised or sunken letters.

A router cuts decorative designs in wood, plastics, and nonferrous metals. It incises or routs out areas for inlays. It cuts ¼″ plywood like a jigsaw.

A router is *the* essential tool for countertop work. With a veneer-trimming attachment, a router flush-trims edges of Formica and other plastic laminates.

With a simple jig, it cuts decorative flutes or beads on a table leg or other piece. The work to be cut is held between the centers on a lathe, or in a jig that has an indexing arrangement so flutes or beads can be spaced accurately.

Attach the router to a supporting table, which you can either buy or build, and it becomes a spindle shaper. One router model has a self-storing carrying case which becomes a shaper table. The router can then cut chamfers, coves, rabbets, and a great variety of other straight or free-form cuts in wood or plastic. Some router tables can be tilted to 45 degrees, with every change in angle producing a different shape with the same cutters.

Builders use a router to cut recesses for hinge butts. Templates are available for matching various hinge styles and sizes.

Remove the router motor from its base and it can be inserted into an attachment that makes it a power plane. It does

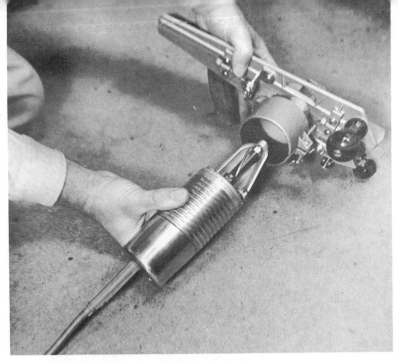

With a special attachment, router can be converted into a power plane. Motor, with cutter in place, is simply inserted into the plane (above). Tool makes short work of tough jobs such as trimming down a window frame (below).

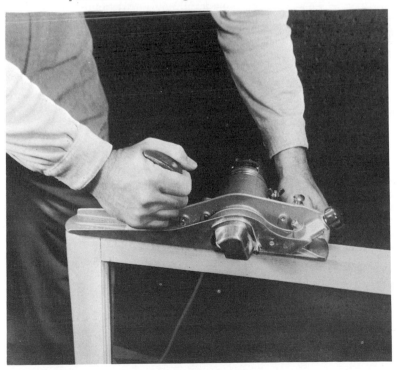

This router kit includes a motor, base, guide, power plane
attachment, and a set of basic bits.

anything a hand plane can do—but easier and faster. It leaves
smooth surfaces that need no sanding. It cuts doors and windows to a fit quickly and effortlessly.

With a trammel point you can cut circles with a router.
The point is used with a rod from the router guide.

Almost an essential is a grinding fixture. It is used for
sharpening router bits and shaper cutters. A variety of abrasive
wheels and points is available for the purpose. For sharpening
plane cutters there is also a plane-cutter grinding attachment.

A bench stand is available which holds the router motor
so it can be used for sharpening bits, cutters, chisels, punches,
even kitchen knives.

A basic router is not expensive, as power tools go. But by
the time you add necessary and desired attachments, extra cutters and sharpeners, a carrying case and other extras, the initial
cost quickly doubles or triples.

35 | The Wood Lathe

The wood lathe was once the most popular power tool in the shop. Often it was the *only* power tool in the shop. When tastes for elaborate wood turnings changed, however, the lathe began collecting dust. Then, as its virtues and possibilities were rediscovered, it made a comeback. The wood lathe can do things no other shop tool can.

If you are an artist at heart, a lathe may very well be your favorite. It's really a sculpturing tool. With it, you can turn out such diverse items as chess men, salad bowls, pepper mills, lamp bases, gunstocks, candle holders, lazy Susans, center-pieces. You can turn bowling pins, and produce a credible match for a broken baluster. You can turn plastics on a lathe, and the larger wood lathes can be equipped for many metal-working operations.

LATHE ANATOMY. A lathe consists of a fixed headstock and a movable tailstock. The work is supported between the two on spindles. The diameter of work a lathe can turn determines its size. If it has enough clearance to turn a piece 12″ in diameter, it is a 12″ lathe. Sometimes a lathe bed has a gap near its headstock so that it can clear larger work than it would otherwise.

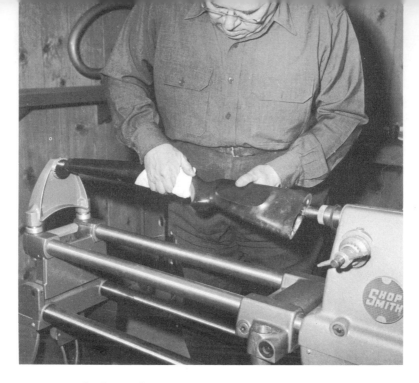

Lathe is the only power tool that can carry a project through from beginning to end. Here finishing touches are applied to a gunstock which was turned on the lathe.

The tailstock moves on the lathe bed or tube, as does a tool rest. The motor that runs the lathe is usually mounted on a bench at the rear of the headstock or below on the bench shelf. Typically, it is connected by a ½″ V-belt, and if the lathe is mounted on a bench, the belt travels through a slot in the bench. A hinge mount for the motor makes it simple to shift the belt to different pulley stops to change the speed of the lathe. With a four-step motor pulley that's the same size as the one turning the spindle, a 1750 rpm motor can deliver speeds ranging from 875 to 3450. The lower speeds are for larger diameters and roughing work, the higher speeds for finishing and smaller diameters. For average use, a ⅓ hp motor does nicely. For continuous heavy-duty use, a ½ hp motor is recommended.

The lathe may be mounted on a bench, or on steel legs. The spindle should be approximately at waist level. You can buy a pedestal stand 30″ high for a wood lathe. This puts the spindle at approximately the right height for most men.

CHOOSING A LATHE.   Here's what to look for. How well is it engineered? Is it rugged? Can its movable parts be positioned easily and locked securely? What length and diameter stock will it handle?

Does it have a built-in indexing mechanism? You need this for such operations as fluting and reeding. The index head spaces reeds and flutes exactly.

Turn the spindle by hand. What does it tell you about the bearings and the precision of the machine? A tool that bears the name of a reliable manufacturer may mean that replacement parts will be available indefinitely. That's important, for a lathe is a tool that will be in use for years and years. What kind of accessories come with it? If you're buying a secondhand lathe, will there be accessories and replacement parts available to fit it?

THE CHISELS.   Cutting stock on a lathe is done with five basic types of chisels. In cutting, these chisels are supported on a tool rest which slides along the lathe bed.

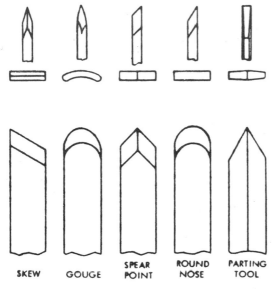

| SKEW | GOUGE | SPEAR POINT | ROUND NOSE | PARTING TOOL |

Five basic types of turning chisels used in lathe work.

Turning chisels can be hung on nails on a rafter above the lathe, or kept in removable tray in box for accessories.

The most important chisel is the gouge. It is a round-nose hollow chisel, available in such sizes as ¼″, ½″, and ¾″. The ¾″ is most important, but you will want all three sizes. The skew, usually ½″, but also available in ¾″ and 1″, is a flat-ground cutter used for tapers. A ½″ spear point (or diamond point) and a ½″ round-nose tool are commonly used for scraping operations. A ⅛″, ¼″, or ½″ parting chisel is used for cutting loose completed work.

If you cut plastic, aluminum, and brass, in addition to wood, you will want to get a set of carbide-tipped tools. They stay sharp many times longer than tools of ordinary steel.

ACCESSORIES. A faceplate attachment is for work that can't be mounted between centers. If it's for work too large to swing above the bed, the plate can be attached outboard. A 3″ diameter faceplate is for small and medium work, a 6″ diameter is for large work. An 8″ diameter combination faceplate and sanding plate of cast iron will fit many models and is readily available.

With the use of screw-on arbors, a lathe can be used for sanding, wire brushing, grinding, buffing, and polishing. Arbors are available in both right- and left-hand threads to fit either end of the lathe spindle. With an arbor, sanding drums and sleeves of various kinds can be used for sanding irregular and curved surfaces.

A sanding table is a handy accessory. You may be able to get one to fit your lathe, but if you can't, you may be able to improvise one out of wood.

Tool supports of various kinds and sizes are available to make work easier. A right-angle support is used in faceplate work. Its special advantage is that it gives support for working on both the face and rim of a turning.

A 12″ tool support is for average work. For extra-long turnings, a 24″ support is useful, but it requires an extra base support. For miniature work, there is a 4″ tool support.

With a "compound slide rest," most metal-turning opera-

On this bench, grinder is installed below the lathe where it is accessible for keeping turning chisels sharp.

tions (except screw cutting) can be done on the lathe. When a lathe is used for metalworking, a special holder for boring bars and tool bits is required. A set of bars for boring metal usually includes ⅛″, ³⁄₁₆″, and ¼″ sizes. A set of high-speed ¼″ bits should include roughing bits, finishing bits, right and left corner bits.

A "steady rest" is for supporting long, thin turnings. It keeps work from vibrating. It has sliding jaws which adjust to the diameter of the work.

Drive and cup centers are for mounting all spindle turnings. A screw center is for quick and easy mounting of small faceplate turnings. There is also a ball-bearing center for use in metal spinning.

This lathe bench features a folding top which covers the lathe when it's not used, storage space below, and a closet built onto the bench for a shop vacuum. Plans are available from Rockwell Mfg. Co.

A chuck makes it possible to use the lathe for horizontal drilling and reaming.

A hand wheel is available for mounting on the outboard end of the headstock spindle. It is useful in positioning work and for stopping work when the lathe is switched off.

36

Motors

Motors not only power workshop tools, they run almost everything else around the house. To get the most out of them, and to fix them when they talk back, requires knowledge of only a few basic facts.

Torque, or turning force, is what makes motors run. The more torque a motor has, the more powerful it is. Most household motors are one horsepower or less. That is why they are called fractional horsepower motors. Typically, they may be ¼, ½, or ¾ horsepower. This fact is marked on the motor's specifications plate. If there is no indication of horsepower, you can assume it's less than ⅛.

Often a motor will be rated in amperes. This is even a better clue to its actual horsepower than the manufacturer's statement. A motor requires far more horsepower to start turning than after it is running. It may require five to eight times as much power to start and this is sometimes given as its "horsepower rating." When it is stated that a motor "develops 2½ horsepower," it means that this is its initial surge. Under normal running conditions its power may be only ½ horsepower.

It's easy to calculate horsepower if you know amperes. Take a motor with a 3½ ampere rating. Multiply 3½ by the voltage (115) and you get 402.5, its input in watts. Since fractional horsepower motors are about 68 percent efficient, multiply its watts input of 402.5 by .68 and you get 273.7 watts output. There are 746 watts to a horsepower, so divide 273.7 by 746 and you get .36 horsepower. Don't be surprised if the plate lists the motor as ½ horsepower. Manufacturers often set their own rules when it comes to calculating.

TYPES OF MOTORS.   Three different types of motors are commonly found around home and shop: universal, split phase, and capacitor start.

The universal motor gets its name because it runs on either A.C. or D.C. current. It is the kind commonly used on electric drills, sanders, vacuum cleaners, and on many small appliances. Universal motors are characterized by having brushes. Brushes provide the electrical connection to the "rotor," the moving part of the motor. The part of the motor that doesn't turn is called the "stator."

In split-phase and capacitor-start motors, there is no electrical connection to the rotor. Power is transmitted to it by "induction," and these are commonly called induction motors. They work on A.C.

Universal motors are self-starting. Induction motors have separate starting mechanisms. In a split-phase motor this is a starting winding which is disconnected by a centrifugal switch after the motor reaches speed. A capacitor motor, recognized by the small cylinder or hump riding atop it, includes a capacitor or condenser. This provides extra voltage to the starting winding and increases its starting torque.

Split-phase motors are more likely to cause lights to dim momentarily when they start. A capacitor eliminates this dimming. If lights do dim, it may not be the motor's fault. It may be due to inadequate wiring that lacks the capacity to carry current equal to the demand the motor makes upon it.

TROUBLESHOOTING.   A prominent manufacturer says that it doesn't pay to repair small worn-out motors, that it's

When a motor stops and you've determined that it's properly plugged in, pushing button of thermal overload protector may be all that's needed to start it again.

cheaper to buy a new one. Nevertheless, there are many motor repairs that are simple to make, and you'll learn about motors in the process.

Many motor troubles are outside the motor itself. If a motor is completely dead, first investigate its socket, switch, and connecting cord. Plug a lamp into the socket to verify that you have current there. If the motor has a "manual reset button," press it in firmly. To protect against excessive heat, some motors have built-in "thermal overload protectors." In some cases, when the motor cools off, the protector automatically snaps the current back on. In other cases, you must do it manually.

If the motor is plugged into a live outlet and doesn't run, remove a plate or whatever else is necessary to get to the wiring strip where the cord connects to the motor. Use a test light to verify that current is getting to this point. If the outlet is live, and there is no current at the terminal strip, you know the trouble is in your plug or connecting cord.

Check the brushes. This can usually be done without taking the motor apart. Merely unscrew the small plastic button on either side of the commutator (the copper end of the armature or rotor). A brush consists of a spring and a carbon block. Sometimes by stretching out the spring, its action can be strengthened and the brush contact improved. If the brush or brushes are worn out, take them to an electrical supply store

When motor stops, and a plugged-in lamp at the outlet tells you there's a supply of current, check to see if the current is getting to the motor by touching the leads of a test light to the motor terminals. If the light comes on, it indicates that the plug and cord are good and that the trouble is in the motor itself.

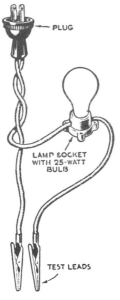

PLUG

LAMP SOCKET
WITH 25-WATT
BULB

TEST LEADS

Simple test light is easily made with a plug and weatherproof socket, although a porcelain one will do if you tape the exposed terminals.

Worn brushes, a common cause of motor failure, can often be replaced without taking the motor apart. Merely unscrew the small plastic heads on the motor face. If a brush makes poor contact, stretching the spring may improve it.

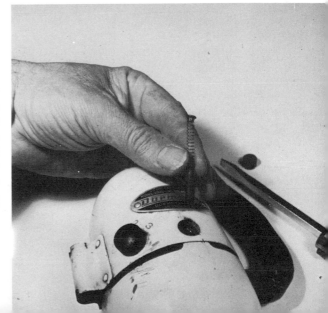

A commutator should be bronze in color, not black. Over-oiling a motor, or oiling it where oil is not supposed to go, can gum up a commutator. Carbon tet and a toothbrush are the best cleaning agents, but exercise caution. Carbon tet vapors can be deadly. Use only in the open air, and avoid breathing the vapors. If the commutator isn't gummy, clean it with very fine sandpaper (5/0 or 6/0). Do not use emery paper or coarse sandpaper.

If a motor hums, but won't start, check for jamming. Disconnect the belt, or any load. Try turning the shaft by hand. It should turn freely. On a capacitor motor, if the motor hums but won't start, wrap a length of twine around the motor shaft and give it a fast spin while the current is on. If it runs now, indications are that the trouble is in the capacitor or starting windings.

If a motor runs hot, check for blocking of air and ventilation holes. On an induction motor, check the centrifugal switch. If it's stuck in the closed position, this would cause overheating. If a motor requires replacement of a bearing or rewinding of a field, get a price at a motor repair shop and then decide if it is worth repairing or if you are better off buying a new motor.

The motor's rotating shaft is supported by bearings. These may be either sleeve bearings or ball bearings. Bearings may

If a motor hums but won't start, it may be due to a dead capacitor. Replacing the capacitor with a new one is a simple soldering job.

be stiff due to lack of lubrication or to wear. Overheating may reach such a point that bearings fuse. A motor may also overheat because of an overlong extension cord. A motor may run on an overlong or inadequate extension cord, but continuous operation on voltage more than 5 percent below what is specified on its plate will damage it. The accompanying table shows the maximum cord length for different gauges of wire with motors of different amperage. Also, follows the manufacturer's direction for motor care and lubrication.

MOTOR AMPERAGE	WIRE SIZE	MAXIMUM LENGTH OF CORD
3.5 amp	16 gauge	100 feet
5 amp	16 gauge	75 feet
5 amp	14 gauge	100 feet
7 amp	16 gauge	50 feet
7 amp	14 gauge	75 feet
10 amp	12 gauge	100 feet
12 amp	14 gauge	50 feet
12 amp	12 gauge	75 feet
15 amp	12 gauge	50 feet

If a motor has been inundated by a basement flood, or otherwise soaked, it must be dried out before starting. It is best to have a wet motor dried out at a motor shop. If you attempt it yourself, put it in an open oven set at its lowest temperature. Bake the motor until it stops steaming. Another technique is to put it over a warm-air register.

A word of caution about disassembly of motors. Mark bell ends and housing, so the ends can be replaced in exactly the same position they had originally. Don't rely on memory for correct replacement of wires on terminal strips. Number the terminals and put matching number tabs on each wire.

Motor belts that are too tight, or extreme pulley ratios, put an excessive load on motors. Match the motor to the load. An overworked motor will cause you trouble. If your motor regularly blows fuses, switch to slow-blow fuses.

If a motor overheats, first check to see if its air holes are clogged. Blow them out with an air hose, or suck up the dust with a vacuum.

A split-phase motor is cheap, but it can offer only about $1\frac{1}{2}$ times its full-power torque in getting a load started. It can make a tremendous demand on current to get started if it is overloaded. With far less starting-current demand, a capacitor motor delivers much higher starting torque. It is less likely to blow fuses. Capacitor motors also deliver more horsepower per watt when running. If you can install a centrifugal clutch between the motor and its load, you can let the motor get up to speed before connecting to the load. That may help you to do the required job with a less expensive motor.

A split-phase motor requires 5 to 7 times more electric power to start than to run. A capacitor motor needs only about four times as much.

If your motor is one that can run on 230 volts, as well as 115, give it 230 if you can. At 230 volts a motor draws only half as much current for the same power.

Higher voltage cuts down on the amperage a motor needs, and there is far less strain on its electrical windings. It will run cooler.

A motor may run even if it has a short in it, but it won't be running at full power and it is a shock hazard. Use a test lamp to check a motor for shorts or burned out (or open) windings. First, remove all connections from the terminal strip. You can quickly tell the difference between running (or main) and starting windings. The former is made of bigger wire.

A motor that has been submerged in water should be dried out before being used again. To do the job at home, bake it in the oven at the lowest setting. The oven should be warm, not hot.

Put a test lead from the bulb to each terminal of the coil. The bulb will light if the coil has no break. If you can see a break, you may be able to repair it by splicing, but be sure to insulate it well. If you can't see the break, rewinding or replacement of the coil is required.

Check for a short between the windings and the frame. If your bulb lights when one clip touches the frame and the other touches either winding lead, there is a short. Check between separate windings by touching a clip to a lead of each. If the bulb lights, there is a short between the windings. With luck, you may be able to locate it and correct it.

37

Belts / Pulleys / Motor Mounts

Belts transmit power from motor to tool. They offer a means of braking, clutching, and changing speeds.

Most belts come in ⅜″, ½″, and ⅝″ widths. Manufacturers have a code method for indicating belt widths and lengths. For example, a 3L340 means that a belt is ⅜″ wide, light duty, and 34″ long. The first figure is the width in eighths of an inch. The "L" stands for light duty. The next two figures are the size in inches. The last 0 indicates that there is no fraction.

In replacing an old belt, to measure the pulley length required, run a tape around the outside edge of the first pulley, over to the next pulley, around it, then back to the starting point. Don't measure the belt itself. If it's old, it will have been stretched. A belt gets its traction against the angled sides of the pulley. It must never ride in the bottom of the pulley groove.

It is important that a belt be neither too tight nor too loose. You should not have to pry a belt onto a pulley, for if you do you'll damage the belt. If, when a belt is in place, you can pull it up more than 1″, it's too loose. If you can't pull it up 1″, it's too tight. The correct slack is exactly 1″.

Here is another way to test belt tension. Midway between

When replacing a worn belt, determine the correct size by running a tape around the outer rims of the pulleys back to the starting point. Don't measure the belt; it will have been stretched through wear.

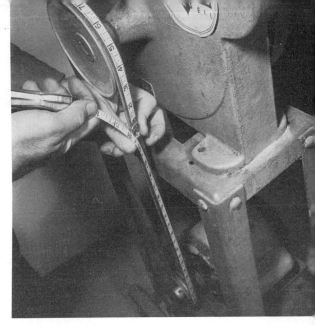

the pulleys squeeze the belt with two fingers and twist. If it's correctly tensioned, you won't be able to twist it more than half a turn. A good motor mount will maintain belt tension automatically and deliver better power.

It is important that the driving shaft of the motor and the driven shaft of the tool be exactly parallel. In addition, the pulley on each should be in exactly the same plane. A simple way to get them in the same plane is to loosen the machine pulley. Start the motor up and let it run briefly. You will find that the pulley automatically adjusts to the same plane as the other. Tighten it there by turning the set screw.

PULLEY SIZE AND SHAFT SPEED. Power tools come with a pulley. The manufacturer's instructions will tell you the

Belt is properly tensioned when you can take up exactly 1″ of slack.

Pulley size is determined by measuring diameter from rim to rim.

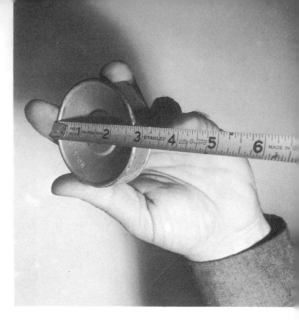

correct speed at which the tool should be run and the size of the motor pulley needed to achieve this speed. However, if this information is not available, you can calculate the size of the pulley needed and the speed it will deliver.

Most induction motors run at 1750 or 3500 revolutions per minute. A few run at 1725 or 3450 rpm. You can modify motor speed by using the appropriate pulleys. You will need high speed for a shaper (10,000 rpm) and jointer (7000 rpm). You will need relatively slow speeds (600 to 850 rpm) for a band saw. A table saw may require a speed of 3500 rpm. The accompanying table explains how to calculate pulley sizes and shaft speeds.

HOW TO CALCULATE PULLEY SIZES AND SHAFT SPEEDS

IF YOU KNOW	AND WANT	DO THIS
Speed and diameter of driving pulley, and diameter of driven one	Speed of driven pulley	Multiply speed of driver by its diameter; divide by diameter of driven pulley

Example: A 2″ motor pulley turns at 1750 rpm to drive a 3½″ pulley on a jigsaw. How many strokes a minute will result? Multiply 1750 by 2; divide by 3½. Answer: 1000

IF YOU KNOW	AND WANT	DO THIS
Speed and diameter of driving pulley and required speed of driven one	Diameter of driven pulley	Multiply speed of driver by its diameter; divide by required driven speed

Example: A countershaft is to turn at 1650 rpm when driven from a 3″ pulley on a gas engine governor-controlled at 2200 rpm. What size pulley is needed on the countershaft? Multiply 2200 by 3; divide by 1650. Answer: 4

IF YOU KNOW	AND WANT	DO THIS
Required speed and diameter of driven pulley, and speed of driving shaft	Diameter of driving pulley	Multiply required speed of driven pulley by its diameter; divide by speed of driving shaft

Example: A cut-off wheel to run at 4000 rpm has a 1¾″ sheave on its arbor. What size driving pulley is needed on a 1750-rpm motor? Multiply 4000 by 1¾″; divide by 1750. Answer: 4″

IF YOU KNOW	AND WANT	DO THIS
Diameters of both pulleys and required speed of driven shaft	Speed of driving shaft	Multiply diameter of driven pulley by the required speed; divide by diameter of driving pulley

Example: A gas engine with a 3″ pulley is to drive a circular saw at 3600 rpm. The saw shaft has a 2½″ pulley. At what speed must the engine run? Multiply 3600 by 2½; divide by 3. Answer: 3000 rpm

REVERSING MOTOR DIRECTION. It is best and most convenient to have a separate motor for each tool. Often you can salvage a motor from an old refrigerator or an oil burner. Most motors run in a clockwise direction when you face their

The bigger the pulley on the motor and the smaller the pulley on the tool, the faster the tool will operate. This triple pulley arrangement permits running tool at three different speeds.

Lever on lathe acts as a clutch, takes tension off pulley connection between motor and tool (left). More complex lathe (below) has interchangeable gears and pulley belts for thirty-two speeds.

pulley. You may find this requires an inconvenient kind of mounting and that it would be better if the motor ran in a reverse direction. It is simple to reverse motor direction.

In a split-phase or capacitor motor the starting winding determines the motor direction. One lead of the starter winding goes to the terminal board, the other to the starting switch. Unsolder and reverse these leads and you will have reversed the motor direction.

In a universal motor, change direction by interchanging the connections to either the armature or the field winding. It is usually easiest to change the armature connections. It can be done at the brushes.

MOTOR MOUNTS.   When a motor is being used for a single tool only, you can use inexpensive adjustable motor rails as a mount. Belt tension is adjusted by adjusting bolts. If you wish to move a motor from one tool to another, you can use a floating motor rail. At each point of use the motor rail is held by two

DROP-IN MULTI-TOOL MOUNTS

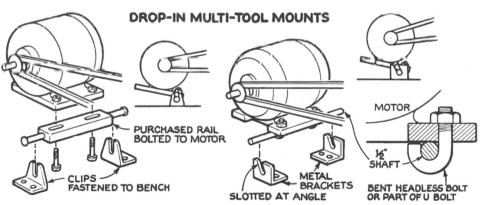

PURCHASED RAIL BOLTED TO MOTOR

CLIPS FASTENED TO BENCH

METAL BRACKETS

SLOTTED AT ANGLE

MOTOR

½" SHAFT

BENT HEADLESS BOLT OR PART OF U BOLT

One motor can be used for several power tools if you install brackets for a drop-in mount at each tool. The floating motor rail in the setup at left is sold by Sears, Roebuck. Bolted to the base of the motor, it slips into the brackets, or clips, fastened to the bench. The belt must be short enough to tilt the motor well up; if it hangs nearly flat, it may put excessive strains on the belt and bearings and cause rapid wear. Homemade mount at right has angled slots that keep the motor from jumping out at starts.

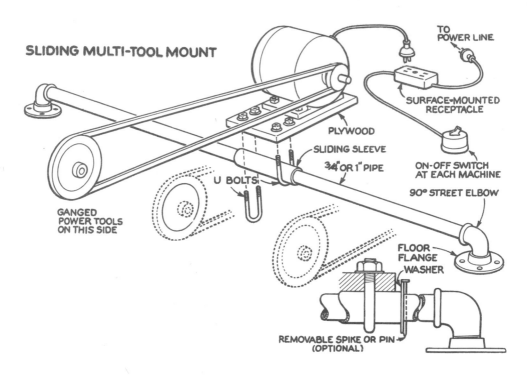

SLIDING MULTI-TOOL MOUNT

TO POWER LINE

SURFACE-MOUNTED RECEPTACLE

PLYWOOD

SLIDING SLEEVE

¾" OR 1" PIPE

ON-OFF SWITCH AT EACH MACHINE

90° STREET ELBOW

U BOLTS

GANGED POWER TOOLS ON THIS SIDE

FLOOR FLANGE WASHER

REMOVABLE SPIKE OR PIN (OPTIONAL)

When power tools can be ganged on a bench, the motor may slide from one to the other on a long rail. Several belts may be needed. Should the motor tend to shift, spikes may be dropped through holes in the rail to keep it aligned. Make it safe—and handy—by mounting a permanent switch near each tool. Connect only a short cord and plug to the motor. To guard against shock hazard, run a ground wire to all the motor brackets or use approved grounded plugs and receptacles.

clips. You buy added pairs of clips for each desired location.

The position in which you can mount a motor may depend on its bearings. Ball bearings are better than sleeve bearings. They take more abuse, run quieter and longer. They may be sealed in grease so that no lubrication is required, and they usually may be run in any position. Motors with sleeve bearings are unsatisfactory in a vertical position. Their lubrication runs out.

If you are using a salvaged motor and it has no base you

SIX MOTOR MOUNTS TO INCREASE BELT TENSION

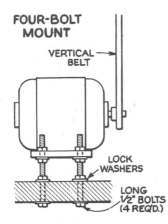

FOUR-BOLT MOUNT

VERTICAL BELT

LOCK WASHERS

LONG ½" BOLTS (4 REQ'D.)

Pulley belts eventually stretch, so a motor mount must be adjustable to take up the slack. This four-bolt mount, for vertical drives, permits lowering motor to increase belt tension.

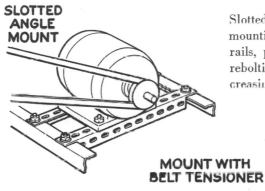

SLOTTED ANGLE MOUNT

Slotted angle, useful for mounting motor on tool-stand rails, provides openings for rebolting the motor and increasing belt tension.

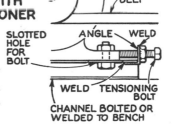

MOUNT WITH BELT TENSIONER

BELT

SLOTTED HOLE FOR BOLT

ANGLE WELD

WELD TENSIONING BOLT

CHANNEL BOLTED OR WELDED TO BENCH

In awkward situations, where the motor can't be moved by hand, a bolt turning in a bracket will push it back and put tension on the belt.

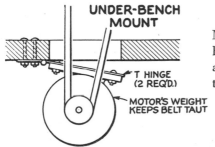

UNDER-BENCH MOUNT

T HINGE (2 REQ'D.)

MOTOR'S WEIGHT KEEPS BELT TAUT

Motor hung under its support on big T hinges will keep the belt taut automatically. Enlarge or drill extra holes in the hinge as needed.

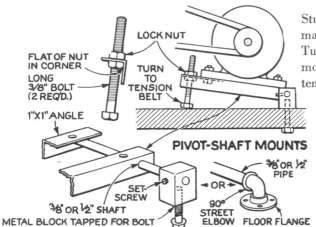

Sturdy tilting mount can be made of angle iron and pipe. Turning bolt at the front of mount raises the motor and tensions the belt.

may be able to buy a clamp-on base or mount the motor to a wooden base with strap-iron bands.

To run a motor free of its load and connect it to its load after it reaches speed, use a centrifugal clutch in place of a plain pulley. (*Note:* Electric motor clutches are different from gas-engine types.) If you have a motor on a tilting base, you can lift the motor to disengage the load, let it rest back to take up the load. It is not difficult to rig control levers to do the tilting of the mounts. A lever attached to a cam is a good method.

Two smaller motors can be hooked up to work together and do the work of a larger motor. You may be able to connect the shaft of the two motors with a flexible coupling. This can be done if one of the motors has a double-ended shaft, for the drive pulley can then be put on the outer shaft end. If this is not practical, you can use two belts and identical pulleys.

Part **4**

SHOP AIDS

38

Sawhorses

Build yourself a couple of sawhorses, and you're off at a gallop. You'll use them to support work of all kinds. A sawhorse that's broad across the beam can be your workbench away from the shop.

You can buy sawhorses already assembled and ready for use. One kind is all metal, another has metal legs and a wood top. Both kinds have folding legs so they can be stored in minimum space.

The easiest way to make sawhorses is to use steel brackets manufactured for the purpose. One type of bracket eliminates the need for nailing. You merely insert 2-by-4s and tighten wing nuts. Some steel brackets are hinged so that the sawhorse rail can be removed and the legs folded for storing.

A-FRAME SAWHORSES. The classic type of sawhorse is an A-frame with a 2-by-4 set on edge as a rail. The legs, also of 2-by-4s, are mitered to fit the rail. To get the correct slant for the legs, cut the end brace first (out of 1″-by-8″ stock), and make its top edge 5″ and its bottom 8″. If you line the legs up with the brace sides, they will have about the right spread.

If you want a horse instantly, and without the work of miter cutting, nail a 1-by-4 to the top and bottom of a 30″

All-steel folding sawhorse is designed so you can attach your own wood top. Covering top with carpeting protects fine cabinetwork or paneling from damage.

Steel brackets are available for making strong, wobble-free sawhorses out of 2-by-4s. Absence of cross brace on legs allows you to stack them compactly in the shop.

length of 2-by-4 set on edge. Nail 1"-by-4" legs to the rail so they fit tightly under the top board. Apply 1"-by-4" cross braces to the legs—and the job is done.

For an extra-sturdy sawhorse, build your equine friend out of 2-by-6s. So he won't look clumsy, taper his 2"-by-6" legs to slim down about 2" from top to bottom. Mortise them into the top rail (which is set flat and stiffened by a 2-by-3), and mortise braces into the legs.

Tack a yardstick along one edge of the rail of your sawhorse for quick measuring of stock. Install a swing-up clamp on the rail's underside to hold boards in place. Cover the rail with fiberboard or carpet to prevent marring the work.

Classic A-frame sawhorse has been the carpenter's friend for generations. Legs are mitered to fit the rail. Cleats at the ends may be surface-mounted, as on this model, or recessed for greater rigidity.

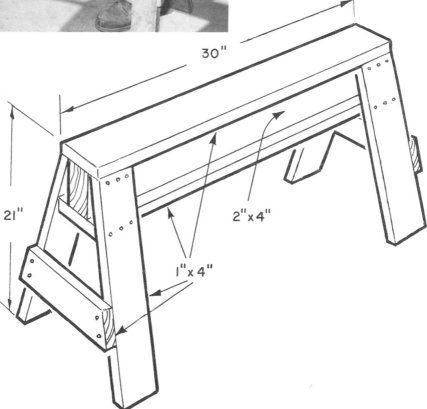

Instant sawhorse can be built by nailing 1-by-4s to top and bottom of a 2-by-4, nailing on 1″-by-4″ legs and cross braces. It's not necessary to miter the legs.

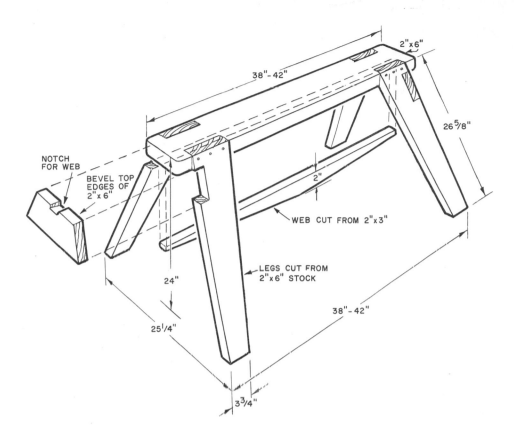

2"x6"

38"- 42"

26⅝"

NOTCH
FOR WEB

BEVEL TOP
EDGES OF
2"x 6"

2"

WEB CUT FROM 2"x3"

LEGS CUT FROM
2"x6" STOCK

24"

38"- 42"

25¼"

3¾"

Extra-sturdy sawhorse is built of 2-by-6s. Recess tapered
legs in notches cut in the top rail, which is braced by a
web cut from 2"-by-3" stock. Cross braces, notched for the
web, fit into notches on the legs.

KNOCKDOWN SAWHORSES. If you have a space problem, or don't want sawhorses standing in the shop area when
not in use, build collapsible ones out of either solid stock or
plywood.

The plans for a solid-stock sawhorse show how the crossbar, or rail, is slotted so that it fits tightly into the opening at
the top of the legs. If the opening is tapered slightly, it helps
insure a tight fit.

You can build collapsible sawhorses from ¾" plywood.
A single 4'-by-8' plywood panel will make two sawhorses. The
assembled horse is locked together by 20d nails inserted in

Plywood knockdown sawhorses have double rails which serve as a convenient slot for sawing. The rails are held in the slots by 20D nails inserted in drilled holes.

drilled holes. Make cuts accurately to insure that parts fit smoothly. Finish with two coats of paint, or resin floor hardener. Apply soap or paste wax to the joints and the pieces will slide together easier.

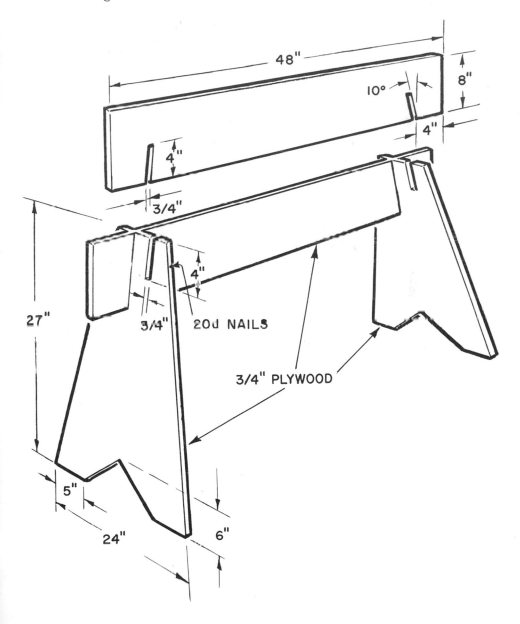

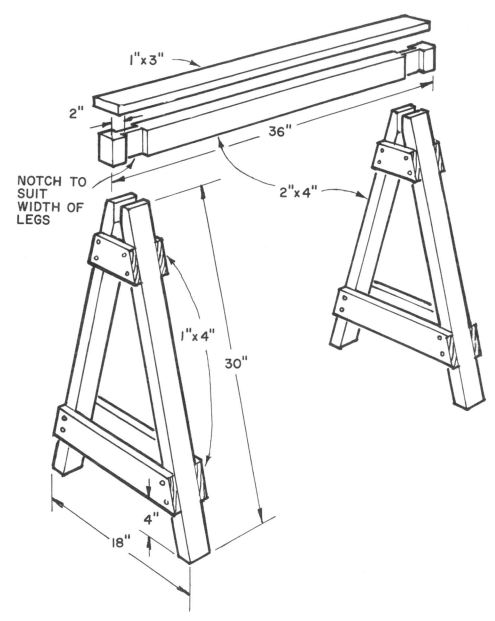

1"x 3"

2"

36"

NOTCH TO
SUIT
WIDTH OF
LEGS

2"x 4"

1"x 4"

30"

4"

18"

Knockdown sawhorse has a detachable rail which fits in slots formed by the legs. Make the legs and rail of 2-by-4s, the cross braces of 1-by-4s, and the top of a 1-by-3.

39

Riveters / Staplers / Stud Drivers

RIVETS were invented 4000 years ago, but it wasn't until the relatively recent development of the squeeze-type or "pop" rivet that they became foolproof easy-to-use fasteners for the homeowner. The squeeze rivet is clinched by squeezing a handle instead of hammering and this is now what makes rivets as easy to use as screws.

Squeeze rivets are set much faster than hammer set tubular rivets, and they hold better. They do not hold as well as solid rivets, but they hold well enough for almost any household job.

A special advantage of squeeze rivets is that you don't have to have access to the back side of the material to fasten them. They are secured without getting in behind.

This "blind-setting" is made possible by the ingenious way in which the rivet's other head is flared. The squeeze rivet looks like a regular tubular rivet except that there is something that looks like a finishing nail extending through it. It has a bulbular head and a thin stem. The head end goes through a hole made in the material being fastened. The stem end goes into the riveting tool. When you squeeze the handle of the tool, the stem pulls the bulbular end up into the tube, flaring out the rivet's other end. A final squeeze and the stem snaps off.

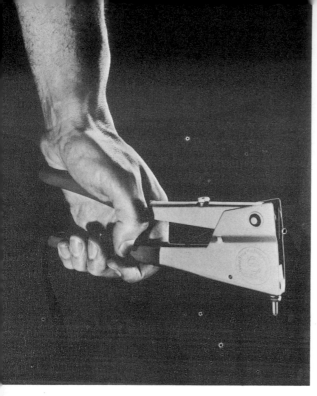

With rivet inserted in nose-piece of tool, it is ready for placement in holes predrilled in materials to be fastened together. Squeezing tool handles breaks stem and flattens rivet, joining the parts.

If you want to remove a squeeze rivet, you merely drill out its head. There is little danger of marring work, as in removing most solid rivets.

Rivets can be used in place of sheet-metal screws, nuts and bolts, soldering and brazing. They won't shake loose even under vibration, the way sheet-metal screws and nuts and bolts sometimes do. By riveting instead of spot welding, you avoid the dangers and possible damage of heat. Paint isn't blistered, and you don't have to worry about fire or explosion if you're working on a gas tank.

Squeeze or pop rivets are made in a variety of diameters and lengths and can be used to fasten materials up to ½″ thick and over. They adapt to variations in hole size and pull up tight whatever the material thickness. Riveting tools have interchangeable nose pieces or nozzles to accept rivets of different diameters.

Most popular rivets are aluminum, but rivets also come in steel and copper. Copper rivets are for repairing and fastening flashing, gutters, downspouts, dry sinks and other copper items.

Some rivets are closed for making a liquid-tight and gas-tight seal in fuel tanks, sinks, and water tanks. There are countersunk rivets which set flush with the surface. You can get white aluminum rivets for repairing white aluminum gutters, downspouts, siding, metal cabinets, and other white articles. You can get rivets with extra-large flanges for large holes in soft materials. You can get threaded aluminum rivets for setting threaded holes into metal, hardboard, and plastic sheets. These rivets come with a reusable mandrel.

Backup plates or washers are recommended for use with rivets in soft materials, like leather and canvas, or when predrilled holes are oversized. The backup plates give added holding power. Backup plates may be steel or aluminum.

STAPLING TOOLS.   Staples are 2-pointed fasteners made of wire. For many fastening jobs, they do just as well as nails and are driven much faster. A good stapler will drive heavy-gauge staples into composition board, plywood, soft- and hardwoods, plastics, even soft metals.

Three types of stapling tools or tackers have application in the home workshop and around the house: 1) the staple gun; 2) the plier stapler; 3) the hammer tacker.

The stapling gun is for jobs like attaching insulation, vapor barriers, building paper, ceiling tile, upholstery materials, screening. It can staple tags on wooden boxes. A good size for the homeowner is a stapler that can use staplers with leg length up to ½".

If you buy a stapling gun kit, also included may be a special screen attachment to pull screening taut when you drive the staples, a wire attachment for centering over bell, thermostat, telephone, intercom, and other small low-voltage wires, and a window-shade attachment to fit round shapes. You'll also get a staple lifter for removing staples.

There are many specialty staple tackers. One shoots a flared staple which enters soft material and locks inside without penetrating through. Another is for fastening electric wires, cables, and copper tubing up to ½" in diameter.

Stapling gun is an all-round fastening tool which finds many uses in shopwork. Special attachment hooks onto screening and pulls it tight when staples are driven.

If you get a light-duty stapler and then find you want to do a job like installing ceiling tile, you can rent a heavy-duty stapler (often without charge) where you buy the tile.

Plier-type staplers are for use in fastening thin sheets of material together. Both sides of the material must be accessible. The tool bends the staple legs closed on the reverse side. With some exceptions, plier staplers cannot be used for nailing.

A hammer tacker is a stapling tool that is swung like a hammer. When it hits, it automatically drives a staple. It makes "nailing" a one-hand operation, and is especially good for such jobs as tacking up building paper, attaching undercourse

Heavy-duty hammer tackers are used for attaching composition roofing and undercourse shakes on house walls. Swung like a hammer, the tool staples when it hits.

shakes, vapor barriers, etc. You don't have accurate aim with a hammer tacker, as you do with a gun tacker, but for the jobs it does you don't need it.

Almost always, a stapler—whatever the variety—will take staples made only by the manufacturer of the tool. Staples of other manufacturers won't fit. Thus it is important not only to get a good stapler, but also one that will take all the sizes and kinds of staples you want to use.

STUD DRIVERS. When you want to fasten to concrete, bricks, or soft metal, you don't have to drill a hole and use expansion shields, plugs, or toggle bolts. A drive tool can do it. It's designed to give the control and support needed to hammer threaded studs or pins into all these materials.

Some of the kinds of things you can fasten to masonry are plumbing pipes, furring strips, paneling, perforated board, shelves, brackets, door sills, porch and stair railings, mail boxes, lighting fixtures, house numbers, awnings and shutters.

Drive tool pounds tempered steel studs which hold materials to concrete, block, and brick. Stud is placed in bottom opening and held against work, then driven home with a hammer blow on the driver.

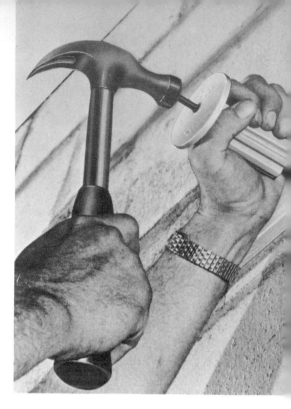

Stud fasteners are available in sizes from ¾″ to 3″. Fasteners should be long enough to penetrate ¾″ into hard concrete and 1″ in masonry or mortar. In fastening 2-by-4s to any material, allow for 1¼″ penetration. Though studs can be driven with an ordinary hammer, a 2- or 3-pound hammer is recommended, especially if you have a lot of driving to do.

40

Cleanup / Maintenance

Plan your shop with an eye toward saving work. Eliminate the traps that keep shops looking messy and disorderly, and that make them hard to clean.

As an example, avoid having too many open shelves. Put them behind sliding panels or swinging doors to keep out sawdust. Sliding panels are especially easy to install. They can be made of plywood or hardboard (⅛" or ¼") and can slide in metal, plastic, or wood track, available at almost any lumberyard.

A crowded, cluttered shop is hard to maintain. Get rid of what you really don't need. Occasionally you will throw out something you will need the following week, but most times it will never be missed. The space, comfort, and pleasure gained by having a more orderly shop is worth far more than you can save by salvaging junk. Time is your most expensive commodity. Put your time in dollars-per-hour terms and you'll discover how expensive salvaged materials really are.

Provide a floor that's easy to maintain. Vinyl asbestos tile is one of the best and least expensive covers for concrete. It tends to disguise soiling. It isn't bothered by grease.

A floor that's thoroughly clean is easier to keep clean. A variety of cleaners specifically designed for concrete floors and

It's natural for a shop to become littered when you're working—but it should be cleaned after each session. Facilities for orderly storage can help eliminate clutter and minimize mess.

driveways are especially helpful in removing grease stains and preparing concrete floors for applications of enamel. You'll often find them at service stations and auto supply counters. Trisodium phosphate, Spic and Span, Soilax, and Oakite are all good heavy-duty cleaners for shop use.

HOW TO STOP SAWDUST. You can't avoid creating sawdust, but you can stop it from spreading. A saw is about the biggest sawdust producer. Sanding machines, shapers, planers, and other chip and dust producers are also troublemakers. Provide them with hoods, traps, or boxes to collect their pollutants as fast as they are produced. If you're buying a sander, get one with a vacuum or provision for attaching one.

You need a sawdust collector under a table saw. Some saws come with sawdust drawers. You can make your own drawer. Easier than that, provide a box of appropriate size. For some saws a scrap bin at the rear may work out better than one directly under the table. Extend the rear of the bin upward to support a roller, with the top of the roller fractionally below the level of the table, and it can also act as a support for ripping long boards.

Enclosed storage areas which extend to the floor protect tools and supplies from sawdust and leave no space under the bench where sawdust and scraps can collect.

Lumber should be stored neatly out of the way. This cradle support is hung from ceiling joists, holds an ample supply of lumber.

Box under table saw is a good dust collector. Plywood cover when saw is not in use is a good idea if you have a cat.

SHOP VACUUMS. Ordinary household vacuum cleaners aren't powerful enough and rugged enough for shop work. They can't handle rough shop materials. Unless you have a built-in central vacuum system, with one or more shop outlets, you need an industrial-type shop vacuum.

A shop vacuum will pick up all the sawdust, wood scraps, bits of plaster, rust, and paint chips you can feed it. It will remove dust from grinders, sanders, finishing tools. You can attach it directly to a variety of power tools, including saws, sanders, routers, shapers, and jointers. Besides that, you'll find

Sawdust from radial saw sprays toward the rear, and this hood (above) stops it from spreading while a vacuum hose inserted in rear wall collects it (right).

Chute directs shavings from jointer-planer down to collector box, which is attached to tool stand with hooks and eyes so it can easily be removed for dumping contents.

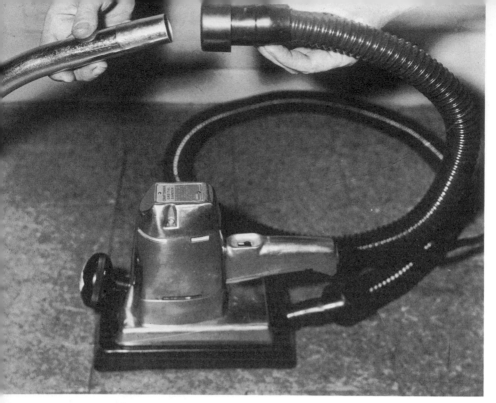

Many sanders come with dust-collecting devices such as a connection to any vacuum hose (above) or a zippered dust bag (below).

Shop vacuum is built to pick up sawdust, scraps, and paint chips. It comes with an assortment of nozzles and may operate wet or dry.

it useful around the house in the maintenance and cleanup of such other things as fireplaces, furnace flues, ventilators, etc.

Some vacs operate wet or dry. The wet feature is a great help in scrubbing, or if your basement is subject to flooding. Some vacs can be converted to handling water by means of an adapter.

Most vacs have hoses ranging in diameter from 1¼" to 3". The typical hose size is 2½". However, you can get an adapter so that you can use 1½" or 1¼" hoses and accessories.

Standard equipment is a triangular or rectangular nozzle. In addition, you may want a floor nozzle, a wet nozzle, a crevice nozzle. A round nozzle is good for use when you reverse the action and blow instead of vacuum. A fishtail nozzle or a square dust hood is especially designed for attaching to power tools. A round brush is useful for many cleaning operations. A good set consists of a blower, a brush, and a crevice tool.

Shop vacuums are available with drum capacities of from 5 to 55 gallons. A 10-gallon drum costs only a little more than a 5-gallon one and it means less frequent emptying. Drums are usually lightweight steel or fiber. Some vacs come with dollies. For others, you have to provide the dolly separately. Get a dolly and spare your back.

OTHER CLEANING EQUIPMENT. A vacuum does not eliminate the need for brooms or brushes. A hair pushbroom is usually most satisfactory for floors. It doesn't raise as much dust as a straw broom and it covers more area and in faster time. Hair is better than fiber because it gets the fine dust. Save the fiber broom for rougher work, like sidewalks. A dustpan and brush are needed for keeping the workbench and tool tables clear.

Large metal or plastic wastebaskets are attractive, but you can get by with drums in which soap powders or swimming pool chemicals are packed.

Plastic trash cans have much to recommend them over metal. They're silent, they don't dent, and they don't rust. Being seamless, they're also easier to clean.

You may prefer plastic rectangular cans to round ones. They hold more in less space. They snug up closer to the bench or wall, and in some cases they come mounted on their own wheels.

Provide a box for collecting wood scraps, preferably on a dolly. With a place to throw scraps, they are less likely to land on the floor.

Apron, dustpan, brush, and wastebasket are essential cleaning equipment (left). Brush is handy for keeping table saw free of bothersome sawdust (right).

A good collection of cleaning rags is always useful. Provide a covered hamper or a bin for them. You'll find just what you need in a housewares department. If you keep oily rags, to avoid fire hazard store them in a metal container with a tightly fitting lid.

Provide a roller for paper towel. Paper towel is almost a shop necessity. A roll of aluminum foil also makes sense. Line a paint tray with it and it saves a cleaning job. Wrap brushes in foil for overnight storage and it can also save on cleanup time.

RUST PREVENTION.   After dust, the biggest shop nuisance is rust. If it can't be prevented, it can at least be minimized. Coat vulnerable metal, like saw tables, with paste wax. Paraffin is good, too. Occasionally wipe rust-prone tools like handsaws and planes with a lightly oiled rag.

If conditions of humidity and condensation are severe, consider the installation of a dehumidifying unit. Besides stopping rust, a dehumidifier in summer can make working conditions more comfortable and can take the load off air conditioners, or even eliminate the need for them.

During especially humid weather cover power tools with dust covers, either cloth or plastic. They will help stop condensation of moisture on metal. Bags containing silica gel are also effective in absorbing moisture. Put one in a cabinet or toolbox. In some cases, a little added heat can dry up the moisture. In cool weather, run your heating plant briefly. In confined spaces, a 7½-watt bulb kept burning may do the trick. Even a 25-watter kept burning can pay for its cost with the damage it prevents.

Products like Chrome Guard and Silver Guard apply a clear coating that protects all metal against atmospheric corrosion and tarnishing. They offer year-round protection against rust. Silicone sprays and penetrating oils are also helpful in driving out moisture and preventing the destructive effects of rust.

OIL, SOAP, SOLVENT.   A little oil goes a long way toward keeping tools and equipment operating. It's preventive medicine at its best. Keep a checklist on tool maintenance. Every power tool you buy and many hand tools will come with suggested maintenance procedures.

As important as oiling is getting the oil where you want it to go. The can that oil comes in is not always the best applicator. A trigger oiler—typically with a 6″ spout—helps you get oil in the right place. It's the oiler for most household and small jobs. A pump oiler offers force feed and is usually best for machinery. It generally has an 11″ spout and 1-quart capacity.

Lubricants in your arsenal should include penetrating oil for rusty joints; silicone spray for rubber, metal, and wood; gear-case lubricant for electric tools; and grease for general purposes. You can get all-purpose lithium grease in a dispenser can.

Besides cleaning your shop, you have to clean yourself. As in the case of the shop, prevention is better than cleanup. If the job doesn't warrant getting into old clothes, or pulling on coveralls, use a shop apron. If the job isn't one where wearing gloves is convenient, use protective creams to prevent grime and grease from clinging and from getting under your fingernails.

The best soap for hand cleaning is Lava with its content of fine pumice. Better, however, in many cases are waterless hand cleaners because they can be used without the problem of dirtying the washbasin. Thoroughly masage the hands with the cleaner, then wipe it away with paper towel.

Your collection of solvents for cleanup (both of yourself and equipment) should include turpentine, paint thinner, denatured alcohol, lacquer thinner, and methylethylketone (MEK).

41

Shop Safety

A workshop may not be as dangerous as an automobile, but it's still in the high-hazard category. Shocks, falls, cuts, splinters, burns, dust, poisons, explosions—these are a few of the dangers you face in a workshop, and in maintenance and building operations outside it.

Beginners have a safety advantage. They are afraid. They respect tools. As they become more familiar with the hazards involved, however, the fear begins to fade. Familiarity breeds contempt, someone once said, and that's why pros, rather than amateurs, have the most accidents.

POWER TOOLS. The blade of a power saw travels 3800 rpm and doesn't care what it cuts. At 3800 rpm, the edge is invisible. It may be a half inch closer to your flesh than it appears to be.

Read the instructions that come with the tool. Then read them again. Don't throw them away after that. Keep them handy so you can review them in the future and refresh your memory.

Leave all power-tool guards in place. Use all the safety devices the tool provides. For example, a radial saw may have

Can You Find Eight Sins Against
Safety In This Photo?

1. Child in shop and, worse, handling tools. 2. Not concentrating on work. 3. Not using safety guard on saw. 4. Saw table cluttered. 5. Beer. 6. Loose clothing. 7. Blade too high for work. 8. No push stick.

a "splitter" and "anti-kickback dogs." If you rip a board without them, you may get away with it—but you may not. The tool may hurl the ripping like a deadly spear. Too bad if anyone is standing in its path. A table saw can hurl things too, unless they are properly secured. A drill press has other tricks: it can grab work and become a battering windmill.

Never fight a tool. Don't force it beyond its capability. Don't use it in ways or for purposes for which it is not intended. Don't attempt freehand cuts, or cuts without proper support. If an operation seems to hold special hazards, don't attempt it without thinking for a moment what the price may be.

Keep out of line of the saw blade, front and rear, and see that no one else ever moves in line with it. This is the area where those deadly spears are seeking a target. Let only enough blade project on a table saw or portable saw to cut the work. The saw cuts better that way, binding is minimized, and the chances of throwing wood spears are reduced.

If you find yourself daydreaming as you work, snap out of it or postpone your efforts to a time when you feel more alert. When you daydream, you're not thinking of what you're doing. You are also more likely to be startled. Even when you are alert, when you are using a power tool you aren't apt to hear the approach of a visitor. Instruct your family to wait

Warning banner on chuck key is a reminder to remove the key before starting the drill press. Otherwise, key would be hurled across the room with dangerous force.

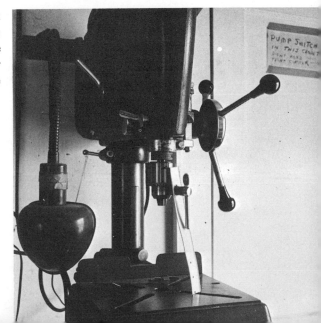

until anyone using a power tool has finished what he is doing and can't be imperiled in case he is startled.

Distraction causes accidents. That's why it a good idea to ban children from the shop, or from areas where power tools are being used.

Almost as dangerous as children underfoot, is clutter underfoot. Some shop floors get to look like an obstacle course. Keep the floor clear.

Also keep your head clear. A beer or martini at the saw table would make a pleasant companion were it not that alcohol slows reflexes.

Working in poor light is inviting an accident. Make sure that all power tools have sufficient illumination, as shown in Chapter 2.

Never leave a running power tool unattended. If there are children around who may get into mischief, lock the shop when you leave. It's also a good idea if there is a separate switch so you can turn off all shop electricity and prevent unauthorized use. If the switch is lockable, so much the better.

ELECTRICITY.   A large sign in a well-known research laboratory carries this warning: "Touch electrical equipment with one hand only."

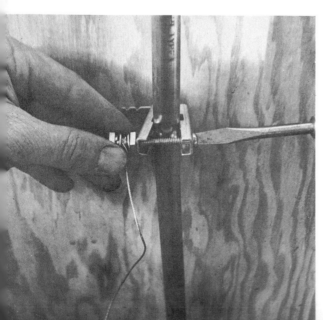

If stationary power tool lacks grounding plug, you can ground its metal frame by running a wire to a cold-water pipe.

This is the old one-hand-in-the-pocket trick. It works this way. If you touch a hot line with one hand, the jolt will travel down your arm and through your body to the ground. You'll feel it, but it won't kill you. But if you touch with both hands the jolt passes up one arm, across your body, and down the other, completing the circuit. The path goes right through your heart.

An insidious thing about electricity is that it can paralyze your muscles. You may not be able to open the hand that clutches a hot wire, and let go. You may be conscious, but helpless to do anything to save yourself. So avoid getting into such a predicament. Switch off power at the service entry box before you work on a line. Turning power off at the room toggle switch is not enough; sometimes fixtures are incorrectly wired and may be hot even when switched off. The switch may be on the ground line instead of on the hot line.

Always ground power tools that have provision for grounding. Usually this means using either a grounding receptacle or a grounded adapter. An adapter doesn't do any good, incidentally, unless its wire is firmly seated under the brass screw of the receptacle plate.

Make it a rule never to use power tools in wet locations, such as in a flooded basement. The only exception to the rule

Switch that can cut off all electric power in the shop is a good precaution in a home with children. Placed high and near the door, it is out of their reach and reminds you to turn off power when you leave the shop.

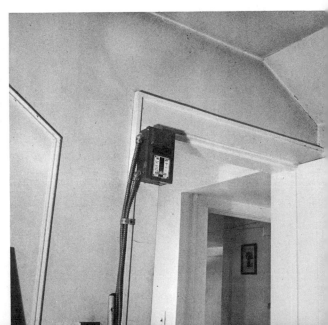

Never stand on the top rung of a stepladder. This may happen to you.

is a battery-operated drill. Never hold onto a pipe for support, or touch other metal, when using a power tool. Promptly replace electric cords when they become frayed.

LADDERS. If a ladder has bad rungs, poor footing, or is rickety or improperly slanted, don't climb it until these hazards are corrected. If a ladder slips or moves as you climb, it's not placed properly. If you're using a straight ladder, its base should be away from the supporting wall a distance equal to one quarter of its height.

Before getting on a step ladder, see that it is fully opened and its braces locked. When you get on, don't climb higher

Don't try to reach for out-of-the-way tools when on a ladder. More people fall from a low position on a ladder than from high.

than the second step from the top. Never, never stand on the top platform.

In climbing a ladder, carry tools in your pocket, scabbard, or other tote device, but not in your hand. When working on a ladder, try at all times to keep one hand free. You may want to grasp the ladder. If your ladder is set in a doorway, see that the door is open, or that it is locked. Then no one will bump the ladder and bump you off. Before you move a step-ladder, be sure you haven't left your hammer on its top. It may come sailing off.

The light weight of magnesium or aluminum ladders is an asset, but the lightness and the metal can also be hazards. A strong wind can blow them down and leave you stranded on a roof. And since magnesium and aluminum conduct electricity, they are risky to use around electric lines and during electrical storms.

LIFTING.   A back injury may not kill you, but it can give you uncomfortable moments the rest of your life if you slip a disc, tear a ligament, or pull a tendon. The rule for avoiding back injuries when lifting is to bend the knees, keep the back straight. You have to bend your back a little, of course, but minimize it. When you have a lifting job that's just too awkward or heavy, get help—a block and tackle and/or a neighbor.

Avoid lifting heavy tools by using rollers to move them. Here a length of pipe serves as a roller, enabling one man to move a heavy piece of machinery without danger.

MENACES MISCELLANEOUS. When you saw, don't use your knee to brace work. When you hammer, hold the nail you're driving only long enough to start it, and make the starting hammer strokes slow and measured so you can't miss. When you drill, keep your hand away from the bit. It may jump. The same goes for a screwdriver, especially one of the wrong size, or one whose tip has become rounded.

Use goggles or a mask to protect your eyes when grind-

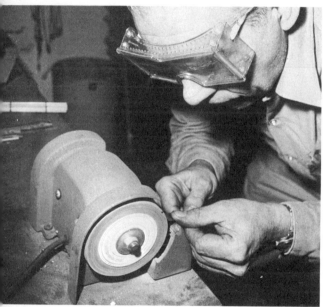

Always wear safety glasses when working at the grinder to protect your eyes against richochets from the side.

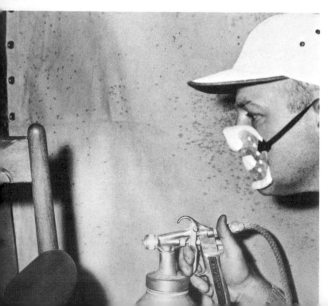

Solvents used in paint sprayers are dangerous to the lungs. Wear a mask when you spray to guard against inhaling the fumes.

Low overheads present a hazard in many shops. Use reflective tape as warning markers in these areas and you'll spare yourself a few bumps on the head.

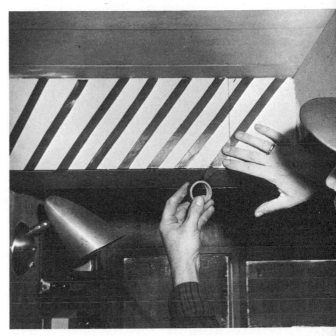

ing, when sawing metal, when sawing overhead. Use gloves to protect your hands when handling broken glass or rough masonry.

If your shop is in a basement or attic, and there is a low overhead en route, identify the hazard plainly, so no one could possibly be unaware of it. Avoid having a door that opens onto a downflight of steps. It should open away from the steps. Repair loose or broken steps and handrails as soon as you discover them.

Store inflammables outdoors. Keep oily rags in a sealed can. They sometimes catch fire by spontaneous combustion.

Water is best for putting out wood or paper fires. Dry-chemical extinguishers are best for oil and electrical fires. In the event of fire, people—not property—are most important. First, see that everyone is safely evacuated. Second, call the fire department.

Fighting fires is for professionals. It is definitely not a do-it-yourself undertaking. Extinguishers are only for dousing the first flames before a fire can get started. It is for squelching incipient fires. Don't be misled or lulled into thinking they are capable of doing any more than that.

42

Shop Data

ABRASIVES are available in both paper- and cloth-backed sheets. Coatings may be "closed" for fast cutting, or "open" to resist clogging.

Aluminum oxide is the toughest abrasive known. It cuts faster than either flint or garnet and is the most popular of the "electric furnace" papers. It is almost ten times as expensive as ordinary flint sandpaper, however, which is cheapest. Flint, therefore, is commonly used for work that rapidly clogs the abrasive sheet. Garnet grits are popular for fine finishing and are available in wet or dry paper for use with water or rubbing oil on wood or metal. Silicon carbide, another of the electric furnace-formed papers, is also offered in "wet or dry" for such jobs as removing rust and polishing metal. Emery cloth is used mostly in fine grades for cleaning and polishing metals.

Abrasive powders, such as pumice and rottenstone, are used in producing hand-rubbed finishes on wood. Pumice is the faster cutting of the two, but rottenstone will produce a higher gloss. Steel wool (fine grade) is used in toning down lustre. It is also useful with paint remover in refinishing projects, and in rust removal. Rouge abrasives are used in putting a high polish on metals.

ADHESIVES. The Glue Guide on page 430 tells you most of what you need to know, but observe these points particularly.

White, or polyvinyl, glue is the easiest to use and the most popular. But it is not the best glue for wood that is under stress. For a stronger bond, use plastic-resin glue. When a joint is not dependent on the adhesive for its support, such as in mortise-and-tenon and dovetail joints, white glue is generally satisfactory. Don't use excessive pressure with white glue. You'll force out too much glue and weaken the joint. Don't use at temperatures below 60 degrees F.

Epoxy cement has little application in woodworking. Almost any of the other less-expensive adhesives will do a better job. Epoxy works best with rigid materials like metal, plastics, ceramics, and masonry.

BLUEPRINTS. The symbols in the chart (p. 433) will help you read architect's drawings, as well as draw up your own. You don't need a fancy drafting set, or even talent, to make presentable drawings. Get a small plastic template of architectural symbols and you can quickly and accurately trace doors, bath and laundry equipment, electrical symbols, etc.

A plastic triangle and a T-square are other worthwhile additions to the basic equipment of a good straightedged ruler, a pair of compasses, and a good eraser.

ESTIMATING LUMBER COST. The price of lumber is usually on board feet. To calculate board feet multiply the square feet measure of a board (width in feet by length in feet) by its thickness in inches. For example, a 2-by-6 that's 12' long contains $\frac{1}{2}$ x 12 x 2, or 12 board feet. If a board is less than 1" thick, it's still figured as 1".

Usually, 16' is considered as the maximum standard length for boards. You can get longer sizes, but you'll pay a premium charge.

Save by using the best size board to do a job. For example, a 2-by-10 contains less lumber and costs less than a 4-by-6, but it's considerably stronger. To determine the loadbearing strength of a board, square the dimension that will take the stress and multiply it by the width. For a 2-by-10, you would multiply 10 x 10 x 2, or 200. For a 4-by-6 you get 6 x 6 x 4, or 144. Under equal loads, the 2-by-10 will also bend less than the 4-by-6. Figuring stiffness is done by cubing the direction of the stress and multiplying it by the width. For a 2-by-10, you get 10 x 10 x 10 x 2, or 2000. For a 4-by-6 you get 6 x 6 x 6 x 4, or 864. These proportions indicate that the 4-by-6 will sag more than twice as much as the 2-by-10.

PAINT, EXTERIOR.   Five hundred square feet per gallon is approximate average coverage.

Add 10% for narrow lap siding

20% for rough or porous material

30% for corrugated material

50% for first coat on concrete block

In calculating square footage, add 2' to average house height, multiply that figure by total length of all sides.

WALLPAPER is sold in double rolls 16 yards long, 18" wide. Waste is mostly in matching patterns. Multiply perimeter of room measured in yards by 2 and you'll get number of strips needed. Then figure how many strips you can get in each 16-yard roll. If your room is 8 feet high, and there's no waste, you'll get 6. But there will be waste so allow some extra and save an extra trip to the store.

KEY TO SHEET ABRASIVES

ABRASIVE	COLOR	USE
Crocus cloth (iron oxide dust)	Red	Metal
Silicon carbide (sand and coke cinder)	Shiny black	Soft metals (aluminum, bronze, etc.), glass, stone, plastics, leather
Garnet	Reddish	General woodworking, all-purpose
Aluminum oxide	Brownish purple	Hardwood, iron and steel, rust and peeling paint removal
Flint (white quartz)	Tan	Paint, gummy wood, quickly clogging materials
Emery	Black	Cleaning and polishing metals, rust removal

COMPARATIVE GRIT SIZES

FLINT OR SANDPAPER	GARNET, ALUMINUM OXIDE, SILICON CARBIDE	EMERY CLOTH
Ex. fine	150 (4/0)	2/0
Fine	120 (3/0)	
Med. fine	100 (2/0)	½
Medium	80 (0)	1
Med. coarse	60 (½)	
Coarse	40 (1½)	

Above sizes are most common, but complete range of coarse grades is to 12 (4½), and fine to 600 (10/0).

GLUE GUIDE

ADHESIVE	APPLICATION	GENERAL INFORMATION			
		TYPE	CLAMPING	SETTING TIME	WATER RESISTANCE
EPOXY GLUE	Heavy-duty household repairs: china, glass, metals, plastics, porcelain. Concrete to concrete, wood, masonry; metal to metal, wood, masonry	Resin and hardener: easily mixed	Not required	Overnight	Waterproof
CONTACT CEMENT	Light-duty household repairs: china, glass, metals, plastics, porcelain. Plastic laminates to plywood or particle board; leather to leather, wood	Liquid	Not required	Bonds on contact when dry	High
WHITE GLUE	Wood cabinets, built-ins, furniture, light assembly; paper to paper, fabric, cardboard; canvas, cork or felt to wood	Liquid	Moderate pressure	20–30 minutes	Moderate
PLASTIC-RESIN GLUE	Heavy assembly: wood cabinets, built-ins, furniture; leather to leather, wood	Powder: mixes with water	Required	5–6 hours	Very high
PANEL ADHESIVE	Installing plywood panels on walls without nails	Mastic	Not required	8–10 minutes	High
WATERPROOF RESORCINOL GLUE	Exterior wood, outdoor, furniture, sports equipment, wood to wood, cork, canvas; boatbuilding	Liquid and powder	Required	8–10 hours	100% waterproof

Courtesy U.S. Plywood Corp.

OTHER ADHESIVES

ADHESIVE	CHARACTER-ISTICS	TYPICAL USES	WHAT MATERIALS
HOT MELT	Chalk-size polyethylene-base cartridges used in electric glue gun. Fast-setting, waterproof	Spot gluing. Small-job repairs like broken or loose chair rungs, wood-to-metal joints	Wood, paper, cloth, leather, fiberglass, rough surfaces
HOUSEHOLD CEMENT	Crystal clear, waterproof	Mending china and glass	China, galss, metal, leather, canvas, wood
EPOXY STEEL	Epoxy resin and steel powder. For rigid repairs. Fills and mends	Repairing gutters, tools, radiators	Steel, iron, brass, bronze, aluminum, glass, wood, porcelain, concrete
LIQUID RUBBER	For flexible repairs. Caulks, bonds, insulates, rustproofs	Motor belts, weatherstrips, rubber inflatables, tents, tarps	Rubber, fabrics plastics, glass, metal
MODEL CEMENT	Colorless, fast-drying	Building and repairing models, toys	Polystyrene, balsa wood
LIQUID ALUMINUM (liquid solder)	Dries metal-hard. Waterproof, weatherproof, heat-resistant	For plumbing repairs, aluminum ware, tinware, furniture, toys	Metal, wood, concrete, etc.
OLD-FASHIONED GLUE	Liquid hide or fish in bottles or cans	Furniture assembly and repair	Wood, leather, cloth, cardboard, glass, china

OTHER ADHESIVES (cont.)

ADHESIVE	CHARACTER-ISTICS	TYPICAL USES	WHAT MATERIALS
PLASTIC MENDER	Waterproof, flexible mender for most plastics	Swimming pools, rainwear, inflatables	Vinyl, acrylic, phenolic and styrene plastics. Also china, glass. paper, leather, canvas
VINYL SEAL	Repairs vinyl plastic without patches	Seals leaks and rips in pools, rafts, shower curtains, raincoats, beach toys, seat covers	Vinyl plastic
FABRIC MENDER	Use instead of sewing	Repairing rips, tears, burns, reinforcing worn spots in fabric	Cotton, wool, canvas, leatherette, felt
MARINE REPAIR	Nonrusting, flexible	Repairing water or gas tanks, anchoring screws, bolts, fittings, filling gouges and dry rot in planking	Wood, fiberglass, metal
FIXTURE	Weatherproof, waterproof, fast grab	Mounting house numbers, brackets, electric boxes	Wood, brick, concrete, glass ceramic tile, metal
CHAIR FIXER	Use with flexible needle for repairing furniture without disassembling	Loose chair rungs, table legs, drawers, etc.	Wood
RUBBER CEMENT	Fast drying, noncurling	Graphic art, paper	Paper, cloth, wood, leather, rubber

Symbols to Help You Read Architects' Drawings

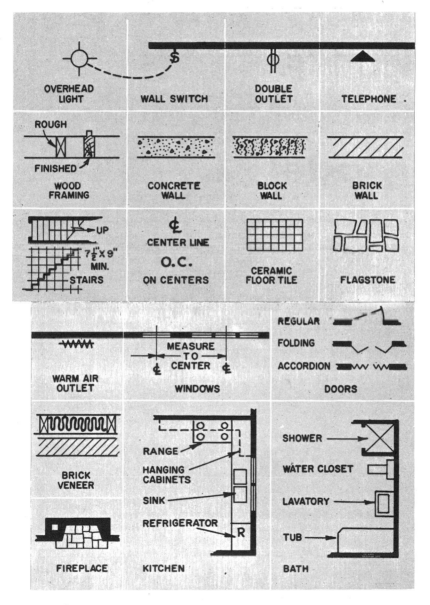

U. S. GYPSUM

BASIC STANDARD FURNITURE DIMENSIONS

ITEM	HEIGHT inches	LENGTH inches	DEPTH OR WIDTH inches
Bed—twin	22–24	78–80	36–42
Bed—double	22–24	78–80	57–60
Bookcase	82–max.	var.	12
Kit. cab. wall	30	var.	14
Kit. cab. base	36	var.	24
Chest	28–36 54–max.	18, 36–42, 60	18–21
Card table	30	36	36
Coffee table	15–18	42	15–18
Dining table	29	28 per place	32–36
End table	24	24	15
Kit. table	28–29	48–60	24–30
Desk	29	42–48	22–26
Lowboy	30	30	18
Highboy	60–84	36	18
Wardrobe or storage wall	65–75	var.	15–18—flat hanging 24–regular

LUMBER FACTS

STRIP—pieces of lumber less than 2″ thick and 4″ wide.
YARD BOARDS—less than 2″ thick, but 4″ or more wide.
DIMENSION LUMBER—2″ or more thick, and 4″ or more wide.
TIMBERS—4″x4″ up.

HARDWOODS		SOFTWOODS	
Ash	Gum	Cedar	Redwood
Birch	Hickory	Cypress	Spruce
Beech	Mahogany	Fir	Pine
Cherry	Maple	Hemlock	
Chestnut	Oak		
Elm	Tulip (Whitewood)		

GRADING OF LUMBER

Select Lumber

1 and 2 Clear — (also called B and Better) Highest quality. Generally clear and free from defects. Suitable for natural finishes and fine cabinetwork.

C Select — May have minor imperfections. One side may be without blemish.

D Select — Lowest finishing grade. Has minor defects and blemishes, but ideally suited for painted finishing.

Common Lumber

No. 1 — May have small, sound knots. Takes paint well. Usable with minimum waste.

No. 2 — Utility grade. Has larger and more numerous knots. Often used for knotted paneling

No. 3 — Numerous defects. Some waste in use.

No. 4 — Lowest grade usable in building.

No. 5 — Bottom quality. Suitable only for crating, rough concrete forms, etc.

NUMBER OF NAILS PER POUND

LENGTH inches	PENNY	Approx. number per pound				
		COMMON	BOX	FINISHING	CASING	FLOORING
1	2	850	1000	1350	1000	
1¼	3	550	630	805	630	
1½	4	300	470	585	470	
1¾	5	255	405	500	405	
2	6	170	235	305	235	155
2¼	7	150	210	235	210	140
2½	8	100	135	190	135	100
2¾	9	90	125	170	125	90
3	10	70	95	120	95	70
3¼	12	60	85	110	85	55
3½	16	50	70	90	70	45
4	20	30	50	60	50	30

Subtract ½″ from a nail's length and multiply by four to determine its penny size

FINISHING NAIL

FLOORING BRAD

CASING NAIL

BOX NAIL

COMMON NAIL

THE NAIL TO USE

MATERIAL	NAIL	MATERIAL	NAIL
1" boards	8d common	$\frac{1}{2}$" or $\frac{3}{8}$" gypsum bd.	4d common, cement
2" planks	20d common	$\frac{1}{2}$" gypsum board	5d or 6d common, cement
2x4 framing	10d common	wood or gypsum lath	3d blue lath
2x6 framing	16d common	baseboards	8d casing
2x10 framing	20d common	jambs	16d casing
$\frac{3}{8}$" flooring	4d casing grvd.	1" T&G paneling	5d finishing
$\frac{5}{4}$" flooring	8d casing grvd.	trim, light	4d common
underlayment	3d grooved	trim, heavy	8d common
$\frac{1}{4}$" plywood	$\frac{3}{4}$" #19 brads	24" wood shingles	4d galv. or alum. box
$\frac{3}{8}$" plywood	4d box, cement	13" wood shingles	3d galv. or alum. box
$\frac{1}{2}$" plywood	7d box, cement	bevel siding over wood sheathing	8d box
$\frac{5}{8}$" plywood	8d box, cement	bevel siding over comp. sheathing	10d box
$\frac{3}{4}$" plywood	10d box, cement	asphalt shingles or roll roofing	1" to 1$\frac{3}{4}$" roofing

STOCK SCREW SIZES

Lengths available—inches

SCREW NO.	HEAD DIA.	1/4	3/8	1/2	5/8	3/4	7/8	1	1 1/4	1 1/2	1 3/4	2	2 1/4	2 1/2	3	3 1/2	4
2		●	●	●	●												
3			●	●	●												
4		●	●	●	●	●	●	●	●								
5			●	●	●	●	●	●	●								
6			●	●	●	●	●	●	●	●							
7				●	●	●	●	●	●	●							
8			●	●	●	●	●	●	●	●	●	●		●			
9						●	●	●	●	●	●	●		●			
10						●	●	●	●	●	●	●	●	●	●	●	
12						●	●	●	●	●	●	●	●	●	●	●	
14								●	●	●	●	●	●	●	●	●	●

ANCHORS AND FASTENERS

FASTENER	BOLT OR SCREW REQUIRED	METHOD, TOOLS	COMMENTS
Plastic anchors	Sheet metal or wood screw	Drill, screwdriver, wrench	Works in any material; excellent all-purpose anchor
Nylon anchors	None, anchor complete	Drill, hammer	Works in any material; fast installation
Fibre anchors	Sheet metal or wood screw	Drill, screwdriver	Works in most materials; anchor for hard materials, pre-expansion for soft materials
Toggle bolts	None, anchor complete	Drill, screwdriver	Works in all materials backed by a hollow
Alum. drive anchors	None, anchor complete	Drill, hammer	Works in all hard materials
Machine screw anchors	Machine screw	Drill, hammer, screwdriver, wrench, setting tools	Works in all hard materials
Lead anchors	Sheet metal or wood screws	Drill, hammer, screwdriver	Works in all hard materials
Steel expansion anchors	None, anchor complete	Drill, wrench, screwdriver	Works in all hard materials
Zinc lag shield	Lag screw	Drill, wrench	Works in all hard materials
Hollow wall anchor	None, anchor complete	Drill, screwdriver	Works in all materials backed by hollow
Self drilling anchor	Machine screw	Wrench, hammer	Works in all hard materials

Courtesy Jordan Industries

HARD MATERIALS: Brick, concrete, block, stone, etc.
SOFT MATERIALS: Plaster, plasterboard, gypsum, fibreboard, etc.

WHAT LUBE TO USE WHERE

PART TO BE LUBRICATED		TYPE OF LUBRICANT	HOW OFTEN TO LUBRICATE
MOTORS	Med. to large	No. 30 eng. oil	Twice yearly or each season
	Small	Household oil	
WOOD, PLASTIC, RUBBER, AND SIMILAR NONMETALLIC PARTS		Silicone in spray, emulsion, or grease form	At first indication of sticking
GEARBOXES	With fittings	Gen.-purpose grease	Twice yearly
	With plugs	No. 50 to No. 90 gear oil	As needed; check after each use
OPEN GEARS		Open-gear grease	Keep well coated
GUNS	After firing	Powder-solvent oil	As needed
	For storage	Gun-oil	
FISHING REELS		Fine reel or instrument oil	Each season; more often if kept wet
CLOCKS AND FINE INSTRUMENTS		Fine reel or instrument oil	Not oftener than once yearly
LOCKS		Silicone or dry graphite	Yearly
HINGES		Dripless oil or dry moly	As needed or at least yearly
PLAIN BEARINGS	Under heat	Dry moly	Twice yearly; more often if in continuous service
	Med. duty	No. 30 eng. oil	
	Light duty	Household oil	
	Under abrasive conditions	Gen.-purpose grease	
TRACKS AND SLIDING PARTS		Dry moly, moly jel, or gen.-purpose grease	Twice yearly
CHAINS AND SPROCKETS		Moly jel	Twice yearly or each season; more often for constant use
FROZEN PARTS		Penetrating oil and rust solvent	As needed
LONG-TERM STORAGE AND RUST PREVENTION OF BARE METAL EQUIPMENT		Household oil followed by coating of gen.-purpose grease	As needed

INDEX

Index

M

Y